GUN CONTROL IN CONTEXT

This book approaches the gun control debate by asking what it takes to achieve acceptance of, and compliance with, gun control regulations in a community thought to be opposed and resistant. It does this by centring this question on the experience of gun dealers who occupy a dual role in the compliance process – subject to its regulations, yet central to the application of all regulatory processes. The findings are surprising in that they demonstrate more support for gun control than opposition among this group, more willingness to cooperate with authorities than resistance, and more possibility for setting the tone for support with the wider gun owning community. This book considers how policy makers in the USA can capitalise on these overtones of collaboration and concern for public safety and learn from the successes and mistakes of the Australian gun control experience.

Gun Control in Context is essential reading for all those engaged across the broad spectrum of the gun control debate and offers a grounded and reasoned approach to the challenges of public policy. It will be of interest to criminologists, legal scholars, and political scientists alike.

Suzanna Fay is Senior Lecturer in Criminology at the University of Queensland. Her current research considers how perceptions of gun regulation by police, dealers, and the community influence debate and enforcement of Australia's gun laws.

GUN CONTROL IN CONTEXT

Learning from the Australian Gun Control Experience

Suzanna Fay

Routledge
Taylor & Francis Group
LONDON AND NEW YORK

Designed cover image: © Getty Images / ericsphotography

First published 2024
by Routledge
4 Park Square, Milton Park, Abingdon, Oxon OX14 4RN

and by Routledge
605 Third Avenue, New York, NY 10158

Routledge is an imprint of the Taylor & Francis Group, an informa business

British Library Cataloguing-in-Publication Data
A catalogue record for this book is available from the British Library

ISBN: 978-1-032-22221-9 (hbk)
ISBN: 978-1-032-22222-6 (pbk)
ISBN: 978-1-003-27164-2 (ebk)

DOI: 10.4324/9781003271642

Typeset in Sabon
by KnowledgeWorks Global Ltd.

For my mum, Helen Callaghan, who taught me the art of survival as a single mother. These lessons have been crucial for a career in academia.
For my dad, Colin Fay, who taught me the value of not giving up just because something is hard.
And
For my kids, Aria, Aidan, Jasper, and Keira. The moral of this story is to never assume the narrative you have been given about someone or something is accurate, helpful, or invariable. Listening to multiple perspectives always builds better character.

CONTENTS

LIST OF CONTRIBUTOR

Amy Templar, The University of Queensland

Amy is currently completing her PhD in criminology in the School of Social Science. Her research explores the link between the identity of perpetrators and victims and the subsequent classification of active shooting events as either a mass shooting or an act of domestic terrorism. Her primary areas of research interests are criminal justice decision-making, firearm-related crimes and terrorism.

ACKNOWLEDGEMENTS

The writing of this manuscript took place on land that does not belong to me or my ancestors. The chapters of this book were written in two primary places across Australia. I acknowledge elders – past, present and future – of the Jagera and Turrabul people while writing in Brisbane, and the elders – past, present and future – of the Wurundjeri Woi-wurrung and Bunurong/Boon Wurrung peoples of the Kulin while writing in Melbourne. I recognise that sovereignty has never been ceded.

I have so much gratitude and thanks for the gun dealers that took part in my study. They had no reason to trust me. An outsider, and an academic wanting to know about guns and their livelihoods. They gave me their time anyway. The gun dealers who participated in this study took large parts of their day to invite me into their place of business, homes, and into a part of their lives that others have routinely criticised. I am thankful for what they have taught me about guns, about community and even about myself as a researcher. This project and this manuscript is unique and unlike much of the writing about gun control that has come before it because of the time the participants of this study dedicated to me. I would like to thank Sporting Shooters Association Australia's Geoff Jones, Tim Banister, Jennifer Maartens and Kate Fantinel in particular. You have all made this project possible with your help in recruitment and contacts for me when I started with none. This project would not have been possible without your financial and in-kind support. I acknowledge the support you have also generously extended to my graduate students.

Gratitude and thanks to the Queensland Rifle Association (QRA). Specifically, I would like to thank Maartje, Brian, Peter and your wonderful team at QRA. Thank you for allowing me to bring my class to your range year after year. My favourite thing about the projects we've worked on together is seeing how much my students have developed a love of learning through interacting with you and your team. Without your generosity to me and my students, it would not have been possible to understand the important contribution your community makes understanding the contentious issues of gun control. Your collaboration has impacted my approach to this research in ways I had not anticipated. Thank you.

To Emma Belgrove. I have no idea what this project would have looked like without you. From the very beginning, you have helped me formulate the big ideas behind this project as well as facilitating the tasks to make it happen. Our travels across the country will always be one of the highlights of my research career and I thank you for coming along for this journey with me.

To Angela Elvery, Kathleen DeRooy and Amy Templar. Each one of you has, at some point, worked on this project and been a valuable contribution to the work, and to me. Kathleen worked on the original report submitted to industry, and without her input and hard work, this project would have fallen behind schedule. Thank you. Angela and Amy have been part of my firearms research team since 2020. As part of that team, you have also been subjected to judgement based on what others, including educated researchers, believe a "firearms researcher" is. You have handled these unfortunate judgements well, although I'm sorry I could not shield you from that better. I have been incredibly thankful that you have been willing to be part of this journey. Thank you. Angela, Amy, Emma and Kathleen, along with my PhD students Natalie Fennell and Thamali Ranasinghe, have also provided me with encouragement during times of doubt and overwhelm. They are a wonderful example of why our graduate students are central to the success of our careers as academics. I have learned as much from them as I hope they have learned from me. Thank you.

Professor Bob Crutchfield is primarily responsible for the academic I am today. He was my PhD advisor and has continued to mentor me throughout my career. But even more importantly, it is his friendship that has had the largest impact on my work. He has read drafts for me, listened to me talk through the elements of the manuscript, helped me make good decisions about publishing and has encouraged me when I didn't think I was capable of finishing. I could not have done this without his mentoring and friendship. I will always be eternally grateful for your support. Thank you.

To my UQ colleagues Sarah Bennett, Robin Fitzgerald, Lynda Cheshire, Jonah Rimer, Emma Antrobus, Amelia Radke, Greg Marston, Ashnil Murray and Cameron Parsell. At some point along this journey, you have either read chapters, encouraged me to keep going, been generous with your time as I worked through my thinking on this manuscript, or helped me prioritise the space to do the deep work necessary to complete it. That space for deep work that we so crave in academic is increasingly difficult to find alongside our teaching and administrative responsibilities so my gratitude in encouraging me to find that space is greatly appreciated.

To the fabulous students of the 2021 cohort of CRIM3039 (Advanced Crime Theory) at the University of Queensland. Your willingness to embrace the collaborative activities at QRA and engage with the challenging and difficult topics of gun control were a source of encouragement at a time I needed it. While some may be surprised that an undergraduate cohort of students could be so influential, you were a reminder that the centre of this book is about learning from others. Thank you.

To my fellow members of the Justice and Society Cluster at UQ Social Science. I'm particularly thankful for the time shared writing in community with you all. Thank you for your encouragement, your comradery and your willingness to embrace the messiness of finding time to write among the increasing workloads of our academic lives.

To Professors Lee Libby and Diana Knauf. Your support, mentoring and influence early in my education have had a long-lasting impact on my career. You both saw potential in me before I saw it in myself. You gave me a long-lasting love of learning, a passion for inquiry and inspiration to do more with life than just publish more stuff. This book is written and inspired by those things you have given me. For anyone who believes that a community college education is somehow less than any other, I beg them to look at the success of my career (of which I am just one example) and know that much of it was inspired by, supported by and the foundation laid by these two professors during my community colleges years when I first moved to Seattle. Thank you.

To Jessica Phillips and Thomas Sutton and your team at Routledge. Thank you for your support in helping me bring this book together. I have very much appreciated the time and engagement with the content you have provided me.

To my wonderful family. Aria, Aidan, Jasper and Keira. You have very much been along for this ride. It's stressful to have to write something so important and I know at times that stress must have shown. And to Wes. My husband and colleague. Thank you for being my unwavering support in this messy process of publishing. I could not have done this without your love and encouragement.

LIST OF ABBREVIATIONS

AR-15	ArmaLite Rifle 15
CGC	Coalition for Gun Control
CMT	Compliance Motivation Framework
GCA	Gun Control Australia
NFA	National Firearms Agreement
NSW	New South Wales
QLD	Queensland
QRA	Queensland Rifle Association
SAFE	Secure Ammunition and Firearms Enforcement Act of 2013
SSAA	Sporting Shooters Association of Australia
USA	United States of America
VIC	Victoria
WA	Western Australia

INTRODUCTION

On April 28, 1996, a 25-year-old male took a Colt AR-15 semi-automatic rifle and killed 35 people, wounding 23 others in and around Tasmania's historic tourist site of Port Arthur. At the time, this incident set the record for the deadliest mass murder in the world – until the Pulse nightclub shooting in Orlando, Florida, in 2016. On April 29, 1996, the shooter was taken into custody after setting alight the guesthouse in which he had held a hostage in an attempt to evade police. He was convicted and given a prison term of 35 life sentences, one for each of his victims, and 1652 additional years in prison to be served concurrently. Today, what is most remembered about this incident in Australia and around the world is the rapid response from the then *conservative* government, which instituted widespread gun reforms, tightening gun control across the country *within 12 weeks* of the Port Arthur incident. Gun control in Australia and the rapid response from the government in the wake of this incident have become a hallmark of Australian identity and have led Australia to become the poster child for gun control around the world.

December 14, 2012, in Newtown, Connecticut, June 11, 2016 in Orlando, Florida, and February 14, 2018 in Parkland, Florida, all mark dates and events that have reignited gun control debates around the world but primarily focus on the US response to gun violence. These events were opportunities for the US States and Congress to respond, as the Australian government had done in 1996, but ultimately resulted in watered-down gun laws that do not appear to have resonated with the public cry for intervention.[1]

DOI: 10.4324/9781003271642-1

The battle for gun reform appears to be steep; the number of guns and ammunition currently owned by US citizens is difficult to measure, and the powerful and influential force of anti-gun control lobby groups makes widespread reform feel impossible. Public discourse about gun control has centred on conversations about the effectiveness of gun control – do more guns lead to less or more crime?[2] – and protection of constitutional rights to own a gun.[3] These are both valuable conversations, but ultimately have not resulted in moving the debate forward on how to achieve gun reform in the US context, how to bring the gun-owning community on board with gun reform, or how to reconcile the availability of guns with gun violence. In addition, gun researchers have primarily focused on the overarching link between gun laws and gun violence rates but have been limited in providing understanding, analysis and direction in the implementation process or how to garner support from the community most impacted by gun reform.[4] This book aims to fill this gap by examining what lessons can be learned, especially for ongoing gun control debates in the US, from the Australian experience of gun control, a place where reform was met with widespread backlash from gun owners and legitimate gun dealers yet has been able to achieve widespread compliance and acceptance with most reforms.

Why Guns and Why Me?

I never intended to be a firearms researcher. My first gun raid with law enforcement took me down this unexpected pathway. I had given a seminar about perceptions of terrorism in the Australian population when two firearms licencing police asked me if I believed the increase in firearms ownership in Australia was due to fear of terrorism. I had no idea that the rate of firearms ownership had been increasing, but I did not think that fear of terrorism was a likely cause. This conversation took place in December 2014, a time when the global "war on terror" had permeated social and political discourse in Australia, perhaps more so than ever before. The Australian city of Sydney had just experienced an event framed as a terrorist act, known as the "Sydney Siege", where an armed gunman took 18 people hostage in a popular downtown café. Hostages were asked to hold Islamic flags at the window and after a long standoff, two hostages were killed along with the gunman. I had no doubt that conversations about terrorism were being held in every household across the country, but even the limited knowledge I had about firearms and gun control, didn't lead me to connect fear of terrorism to a rise in ownership – at least not in Australia.

I spent 12 years living in the USA before I moved back to Australia in 2011 to continue my research on perceptions of crime, communities and violence. None of my prior research suggested that in the Australian context, a perceived increase in the risk of terrorism was leading Australians to arm themselves, though there was some evidence that gun purchases increased in the wake of shooting events in the USA. However, the weapons inspection police were adamant that people were procuring firearms at alarming rates and asked me to take a closer look. I was invited to a "gun raid" in a major Australian city so that I could have a better understanding of the kinds of issues firearms licencing police were dealing with on a day-to-day basis. Though this was a departure from my own area of research, I was curious and agreed to attend. The raid centred on a suburban gun dealer, whom the police were concerned, was in violation of a range of firearms regulations. The "raid" consisted of an audit of all firearms at the dealership, which included checking the type of firearm and its serial number with how they were registered in the system. The police were to confiscate anything unregistered or improperly registered.

The day began with the firearms inspection crew in the parking lot outside the gun shop, waiting for the gun dealer and the lead inspector to negotiate entry onto the premises. The waiting continued while police ensured that the premises were safe to enter. Concerns had been raised about safety given the improper storage of gunpowder and other explosives. I overheard concerns about static in clothing setting off explosives, and, unsure if these concerns were serious or made in jest by season firearms inspectors, I wondered whether this was my wisest research decision. Once inside, I observed a small retail space with an upstairs storage room and office crowded with guns and ammunition. I felt the tension and anger of the gun dealer as the inspection team moved in to set up. Over the course of the day, the inspection team and the gun dealer had a number of heated exchanges, including the gun dealer's threats to shoot himself. Given the sheer number of firearms and ammunition at arm's length, it struck me how easy it would be for him to follow through. Regardless, the inspection team continued with their work clearing firearms, checking serial numbers and comparing dealer records with the registry. Multiple violations were discovered. The most serious of these included firearms registered as "blank fire" that had not been altered to only fire blanks – they could still fire real bullets; a fully automatic firearm that was banned after the 1996 reforms, multiple registration errors and improper storage of firearms – including storing firearms while still loaded. All of these are violations of Australia's gun laws.

I understood the seriousness of these violations and the risk they posed to firearms owners, the dealer himself and potentially the community. However, as I sat back and watched the raid unfold inside the small gun shop, what struck me was the underlying anguish of the dealer, the drive and focus to uncover every and all violations, no matter how small, by registry police, and the complicated inventory process for checking every firearm performed by registry staff. Serious violations were certainly documented, but after reflection, I found myself critical of the narrative I was given prior to attending the raid. The police perspective appeared to assume violations were linked to the purposeful circumvention of the law. Instead, my observations of the inventory process and the kinds of errors that were made by the dealer were that the gun dealer was *not* motivated to disregard the law, supply firearms to those who should not have them or purposely pose a risk to community safety by violating storage or registry regulations. Instead, I saw a business owner who had some sloppy business practices that were not up to date with technological change or the expectations contained in current firearms regulations. The gun shop lacked up-to-date computer technology, was overcrowded with supplies and was short on space, but I could see no real signs of purposeful, underhanded behaviour in relation to selling firearms.

The raid lasted all day, and the small gun shop was often crowded with registry staff, detectives, registry police, the dealer and his wife, the dealer's lawyer, myself and another "firearms expert".[5] In the afternoon, the raid became quieter and less crowded as the inventory process was well underway. This gave me the opportunity to take a closer look at the inventory checking process that registry staff were performing on every firearm. Registry police would take a firearm and clear it to make sure it was not loaded. This was then passed to another registry officer to double-check that it was clear. This officer then read out the serial number, gun make and model to be checked against the dealer's inventory list and the firearms registry. All anomalies were noted, and there were many; barrel numbers listed instead of serial numbers, serial numbers with errors, makes and models mixed up or incorrect and firearms registered under the wrong category. As I watched the registry officer himself struggle to find serial numbers on a range of firearms (even having to pull some firearms into pieces to check), it struck me that the registration process itself is naturally prone to human error. Errors in the registry looked like typos or a misreading of the inventory list (which were often handwritten). Each of these errors, no matter how easy or innocent, was also a potential violation that the dealer could be prosecuted for.

Observing this inventory process also distilled the important role that dealers play in the registry process for gun control in Australia. Each dealer must report every firearm acquisition and sale to the firearms registry. Private gun sales also need to be brokered by a licenced gun dealer. State gun registries track the ownership and use of firearms across the country and heavily rely on gun dealers to populate the registry with information that can then be used to follow the history of the firearm. Yet, while gun dealers clearly occupy a pivotal role in maintaining gun registries – one of the hallmarks of Australia's gun control – they are also subject to its enforcement. Therefore, they are both experts who are relied on by the police to inform the registry and simultaneously subject to police enforcement and scrutiny, highlighting the dual and complicated nature of their roles. Months after the gun raid, I continued to think about this dual role in light of the tense interactions between registry police and the dealer during the raid that day. However, I also observed familiarity between the dealer and registry staff; there was a history, and they were known to each other. Registry police get to know dealers well because the nature of their work requires frequent contact, even if only by phone or email. During the raid, the underlying tension between dealer and police appeared to me to be a result of these dual roles colliding – the expert became the subject of the heavy arm of police enforcement, in which there was also an underlying professional relationship.

Since this raid, I have had the opportunity to talk to many gun dealers, hunters and shooters from around the country. I ask them about their interactions with police, and many of them report feeling as if police are "out to get them" or feel that police are unnecessarily punitive in their role of checking dealer inventories. In fact, the perception that police, the media and politicians were "out to get them" or treated them with suspicion was a frequent part of gun dealer narratives regarding their experiences and feelings about gun control in Australia. I soon received firsthand experience with this kind of guardedness and suspicion, where reactions to my research were sometimes met with caution and the assumption I had fallen in with "those people". Two years from the beginning of this project and five years on from that first raid, my understanding of why the caution and guardedness of the public are prominent is as important to understanding gun control and its effectiveness as the legislation itself.

This book is based on two studies that were inspired by my observations on this first gun raid. The Australian Gun Dealer Study sought to understand the gun dealer's role more fully from their perspective in order to examine and explore their role in the gun control compliance process in Australia. The Firearms Court Study sought to understand how judges conceptualise important questions like "who is fit and proper to own a firearm" or how mental health concerns or domestic violence concerns are being dealt with under the current legislation. As Australia continues to be placed on a global pedestal for its quick action after the Port Arthur Massacre in 1996, it is time to move beyond asking simple questions about the link between gun control and gun-related death rates and crime. A deeper understanding of what gun control looks like on the ground and how to achieve it is critical. This requires an in-depth exploration of those who are most involved and affected by gun control, those who are critical to the process of maintaining compliance and an understanding of the latent and manifest consequences of the enforcement of gun control.

Gun Control Laws Today

A great deal of misperception of what gun control is and what it should look like stimulates assumptions about gun control around the world; "Australia has no guns", "America has no gun control", "the government took away all the guns in Australia" or "anyone can go buy a gun in America", are just a few examples of the mistaken understanding of what gun control looks like. In reality, almost all countries have some form of gun control, even the USA. However, form and levels of restrictiveness vary over time and space. The global debate has been dominated by the American experience of highly publicised mass shootings and the loudest voices in the American gun control debate. This debate tends to suggest that regulating guns is abnormal and a violation of rights. However, if we look at gun control regulations around the world, it is evident that regulation, even restrictive regulation, is common.

In **Japan**, firearms legislation bans automatic and semiautomatic firearms (including handguns) for all civilians unless they are involved in professional shooting sports. All forms of gun ownership require a licence, which includes background checks, training and a written and practical test. Owners must also demonstrate a valid reason to own a firearm.[6] These valid reasons are limited to hunting and shooting sports only. Japan's stance on firearms primarily comes from a prohibitive approach and is considered one of the most restrictive examples of gun control in the world. All gun sales and acquisitions must be through a licenced dealer – even private sales. Penalties for the unlawful possession of a firearm could receive a maximum penalty of 15 years in prison.[7]

In the **United Kingdom**, automatic, semiautomatic, all handguns and armour-piecing ammunition are banned from civilian ownership. Licences are required, and applicants must pass a background check and a character reference. In order to own a firearm, applicants must also demonstrate a *need to own*; hunting, sports and collecting are all considered valid reasons. In addition, gun owners must requalify for ownership every five years. Additional limits placed on gun owners include limiting the number of firearms and ammunition that can be possessed. The maximum penalty for unlawful possession is between 5 and 10 years in prison.[7] The UK's gun control regulations are also considered exceptionally restrictive, and the anti-gun culture is reflective in their policing culture, where foot patrol officers do not carry a firearm while on duty.[8]

In **Switzerland**, the right to own a firearm is guaranteed by law, though fully automatic weapons are banned except in exceptional circumstances. Licences are required for all handguns and semi-automatic firearms. Ownership of shotguns and rifles is regulated, but licences are typically not required. If the firearm requires a licence, then potential applicants also need to provide a genuine reason for possession unless it is strictly for hunting, sport or collecting. This means that outside of these standard reasons, a Swiss applicant must make the case for why ownership is needed. Background checks for criminal and mental health histories are common, and training is required only when an owner wants to conceal and carry their firearm. Private sales are prohibited, once again maintaining the importance of the gun dealer, who must broker every acquisition and sale. The maximum penalty for possessing one of the restricted firearms (not a shotgun or rifle) is 3 years in prison.[8]

Canada bans all short-barrelled handguns, automatic firearms except those made before 1978, and a range of firearms that have been altered from the original model. Licences are required for handguns but not typically for shotguns or rifles, nor are owners required to report a genuine need for these firearms unless they are on the restricted or prohibited list of firearms. Background checks are required for all licences, which include checking mental health, criminal, drug addiction and domestic violence histories. Training in the theoretical and practical use of firearms is also required for all licences. A departure from other examples of gun control, correspondence with the next of kin (partner or spouse) to notify the intent to purchase must occur before any licence is issued. Gun sales can be made by licenced owners who are not obligated to perform background checks on their sales. Gun dealers are required to sell prohibited or restricted firearms, but these dealers are also not obligated to perform background checks. The penalty for unlawful possession of a firearm in Canada carries between 5 and 10 years in prison.[8]

In the **USA**, the right to possess a firearm is generally guaranteed by federal law, but there is a wide variety of levels of these rights from state to state – each state responsible for regulating gun control in their own way. Fully automatic firearms are allowed but subject to federal licencing requirements. In most states, private possession of automatic firearms, including handguns, is allowed and licences are not required. Incidents of domestic violence generally require revocation of firearms and the denial of further firearms purchases. While gun dealers are important, they are not required for private sales, though they are required to make sure customers pass a background check. The maximum penalty for unlawful possession is 10 years in prison.[7] A survey of the US States demonstrates there are various approaches and levels of restriction across the country. For example, Washington State has recently expanded "red flag" laws that allow temporary removal of firearms from those deemed to be a risk to themselves or others, while Missouri allows citizens to conceal and carry firearms in public without a permit.[8]

More detail will be given in Chapter 1 about Australian gun controls and restrictions, but generally, there is much overlap with the countries summarised above. Background checks and licences are required; genuine reasons must be cited; gun dealers must broker every sale and acquisition; and training is necessary for any firearms applicant. Australia's gun laws differ from those of other nations by banning a larger range of firearms from civilian possession. Waiting periods are also used to put space between being approved for the licence and being able to purchase the firearm. Storage regulations and limits of the amount and types of ammunition that can be possessed are common across all the states and territories in Australia. Penalties for unlawful possession could carry a prison sentence of up to 20 years.[8] Australia's restrictions are not radically different from those in Japan, the UK or other nations, which suggests that Australia's position as a leading example of gun control is not just about restrictions and regulations. The popularity of the Australian example is likely rooted in two distinct perceptions: the perceived effectiveness of gun laws to reduce mass shootings and the response by a conservative government to enact gun control quickly after one of the most deadly mass shootings in the world.

Gun Control Research Today

Research on gun control worldwide generally focuses on two main areas of interest: gun control effectiveness and public opinion on gun control. Gun control effectiveness examines whether gun control measures are effective in reducing crime rates, suicides or gun-related injuries/deaths more generally. Public opinion research typically examines patterns of public support for gun control laws in an attempt to understand the pulse of citizens regarding current regulations. Additional research has focused on gun culture, primarily in North America, in order to understand the normative attitudes and behaviours of those who hold strongly to identities involving shooting and gun ownership. However, research has been more limited in regard to the implementation of gun control and how to achieve compliance with gun laws. This book attempts to expand this area of investigation by drawing attention to the implementation processes that are core to understanding the enforcement of and compliance with gun control in the Australian experience. Australia's experience provides lessons, successes and mistakes for gun reform globally, but particularly in the USA, where gun reform is an active agenda item.

Research on the broader links between gun control measures and gun related death rates do not always provide a clear and consistent message about gun control effectiveness.[9] A large portion of existing research focuses on measuring gun control effectiveness in the United States, an outlier in the amount and strictness of gun control around the world. Studies from the US context suggest mixed results in the influence of gun control on homicide and suicide – some suggesting that more gun control increases crime due to the reduction of potential victims being armed, and others suggest no significant impact and effect on homicide at all.[10] However, most US studies find that background checks are the one aspect of gun control that shows the most promise in reducing suicide, homicide and gun related deaths more generally.[11]

Research evaluating the impact that post 1996 gun control has had on gun related deaths, homicide and suicide in Australia is also mixed. The most consistent evidence suggests that gun control has reduced the rate of suicides since the 1996 gun control measures were introduced.[12] A recent systematic review of gun control studies in Australia found that there was no statically significant impact of gun control on homicide rates.[13] In contrast, a cross-national study on the impact of gun regulation on homicide and suicide across 16 European nations finds that stricter gun control reduced gun related homicides, suicides and general (non-gun) homicides and suicides.[14] It is almost impossible to distil the evidence for the effectiveness of gun control by focusing on the broader impact of laws on gun related death alone.

The current literature has a number of limitations that requires researchers to rethink how we look at "effectiveness" and the approach to gun research more generally. First, there is little, if any, consistency on how we measure the concept of gun control. Researchers have chosen a range of proxies for gun control including gun ownership rates, number of regulations and the strictness of regulations.[15] Each one of these has implications for how we could view the meaning of research findings. Second, pointed out by a number of systematic reviews on gun control, the diversity of methods employed to undertake research on gun control does not allow for easy comparison that might generate collective agreement on gun control effectiveness.[16] Third, a large portion of research does not take into account the range of social structural variables (macro level) that are also likely to contribute to gun related death rates overtime; such as innovation in healthcare that reduce the rate of death, welfare provisions or other factors criminologists have demonstrated contribute to overall crime rates. These omissions do not allow for a full examination of the impact gun control legislation has on gun violence. Fourth, and perhaps more importantly for policymakers, while research has concentrated on these broader links between gun control measures and gun-related death rates, research has been limited in examining the micro-level factors that demonstrate how gun control might work or the impact of its implementation on individuals and businesses, all of which contribute to effectiveness and compliance with the law. As a result, we have an inconsistent picture of what gun control looks like, what its effectiveness might be and limited knowledge on who is impacted and what it takes to implement gun control.

Despite limitations in gun control research, the predominant opinion by the public, by politicians, by media outlets and by social scientists in Australia is that gun control has worked. Politicians, journalist and researchers have all pointed to the lack of mass shootings in Australia since April 28, 1996, as evidence that gun control has been effective. However, even this becomes problematic when you consider the number of ways one might define a mass shooting.[17] So, what then explains Australia's placement on a pedestal for gun control? Australia's gun control experience is important because "success" is not just defined as the reduction in gun-related deaths and injuries that regulation and control are primarily used for. Successful gun control is not simply about effectiveness but acceptance by the public, the gun-owning community and conservative governments. Australia's example is useful for understanding how to achieve compliance with laws unpalatable to the gun-owning community.

Australia as the Gun Control Poster Child

On December 14, 2012, a 20-year-old male gunman entered Sandy Hook Elementary School in Newtown, Connecticut, USA and killed 26 people. Twenty of these were children under the age of eight. Despite public outcry for gun control, the deaths of small children were only enough to implement limited gun control legislation, leaving many wondering how bad gun violence must get before the government will act. In the aftermath of the political debates about gun control after Sandy Hook, political comedian John Oliver delivered the first of a 3-part series on gun control in Australia, in which he states "In American, we are told that gun control is not possible, but in Australia, they've shown it is, providing a fantastic lesson for America to ignore". Oliver draws attention to Australian gun control policies by highlighting the swift implementation after the Port Arthur massacre, that it was driven by a conservative government despite it being unpopular with their political voting base, and that even though some gun owners did not like the idea at first, many have come to understand and support gun control. This three-part series has been viewed over five million times online by viewers around the world and still circulates on social media eight years later, often after another mass shooting in the USA, demonstrating the lasting impact that Australia's gun control experience continues to have.

On October 1, 2017, a 64-year-old male gunman shot and killed 58 people from his hotel window looking down onto the Las Vegas Strip, where a large number of music fans gathered for the Route 91 Harvest Music Festival. The media quickly focused on how it was possible for the gunman to injure or kill so many people in such a short amount of time. The use of a bump fire stock, a tool fit onto a rifle in order to utilise the recoil action to change the firing mechanism from semi-automatic to automatic, was found on the firearm after the gunman was taken down. Calls to ban bump-fire stocks quickly dominated the public conversation about gun control. Again, debate called on Australia's example for answering questions about what can be regulated beyond the firearm itself. Many argued that it would be too difficult and too far-reaching for the US government to start banning specific parts of firearms, given that by themselves, without being attached to a firearm, they pose no threat to the community. It was quickly pointed out that though bump fire stocks are regulated inconsistently in Australia, most regulations ban or require permits for any alteration of a firearm more broadly, particularly alterations that change a firearm from semi-automatic to automatic. In response to this global discussion on the use and availability of bump-fire stocks after the Las Vegas shooting, the Australian government moved to ban bump-fire stocks across the country, further tightening Australian gun laws and demonstrating swift government reaction to gun violence even when it's not happening inside Australia.

On March 15, 2019, a 28-year-old male, shot and killed 51 people after a shooting spree at two mosques as members gathered for prayer in Christchurch, New Zealand. New Zealand has a long history of established gun control, not unlike many of the countries discussed above. The question of how the gunman was able to access these firearms was quickly highlighted, not as a failure of adequate gun control but as a failure to properly implement and carry out the appropriate process for issuing firearms of this kind. Yet, the New Zealand government quickly mobilised a review of current legislation and began the process of tightening gun laws. Again, Australia's experience was heavily relied on as a point of comparison for what *should* be done to tighten New Zealand's laws.[18] In the immediate aftermath of this terrorist event, direct comparisons between New Zealand and Australian gun laws dominated the media's focus.

In each of these tragic instances, there was widespread public outcry for a government response to crack down on firearm availability and create stricter gun control. In each of these instances, Australia's experience with gun control is used as a global example to follow when swift and strong gun control is needed. Each time Australia's experience is brought into global debates, it reinvigorates conversations and debates about Australian gun policy and how it is working now in pockets of the Australian population, demonstrating the reciprocal effects that gun violence has around the world. These reinvigorated debates in Australia are not unlike those elsewhere; the loudest voices promote the need for stricter gun control, while others claim gun policy is overkill. These debates also have a tendency to drown out more moderate voices in between and concentrate the debate at the extremes, hampering efforts to move the gun debate forward.

Current Debates about Gun Control

High rates of gun-related crime and a number of high-profile mass shootings in the USA have dominated 21st-century debates about gun control around the world. In the wake of some of those well-known and highly televised incidents, particularly those that involved the deaths of children, the public outcry for something to be done about tightening access to firearms such as high-powered assault rifles has grown. Calls for the creation of a more restrictive gun policy are met with pushback from powerful lobby groups who argue that the US Constitution ensures the right to own a firearm. These lobby groups have been so powerful that they have been able to influence government research strategies, making it hard for researchers to ask and evaluate good questions about what kinds of restrictions might work and how they might be implemented effectively.[19] The push and pull of pro-gun and pro-gun control groups dominate public discourse but inevitably do not move the debate towards solutions. Each has their own motivations and agendas; one is motivated by reducing violence, the other by protecting rights. So easy it has become to assume that pro-gun control activists do not care about rights. Just as it is easy to believe that pro-gun lobby groups do not care about victims of gun violence. This standoff prevents the ability to move forward on any reasonable effort to create a good common-sense policy about guns that would be similar to many other nations around the world. Despite this seeming deadlock, many US states have made slow and incremental changes to policy that incorporate greater restrictions on firearms, particularly since the Sandy Hook massacre in 2012. After Sandy Hook, the State of New York passed the Secure Ammunition and Firearms Enforcement (SAFE) Act, one of the most comprehensive firearms control acts in the country, which sought to institute a wide range of controls, including limiting access to a broader range of firearms and requiring background checks to be done by ammunition dealers, among numerous other provisions.[20] Other states have incrementally followed suit. It appears that, however slow, the US is increasingly responding to the public outcry for preventing gun violence.

In the wake of growing attention to preventing gun violence, a new generation of activists has begun to mount pressure on lawmakers to respond to the increasing number of incidents where firearms are used. In particular, the Parkland, Florida, shooting at Marjory Stoneman Douglas High School, in which 17 people were shot by a lone gunman, spurred young activists to call for the government to respond. Their raw and angry protests have been seen, heard and echoed in many places across the world. The March for Our Lives protest was one of the largest marches of student-led demonstrators since the Vietnam War, with participants estimated in the millions.[21] Furthermore, these protests were joined around the world in support of more restrictions on guns in the US. Marches were held in Vienna, Paris, Brussels, Amsterdam, Melbourne, Sydney and Tel Aviv. The global support for young American protestors marked a turning point for the kind of pressure on lawmakers to act as the gun debate was placed front and centre on the global stage.

In Australia in 1996, though lawmakers were quick to respond to the Port Arthur incident, it was not without public pressure to do so. Two organisations, Gun Control Australia (GCA) and The Coalition for Gun Control (CGC), had previous experience in attempting to mobilise the public to pressure governments for more uniform gun control across Australia as a result of mass shootings prior to 1996.[22] After Port Arthur, the CGC in particular had a ready and waiting base of supporters as well as a newly outraged public to aid in pressuring the conservative government to act. In Australia's case, arguments about the right to bear arms were mainly absent from public debates. Australia's constitution does not award gun ownership as a right, nor is there any evidence that gun ownership in Australia is linked to a culture of fear and self-defence. However, pro-gun groups were concerned about the government's heavy-handed and quick approach that left very little time for people to comply with legislation – essentially making previously law-abiding citizens criminals for owning what they had always owned and, for the most part, used responsibly.

April 28, 2016, marked the 20th anniversary of the Port Arthur massacre, where 35 people lost their lives. Media coverage of the anniversary centred again on the gun control debate, particularly as a reflection of its effectiveness 20 years after the National Firearms Agreement (NFA) had been implemented around the country. Twenty years on, emotions about guns, gun crime and gun ownership remain high, and elements of gun control remain controversial. In 2017, a review of Australia's gun laws commissioned by an anti-gun political party suggests that gun laws have been watered down over time; restrictions on non-licenced individuals to shoot supervised at a gun range have been lifted; and restrictions on accessibility of hunting grounds have been eased.[23] In addition, anti-gun lobbyists often criticise the provision for minors as young as 14 years old to access firearms, even with supervision and strict conditions in place. At the heart of these global and local debates lies a core question: how much freedom do we give up in order to protect the community from serious gun-related violence? In order to answer this question, we need a better understanding of the distinction between guns on the black market and those legally obtained by law-abiding citizens. We need to look at the communities in which young people are learning about firearms, and we need to look at and separate interests of legal firearms owners from the horrors experienced by victims of gun violence. To ignore these nuances in gun control is to relegate debate on gun policy to a static and unresponsive set of policies that results in demonising legal gun owners and re-victimising those that have been affected by gun violence. This book seeks to focus on these nuances that need to be understood as part of the gun control acceptance, implementation and compliance process.

The Australian Gun Dealer Study

The current gaps in literature, the considerable impact that Australian gun laws have on the global gun control debate and the problematic way in which these debates are often framed call for a deeper understanding of gun control and what it takes to achieve it, implement it and deal with the inevitable flow on effects on legal gun owners. The gun dealer study that is at the centre of this book focuses on gun dealers for one important reason: gun dealers are the linchpins in maintaining gun control and ensuring compliance with gun control. Without gun dealer cooperation, the firearms registration system would fail. Without gun dealer cooperation, the ability to achieve any measurable compliance with the legislation would fail. That being said, gun dealers, much like gun owners, are often perceived to be people who are opposed to gun control. This study sought to explore gun dealer views and experiences, which have yet to be considered in the academic literature on gun control. Globally, gun dealers occupy a critical but dual role in the gun control compliance process. Gun dealers are both experts able to inform police and populate gun registries with information, but they are also subject to police scrutiny and are monitored heavily by law enforcement.

While gun dealers may be small in population, they occupy a pivotal role, and therefore their views about gun control become important in understanding how compliance is achieved in the implementation of gun control.

The aim was to recruit as many gun dealers as possible for a 1–2-hour interview. The research team mailed out information sheets to let dealers know that the research was being planned and that they might be contacted to participate. These flyers were sent to every dealer listed in the online yellow pages across Australia. Recruitment focused on gun dealers as opposed to those who sold only ammunition or other kinds of regulated tools, like swords and knives, in order to ensure that we were able to capture experiences with the National Firearms Agreement and its implementation after the Port Arthur massacre. Recruitment was easier in some states than in others. In Queensland, Western Australia, the Northern Territory and Victoria, gun dealers were excited to participate, and we readily recruited 6–10 dealers in each of these states.[24] In others, dealers were sceptical of researchers and were not willing to go on the record in expressing their views. However, with the exception of South Australia and Tasmania, dealers were recruited from all the other Australian states and territories. Overall, we completed 40 interviews.

Preliminary analysis of gun dealer interviews led to an expansion of this project in 2017. A number of issues were raised by gun dealers in regard to mental health concerns for gun owners, how to manage gun licences in the event of domestic violence, experiences of stigmatisation because of gun ownership or gun-related business and how decisions are made by judges and police about licence revocations. To explore these further, I collected all available court decisions from NFA violation cases in Queensland, New South Wales and Western Australia for analysis in order to understand court decision-making in cases brought against legal gun owners. Of particular interest was the examination of how judges made decisions about firearms owners who had mental health concerns, how they constructed the meaning of a "fit and proper person" and whether the relative privilege of this group moderated any stigma of being a firearms owner. These results are also drawn from this book.

What This Book Is and Isn't

This book has been written with the aim of contributing to the academic literature, public policy and public discourse on gun control by understanding how gun control is achieved on the ground. This contribution is important because current literature has ignored in-depth understandings of the realities of gun control compliance from the perspectives of individual gun owners or dealers, who are perceived to be the hardest to convince that gun control is needed. In addition, this contribution provides nuance to the current debate, particularly in the USA, that the presence of gun control is a violation of freedoms and rights and that criticisms of gun control automatically mean acceptance of risks to the community. This study is important because it provides in-depth data on the experiences of some of the most important actors in the gun control compliance process and allows our perspectives on gun control to push past rhetoric and think about the reality of the problem of gun violence and how to solve it. Furthermore, it also aims to provide a broader context for understanding the role that the community of legal and law-abiding firearms owns can and are willing to play in conversations about safety and control – providing a different narrative than one that suggests staunch resistance.

I came into this study with curiosity and the knowledge that my assumptions about gun control would be tested. I was genuinely interested in what gun dealers had to say, but I also knew that I too often succumbed to the assumption that any criticism of gun control was equal to reckless endangerment of the community. I considered myself to be an advocate of gun control – and still do – but I felt that my field of criminology and sociology had more to offer in moving gun control debates forward and moving us beyond dogmatic support for and/or against the regulations of guns. That is, the fields of sociology and criminology can provide a broader and more informed framework for understanding violence and government regulations beyond questions about gun control effectiveness.

This project pushed me out of my comfort zone on a number of levels; I expected to hold politically different values from those I was studying. I was aware that shooting was primarily dominated by men and that it can be an expensive occupation or hobby, and I was therefore entering a community of relative white and male privilege. I knew that many were angry about how firearms owners were treated during the implementation of the NFA by politicians and the media, and I knew that because of that treatment, many would be sceptical of the kind of research I was wanting to do. I expected white, male, right-wing conservative views to dominate my experience of gun dealers and shooters when I began this research. However, this was not my experience. While this group of people is the epitome of white privilege in many ways, I also found that shooting sports are diversifying racially and ethnically, and women shooters are the fastest-growing demographic in gun ownership.[25] I found that political identity and political leanings were diverse – political identity driven by the concerns of shooters is just as common as those with values of environmental conservation, animal welfare and community wellbeing. I did encounter sexist attitudes, racist attitudes and right-wing extremism, but I am unable to use a broad brush to paint this entire population with those labels – I simply found as much diversity in values and opinions as I might experience in the general population. The fact that these things were surprising to me demonstrated my unconscious bias, likely shaped by broader political discourse about gun control and firearms owners that had accumulated in my mind in my 12 years of living in the United States, and my upbringing in Australia – particularly during my formative years in the 1980s and 1990s.

This book is not a pro-gun control or anti-gun control book. It provides lessons from Australian successes and failures in implementing gun control from the perspectives of those critical to its sustainability. This book also aims to provide the possibility of a different narrative about gun control that drives debate away from the extremes towards a more balanced and reasonable conversation about community safety and regulation. These balanced conversations are not possible when the motivations of each side of the debate are perceived to be mutually exclusive. It did not take me long to realise that there is much overlap in the motives of pro-gun groups and pro-gun control groups in the Australian context. The current impasse can be solved by asking good research questions and being aware of the impact of our implicit biases in relation to our research, policy agendas and community platforms we choose to support. To do this, even researchers must remember to reflect on our political positioning in their research. The challenge for us as researchers is to be able to communicate, discuss and collaborate with those who hold different platforms and agendas from our own.

My position and my political values about gun control have not changed as a result of this work. However, they have become more compassionate and more open to listening to the views of others, even though I may not share their same passion for gun sports. I have learned how to hold valuable and inclusive discussions about solutions for gun violence. My experience as an academic over the last 10 years is that our political positions and our research agendas often align. As academics, it is easy, if not common, to advocate for and communicate our research to those who already share our political or philosophical positions. As researchers, we have a responsibility to the public to share and contribute our knowledge and research to those who can use it and put it into action: policymakers, policy enforcers and policy agenda setters. However, we also must remember that those who are foundationally different from our political position are our public too. We cannot begin to communicate with them if we have not stopped to understand their concerns and their positions, even when they make us uncomfortable. This book demonstrates the value of coming to terms with that discomfort.

Notes

1 Jacobs, J. B., & Fuhr, Z. (2019). *The toughest gun control law in the nation: The unfulfilled promise of New York's SAFE Act*. NYU Press.

2 Duggan, Mark. (2001). More guns, more crime. *Journal of Political Economy*, *109*, 1086–1114. 10.1086/322833

Kleck, G., Kovandzic, T., & Bellows, J. (2016). Does gun control reduce violent crime? *Criminal Justice Review*, *41*(4), 488–513.

3 Kleck, G. (2013). Gun control after Heller and McDonald: What cannot be done and what ought to be done. *Fordham Urban Law Journal*, *39*, 1383–1420

4 Killias, M., van Kesteren, J., & Rindlisbacher, M. (2001). Guns, violent crime, and suicide in 21 countries. *Canadian Journal of Criminology*, *43*, 429–448.

Ludwig, J., & Cook, P. J. (Eds.). (2004). Evaluating gun policy: Effects on crime and violence. Brookings Institution Press.

5 Registry staff are often sworn plain clothed police officers who are responsible for the administrative work associated with the firearms registry I and another researcher were present during the raid as "consultants to the registry".

6 Cook, P. J., & Goss, K. A. (2020). The gun debate: What everyone needs to know®. Oxford University Press, USA.

Kopel, D. B. (1993). Japanese gun control. *Asia Pacific Law Review*, 2(2), 26–52.

7 Gun policy. org

8 National Firearms Agreement. Commonwealth of Australia 1996.

9 Killias et al (2001), Ludwig et al, 2004)

10 Cook, P. (1978). The effect of gun availability on robbery and robbery murder: a cross-section study of 50 cities. Center for the Study of Justice Policy, Institute of Policy Sciences and Public Affairs, Duke University.

McPhedran, S. (2016). A systematic review of quantitative evidence about the impacts of Australian legislative reform on firearm homicide. *Aggression and Violent Behavior*, *28*, 64–72.

11 Nagin, D. S., Koper, C. S., & Lum, C. (2020). Policy recommendations for countering mass shootings in the United States. *Criminology & Public Policy*, *19*(1), 9–15.

12 Killias et al (2001)

13 Hahn, R A., Bilukha, O., Crosby, A. M., Fullilove, T., Liberman, A., Moscicki, E., ... Briss, P. A. (2005). Firearms laws and the reduction of violence: A systematic review. *American Journal of Preventive Medicine*, *28*, 40–70

14 Millias et al (2001)

15 Duwe, G. (2020). Patterns and prevalence of lethal mass violence. *Criminology & Public Policy*, *19*(1), 17–35.

16 Killias et al (2001); McPheadren, 2016;

17 Duwe (2020)

18 Every-Palmer, S., Cunningham, R., Jenkins, M., & Bell, E. (2020). The Christchurch mosque shooting, the media, and subsequent gun control reform in New Zealand: A descriptive analysis. *Psychiatry, Psychology and Law*, 1–12.

19 Carswell, S. M. (2019). Have we surrendered to gun violence in urban America? Federal neglect stymies efforts to stop the slaughter among young Black men. *Race and Justice*, 2153368719865306.

20 Jacobs & Fuhr (2019).

21 Zoller, H. M., & Casteel, D. (2021). # March for our lives: Health activism, diagnostic framing, gun control, and the gun industry. *Health Communication*, 1–11.

22 Newman, J., & Head, B. (2017). The national context of wicked problems: Comparing policies on gun violence in the US, Canada, and Australia. *Journal of Comparative Policy Analysis: Research and Practice*, *19*(1), 40–53.

23 'Malley, Nick (5 October 2017). "Australia's tough gun laws have been weakened by the states, new report". *The Sydney Morning Herald*.

24 Only one dealer was recruited in the Northern Territory. This is on par with the limited number of dealers available for participation in this region.

25 Bavas, Josh (May 15th 2016). Women lead the way in recreational shooting resurgence, figures show sharp rise in gun licensing. *ABC News*.

1

GUN CONTROL IN CONTEXT

> *The most important civil liberty ... is to stay alive and to be free from violence and death.*
>
> (John Howard, Australia's Prime Minister, National Summit on Terrorism, 2005)

On March 13, 1996, approximately one month before the Port Arthur massacre in Tasmania, a 43-year-old man from Glasgow entered a primary school in the Scottish town of Dunblane. He was armed with two nine-millimetre pistols and two revolvers, which he owned legally. As he entered the school, he began shooting randomly, primarily inside the school gymnasium, where children were getting ready for a PE lesson. Before turning the firearm on himself, he had shot 32 people in the space of three to five minutes, 17 of whom died from their injuries. Of those casualties, one was a teacher and 16 were primary school students in grade one, aged five to six years.

The UK government took quick legislative action in the wake of the Dunblane massacre and built on existing gun legislation to tighten the control of firearms across the UK. Bans on private handgun ownership and semi-automatic firearms, as well as mandatory registration for shotgun owners, were implemented across the UK by the end of 1997. The public outcry over the loss of so many young lives pressured the government to respond, but the strong grassroots movement led by the Dunblane community, including parents of the victims of the Dunblane massacre, demonstrates how influential the public can be in initiating and

DOI: 10.4324/9781003271642-2

supporting strong and swift government responses. For example, the Snowdrop Campaign, founded by concerned citizens and those who had lost loved ones in the Dunblane massacre, successfully petitioned the government to tighten gun laws when they found that the guns used were legally obtained. The effectiveness of this campaign was likely strengthened by the support of activists affected by a similar massacre in Hungerford, England, in 1987.

The debate about the merits of gun control after the Dunblane massacre bore marked similarities to current debates. Gun-owning groups felt the laws were an overreach and felt they were improperly made scapegoats for gun violence.[1] Prince Philip, the Duke of Edinburgh, famously liken the dangerousness of handguns to the dangerousness of cricket bats, suggesting that any tool could cause violence when it is misused.[2] Similar arguments exist today, 27 years on, where the gun lobby continues to shift the rhetoric towards risky people and potential criminals as opposed to the guns themselves as the centre of regulation.

I sometimes feel Australians forget about Dunblane. Instead, I have found that many adopt the view that Australia is somehow special in its response to mass shootings. But Australia is not unique. Governments globally have responded to mass shootings by tightening and enacting stronger legislation to control the flow and access to firearms in the name of community safety. The nature of the public outcry for a government response to violence is similar, the resistance from the gun lobby is similar and the legislative outcomes are remarkably similar. What is globally unique is its American experience – unique in the amount of gun-related violence and unique in the way in which governments have been unable to be galvanised by public support over pressure from the gun lobby.

Twenty-two years after the Dunblane massacre, a school shooting at Marjory Douglas Stoneman High School in Parkland, Florida, on February 14, 2018, left 17 dead and 17 injured. The 19-year-old former student also purchased his firearm legally in the state of Florida. Among those who lost their lives were three staff members and 14 high school students aged between 14 and 18 years. In the aftermath, parents of the Dunblane massacre wrote a letter of support to survivors and victims' families of the Parkland massacre. Parkland families and students affected by the massacre had begun a campaign of their own with the aim of galvanising support for gun control legislation across the USA. In that letter, the Dunblane family wrote:

> *The gunman owned his four handguns legally, and we knew it had been too easy for him to arm himself with lethal weapons. Like you, we vowed to do something about it. We persuaded British lawmakers not to be swayed by the vested interests of the gun lobby, we asked them to put public safety first and to heed what the majority of the British people wanted. Most politicians listened and acted. Laws were changed, handguns were banned and the level of gun violence in Britain is now one of the lowest in the world. There have been no more school shootings.*[3]

While intended as a message of support, it is also a reminder of how much work needs to be done to solve the problem of gun violence and how little has changed in the span of 20 years in the USA. The American experience of gun violence has had palpable reactions around the world, as we are continually shocked by how much violence and how little legislation has occurred despite examples of other nations responding differently. The American experience of gun violence is exceptional.

In teaching criminology in Australia, I often include a discussion of American exceptionalism. This is primarily because the most influential and enduring criminological theories in our field have been developed and tested in the US context. A context that, despite its similarities in global and western development, has some of the highest crime, violence and incarceration rates in the western world. When I began this project, I was interested in questions of compliance – how do you get the gun-owning community to comply (with relatively high rates) with laws they initially resisted, as we have seen happen in Australia, the UK and elsewhere. Are there lessons that can be learned from the Australian experience? In this chapter, I outline what Australian gun laws look like, what role gun dealers play in the implementation of gun laws in Australia and how the gun debate was framed by the media and lay the framework for understanding how regulatory compliance can be understood in the Australian experience of gun control.

Public Debate and the Media Framing of the Gun Control Debate

Dunblane, Port Arthur and Parkland, all three of these, cases ignited a public debate on the control of guns that has had impact on the global discourse of gun control. Countless other mass shootings have done the same. Despite the current focus on gun violence stemming from the North American experience of crime, the majority of the public will not experience a mass shooting of the kind that we associate with powerful calls for gun control. Mass shootings remain rare, even in the USA, in comparison to other forms of violence.[4] As a result, we typically rely on the media to interpret events for our own understanding. The media, including social media, are important because they provide opportunities for us to read, see and hear repeated narratives about important events. While some media outlets take on the role of "monitoring" current events, describing events to us as observers, others use a "management" strategy to produce or create interpretations of events that fit a particular political agenda.[5] It is not a surprise then that public opinion is so influenced by the media's interpretations of shooting events that the media plays an important role in how shooting events become seen as indicators of a social problem needing an official response, or that they become influential in how officials choose to respond.

Australia's reputation for the rapid implementation of gun control after the Port Arthur massacre is not unique. There are similarities to the way in which the issue of gun violence was portrayed, mobilised and acted on by officials after high-profile mass shootings between Australia, Scotland and even the USA. The way in which the media has framed these events is important for understanding the historical context of the gun debate, why members of the gun-owning community hold specific attitudes towards gun control measures and what kinds of elements from these events get remembered in their legacy. The way in which the media frames these issues is also important for understanding how they become defined as a social problem desperate for government intervention.[6]

The importance of this framing becomes obvious when we look at specific shooting events and how they are reported by the media. In 2002, a student suffering from a serious mental illness took a legally purchased firearm to Monash University in Melbourne, Australia, and fired into his university classroom, killing two students and injuring five others, including the course lecturer. Local and national news sources frame this incident as a matter of gun control, which reignited public debate around gun owners in Australia and renewed calls for further tightening of Australia's gun laws, rather than other elements of the crime, such as the untreated mental illness.

In the immediate aftermath of an event, we see patterns of framing where at first the media cover the horror – easy to do when children are the primary victims of some of these events and events take place in everyday locations we don't expect danger. The following are examples of some of the first media headlines after the shootings in Dunblane, Parkland (Florida) and Port Arthur:

> "TINY VICTIMS OF DUNBLANE" – *Express and Star*, March 14, 1996
>
> *(Dunblane, Scotland)*

> "TERROR, AGAIN, IN SCHOOL" – *The Boston Globe*, February 15, 2018
>
> *(Parkland, Florida)*

> "SUNDAY SLAUGHTER" – *The Sydney Morning Herald*, April 29, 1996
>
> *(Port Arthur, Australia)*

In Dunblane, the headline indicating child victims was posted with a class photo that included a number of victims, solidifying the horror of losing such innocent lives in a place that is supposed to be safe. The Boston Globe showed photos of grieving parents outside the school as they learned about the massacre within. And the Port Arthur massacre's main location at the Broad Arrow café filled with tourists enjoying a meal at the historic and beautiful site of Port Arthur linked the horror to the everyday activities enjoyed by many tourists and locals. These initial headlines set the tone for how we view and respond to the social problem they indicate needs a response.

These initial headlines then gave way to framing the problem as a result of gun law leniency and calling for a government response to crack down on the sale of firearms across the nation.

> "Lay down your arms: After Dunblane many people ant guns to be banned before another tragedy occurs" – *The Guardian*, October 15, 1996
>
> *(Dunblane Scotland)*

> "MR PRESIDENT, PLEASE ACT: We need sensible Gun control to help stop the slaughter" – *The New York Post*, February 18, 2018
>
> *(Parkland, Florida)*

> "IT'S WAR ON GUNS" – *Herald Sun*, May 2, 1996
>
> *(Port Arthur, Australia)*

The call for the government to increase restrictions or create new ones is seen as the only responsible approach to the problem. It is not that other frames aren't available. In each of these cases, the perpetrator's mental illness is part of the way in which we come to understand why these incidents occur. But inadequate health care or mental health services routinely have taken a back seat in our initial interpretations and perceptions about what will prevent future violence.[7]

Governments then respond by making promises to ameliorate the social problem as it has been defined by the media and public outcry. Tighter restrictions are proposed; promises to create firearm bans and sweeping legal changes are considered by the nation's leaders. Each of these reinforces the urgency and importance of the social problem defined as a problem that can be solved by gun control.

> "Labor proposes guns crackdown" – The Guardian, May 13, 1996
>
> *(Dunblane, Scotland)*

> "Howard pledges weapons action" – The Sydney Morning Herald, April 30, 1996
>
> *(Port Arthur, Australia)*

> "Trump warms to Gun Limits, Jolting N.R.A" – New York Times, March 1, 2018
>
> *(Parkland, Florida)*

As the government forms its response to these shootings in the form of promises to keep us safer, those most affected by the new regulations attempt to realign these frames with their own concerns. The debates now become adversarial in nature by framing solutions to the problem of gun violence as those that either risk public safety or take away the freedoms of the legal gun-owning community. We can now see the debate and its respective sides take shape in response to calls for tighter gun control.

> "Fury as Tories reject handgun ban – Dunblane parents, doctors and police attack MP's report" – The Guardian, August 14, 1996
>
> *(Dunblane, Scotland)*

> "PM Takes on the gun lobby" – The Sydney Morning Herald, May 8, 1996
>
> *(Port Arthur, Australia)*

> "Stop Tweeting and get in the N.R.A.'S Face" – The New York Times, February 21, 2018
>
> *(Parkland, Florida)*

These headlines demonstrate a debate between two opposing sides: political conservatives against parents and doctors in Scotland, the government and the gun lobby in Australia and the NRA and the rest of the public in the USA. Calls for gun reform have inevitably and consistently become a place for debate between two distinct sides – two sides with no common goal and no moral overlap, and instead, the gun-owning community is seen as the sole barrier that is impeding community safety. It is often not until a shooter is brought to justice and their mental state is examined by the criminal justice system that calls for mental health care emerge as secondary solutions to violence. These media frames help us understand how two opposing sides emerge. The gun-owning community responds to defend themselves, their livelihoods and their sports as perceived to be targets of reform in response to the massacre. Their professions become linked to notions of danger, risk and irresponsibility.

These media frames also play out in government debates, where proposals and policies are created, debated and ultimately legislated. In Australia, these debates also drew fierce parliamentary debate among political groups who represented the interests of farmers and sporting shooters who felt unfairly targeted by the proposed national firearms guidelines. As politicians represented and relayed concerns from their constituents, it became clear that for the legal gun-owning community, they felt attacked and blamed for the massacre at Port Arthur.

> *There has been a lot of consternation amongst law-abiding citizens who feel fairly hurt that they are being singled out and branded as criminals. Those people that have had guns for years are the ones that are making the biggest sacrifice of all. To some people it is part of their way of life to own a gun, and yet they are going to be the ones that have to surrender their guns, albeit with a compensation for them. It is hard for people to make the sacrifices who believe that they have never done anything wrong, have always been law-abiding and have always treated and used their guns in the utmost safety.*
>
> *(Senator Boswell, Leader of the National party of Australia in the Senate, May 20, 1996)*

Senator Boswell went on to say that despite the objections from their constituents in the gun-owning community, the National Party would support the National Firearms Agreement (NFA) because it was "believed to be in the best interests of society". But he also argued that gun owners cannot shoulder the weight of violence prevention alone. He then called for an attempt to regulate violent movies and video games as potential contributors to mass violence. But it was clear that the rights and privileges of gun owners had to be curbed, even if they are not responsible for violence, but as a matter of sending an important message about the greater good and collective society.

> *I know that there are many gun owners who feel they have been unfairly penalised for the actions of one person. They are concerned that their rights and freedoms are being infringed. There is no doubt that it will impinge on the rights of individual gun owners. The Prime Minister has acknowledged that. He spoke of his regret at that, but what right is more important? An individual's right to own a semi-automatic or automatic weapon or the right of the rest of us to live safe from those guns?*
>
> *(Senator Newman, Minister for Social Security and Minister Assistant the Prime Minister for the Status of Women, May 20, 1996)*

Parliamentary debates, in response to the Port Arthur massacre, was able to achieve sweeping gun reform in the form of guidelines to direct Australia's eight states and territories on their own gun laws. The laws are highly supported by the public and in quieter sections of the gun-owning community. But the ongoing debate about gun control between the public and the gun-owning community even today continues to replay these debates from 1996. The community wants gun reform to keep us safe, and the gun-owning community feels as though they have been unfairly targeted and have to carry the weight of that reform in terms of cost, culture and social stigma.

The National Firearms Agreement

The NFA was put forward as the nation's response to the control of guns directly after the Port Arthur massacre in 1996. While it is not "law" in and of itself, it represented a national guideline that was expected to be mirrored in state and territory legislation across Australia. Since its inception, the state and territories of Australia have taken the NFA and implemented it in their own way. And while there are some differences, the guideline has provided enough of an expectation of how to control firearms that there is relative consistency in the aims and principles of gun laws across the country. In doing so, the NFA guideline provided expectations on how to categorise firearms, what reasons can be used to justify the ownership and use of firearms and what requirements need to be met for the licencing and storage of firearms and for the sale and transport of firearms across the country. The NFA also made room for a national registration system designed to track the importation, sale and movement of firearms from the cradle to the grave. While each state and territory has its own reporting system, the national infrastructure to support a national registration system has yet to materialise in the way that the NFA intended.

While the NFA does restrict the ownership and use of particular firearms across the country, it also recognised specific groups of people for whom the use of these firearms might be legitimate. For example, the NFA restricted the importation, sale and manufacture of semi-automatic long arms and pump-action shotguns except in exceptional circumstances. These circumstances include military use, collectors, gun dealers and theatrical armourers (people who supply inoperable firearms for movie sets and theatres). In summary, these kinds of firearms can only be supplied under specific conditions, most of which relate to employment or, in some cases, sport shooting, in which there are additional conditions for ownership.

In order to align firearm use for specific purposes, the NFA introduced 11 reasons for legitimate possession and ownership of a firearm, thereby forcing firearm owners into specific categories of ownership, each with its own conditions of eligibility. These genuine reasons include the following:

a Sports shooters using long arms;
b Sports shooters using handguns;
c Recreational shooters, including hunters;
d Primary producers (farmers);
e Occupations such as pest control;
f Security employees;
g Collectors where firearms must be made permanently inoperable;
h Heirlooms where they must show lineage and the firearm must be made permanently inoperable;
i Firearms dealers;
j Firearms manufacturers;
k Film and theatrical armourers.[8]

Each of these genuine reasons is aligned with specific firearm types best suited for their respective purposes. Furthermore, each genuine reason has its own set of requirements for establishing sufficient evidence and conditions for approval. For example, people wishing to acquire a licence for occupations such as pest control may only be approved for a category A or B firearm. They would also need to provide proof of employment and adhere to conditions such as only carrying the firearm while on duty. Most notable is the absence of personal protection from the list of reasons one can use to argue that they have legitimate reasons to own a firearm.

> *Section 10. Personal protection is not a genuine reason for acquiring, possessing, or using a firearm.*

The categorisation of firearms allowed regulators to do two things. First, make distinctions between more powerful and less powerful firearms as well as those that are more concealable. For example, all handguns are provided in their own category regardless of whether they are semi-automatic or not, given their smaller size lends themselves to easier concealment (see Table 1.1).

TABLE 1.1 Firearm categories created by the NFA in 1996

	Firearm	*Notes*	*Storage requirements*
Category A	Air rifles Rimfire rifles Shotguns Rimfire rifle and shotgun combinations	Does not include semi-automatic rimfire rifles or pump action/ leaver action shotguns	
Category B	Muzzle-loading firearms Single-shot centrefire rifles Centrefire rifle/shotgun combinations Leaver action shotguns	Includes double-barrelled rifles and repeating centrefire rifles Only includes leaver action shotguns with magazine capacity of 5 rounds or less	Locked receptacle made of wood or steel with non-penetrable thickness If the locked receptacle is less than 150 kg, then it must be fastened to the floor or wall Ammunition must be stored in locked containers separate from firearms (Cat A and B only)
Category C	Semi-automatic rimfire rifles	Only includes semi-automatic rimfire rifles with a magazine capacity of 10 rounds or less	

(*Continued*)

TABLE 1.1 (Continued)

	Firearm	*Notes*	*Storage requirements*
	Semi-automatic and pump-action shotguns	Only includes shotguns with magazine capacity of 5 rounds or less	
Category D	Semi-automatic centrefire rifles designed for military purpose	Includes firearms adapted or made to imitate the look or function of a military rifle	Locked steel safe must be used with non-penetrable thickness Must be bolted to the structure of the building
	Nonmilitary self-loaded centrefire rifles	With magazine capacity greater than 5 rounds	Ammunition must be stored in locked containers separate from firearms
	Semi-automatic pump action and leave action shotguns	With magazine capacity greater than 10 rounds	(Cat C, D and H only)
	Semi-automatic rimfire rifles		
Category H	All handguns	Includes air pistols	

Second, these categories were linked to genuine reasons to own a firearm in order to ensure that the use of firearms matched the type of firearms being used. For example, if your stated genuine reason is for your job as a security employee, only category A and H firearms are available to you. All other categories of firearms (such as pump-action shotguns) are not considered appropriate for that specific, genuine reason. In some states, gun control regulations may also include a "Category R" list of firearms. These generally refer to firearms that are subject to bans and are fully restricted for civilian ownership and use. Machine guns, rocket launchers and silencers are examples of firearms or firearms accessories defined as Category R weapons in the state of Queensland.[9]

Australia's NFA is likely most well-known for its licencing system, which places the responsibility for licensing and registration on states and territories to implement. Firearms licencing in Australia includes background checks and monitors each firearm sale and acquisition. In Australia, to be eligible for a licence, the NFA requires applicants to be at least 18 years of age, be a fit and proper person and undertake mandatory safety training. The licencing system also provides guidelines for how long a licence can be issued without renewal (usually five years), sets out other requirements pertinent to the genuine reason used to justify the need for the licence and outlines the grounds for licence refusal and revocation. Licencing is only the first step in the process of gun ownership in Australia. Once licensed, a permit must be acquired for each and every purchase of a firearm. This permit process ensures that only the firearms available for that type of licence are purchased and that the number of firearms purchased can be monitored.

Along with the requirements to apply for a licence, applicants must also demonstrate that they can comply with the storage requirements for firearms ownership. Also linked to the category of firearm an individual has been approved to own, storage requirements generally require firearms to be stored in a locked receptacle made of steel (wood is acceptable for category A and B firearms) that is bolted to the structure of the building, and ammunition must be stored in a separate locked box away from the firearms (see Table 1.1).

While the goal of the NFA has been to provide guidance on what gun control should look like across Australia, there are some important distinctions between the NFA's expectations and what states and territories have implemented. For example, while the NFA restricts licenses to adults (anyone over the age of 18), all states and territories have provided avenues for youth to be involved in shooting with additional conditions. In Queensland, a shooter under the age of 18 must have parental permission and can only apply for a sport shooting or primary producers' licence. These categories recognise two things: that the farming community includes youth who may need to use a firearm in the context of farming and sports shooting via clubs and organisations have the mentorship needed to socialise youth into responsible gun owners.

What Do Gun Dealers Do?

A firearms dealer in the Australian context is typically anyone who sells or purchases more than 20 firearms in a 12-month period. A firearms dealer's licence is one that allows someone to buy or sell firearms in whole or in part; auction firearms or their component parts; repair, modify or test firearms; and store firearms for the purpose of safekeeping or disposal. Each one of those services comes with a required piece of paperwork (sometimes more than one). This means that the average gun dealers' daily tasks can include selling to new firearms owners – those who have been freshly approved for firearms ownership – which requires dealers to check and confirm all permits and licenses have been issued before handing over any purchased firearms. It could also include taking possession of firearms that are being disposed of or handed over, such as in the case of a death where family members are offloading firearms that belonged to the deceased or are being turned in as part of an amnesty. It could also include the repair of firearms, selling ammunition and holding firearms for those who have had their license suspended or revoked, such as in the case of domestic violence cases or other criminal offences.

The NFA and the respective legislation and regulations enacted across Australia hold gun dealers at the centre of the implementation of the gun laws. As a result, gun dealers are essential for every sale and acquisition of guns, hold reporting duties for sales and acquisitions to the state's gun register and must comply with a higher level of administration as a direct result of the gun control laws. More importantly, gun dealers then become the primary contact for the existing gun-owning community, the prospective gun-owning community, as well as law enforcement. This positions gun dealers uniquely in the gun control compliance process.

While they are subject to the laws they enforce, they also have the ability to be the connection between regulators and the public. Their position in the gun compliance process is therefore critical for understanding why compliance might be so high despite tensions between regulators and gun owners. The NFA recognises the gun dealer's expertise and role in the compliance process. For example, while banning the sale, manufacture and possession of semi-automatic category C and D firearms, there are exceptions made for gun dealers, firearms manufacturers and other groups considered to hold special positions of expertise. By placing gun dealers at the centre of sales and acquisitions, all legal gun sales in Australia pass through a gun dealer's hands, cementing their importance and relevance in understanding how gun laws are enacted and translated to the gun-owning community.

Gun Dealers as Street-Level Bureaucrats

I once referred to gun dealers as "street-level bureaucrats" in a paper published in an academic journal.[10] I was concerned about the use of the term "bureaucrat" in particular, as it is a term we colloquially associate with negative interactions – especially in my academic circles. However, the use of the term served an important purpose – to highlight the bureaucratic nature of the roles that gun regulation imposes on the gun dealer's daily life and to situate the role of gun dealer in the larger system of gun regulation and as those that work alongside law enforcement to enforce regulatory compliance. The research and commentary on street-level bureaucracy in the field of sociology aimed to increase our understanding of front-line government workers by focusing on how public servants function within a system that gives them limited discretion but seemingly a lot of power.[11] I saw parallels between public servants and gun dealers in Australia in terms of their role in the inaction of gun control.

The level of the gun dealer's involvement in assisting in the implementation of gun control regulation in Australia means that they serve on the front lines of policy enactment. Their front-line work consisting of processing paperwork for each firearm acquisition and sale, interacting with the public and enacting decisions made by law enforcement with regard to approvals of gun licences is part of their daily business tasks. And their work to populate gun registers that allow gun sales to be tracked and traced is central to Australia's gun control system. As such, the accuracy and reliability of that gun registration system heavily rely on gun dealers to perform their jobs effectively. While police manage the licencing of gun owners, gun dealers become the primary contact for new and existing gun owners because they are tasked with managing the paperwork for the registration of new firearm purchases. Therefore, gun dealers, much like government public servants, are on the front line of the implementation of regulations and laws. While not employed by the government, they are legislatively compelled to facilitate compliance for their clients by ensuring that the appropriate paperwork has been filled out and is passed on to authorities. This role makes gun dealers akin to sociologist Michael Lipsky's "street-level bureaucrat"[12] due to their daily activities in implementing the law and contributing to compliance with that law. Lipsky saw street-level bureaucrats as the typical front-line workers who primarily interact with the public and become the first point of contact in the delivery of government goods and services. For Lipsky, these front-line workers are not just a formal first port of call for government clients; they are also part of an informal process of socialisation whereby government workers "teach" clients how to behave and what is expected of them in relation to the service they are seeking or the policy that is being enacted.

Gun dealers also play an important role in the socialisation of new and existing gun owners through their role in policy enactment. They socialise gun owners by communicating legal requirements and what is expected of them, and they are compelled to only sell to those who have licences and permits approved by law enforcement. And while gun dealers have limited discretion in their day-to-day decisions on who to sell to, the private nature of their business means they do have the power to turn people away or report them to police if they perceive a client to be a risk to themselves or others. As such, gun dealers sit alongside law enforcement to implement and enact gun control policies in Australia.

Unlike Lipsky's street-level bureaucrats, gun dealers hold the unique position of being members of the community which they serve and help to implement regulations. As members of the community they serve, gun dealers and gun owners also share concerns and frustrations about how policy is enacted. Gun dealers do not have the luxury of being disconnected from the community they serve. As such, gun dealers can provide important insight into how the gun-owning community is reacting to, feeling about and complying with the law. Their positioning as leaders in their community holds important implications for what role they can play in motivating compliance with the law among a group with a rocky history of gun control support.

As members of the gun-owning community, it may not be surprising that gun dealers, like gun owners, hold some level of frustration with gun laws. These frustrations are well documented here in Australia and abroad. For gun dealers, the creation and revision of gun regulations mean they are the first to have to implement those changes. New regulations may mean they need to shift business practices in order to comply with those new regulations, often at considerable cost to the dealer. Frustrations felt by gun dealers have the potential to be translated to the community during the process of their interaction with clients. Where support for the law can be communicated to the community they serve, so too can frustrations and tensions gun dealers experience in the process of their daily tasks related to gun control compliance.

Australian gun dealers' front-line role in gun policy implementation and enactment is not unique. Gun dealers hold these important formal and informal roles around the world. In Japan, Switzerland, Germany and even parts of the USA, gun dealers are used to facilitate each acquisition and sale to ensure components of gun control legislation are complied with.[13] As a result, questions about how effective gun laws might be and how to understand compliance with gun laws likely require a better understanding of those from the gun-owning community who have been placed front and centre of gun control policy enactment.

Why Examine Gun Control Compliance?

The question of how we can get people to comply with laws that are unpopular or unpalatable for some groups matters for questions of gun control effectiveness in Australia (and elsewhere) because compliance rests on the ability of gun dealers and registry police to work together. In addition, the political powers of pro-gun groups influence gun law and enforcement, and anecdotal national growth in the number of gun owners has increased concern over violence and security. These trends keep questions about gun law effectiveness and usability central to policy and governance debates and central to understanding how and why people comply.

Gun registry police rely on dealers to report accurate information on gun acquisitions and sales in order for gun control to be effective.[14] However, compliance with the NFA has a significant impact on gun dealer business and thus their livelihood, suggesting that they may not always be allies of gun law compliance.[15] While Australia's gun legislation has largely been heralded as a success,[16] this success has been primarily based on the observed drop in gun-related violence since the NFA was enacted. Yet, few scholars in Australia or elsewhere have examined the necessary cooperation between gun dealers and police or the process of compliance.

Gun control compliance is important to understand, given that pro-gun political parties hold considerable political power and successfully influence the weakening of and support of gun laws. Over the last 10 years, pro-gun lobby groups and political parties have gained considerable political power in Australia, just as we have seen in the USA, though not to the same extent. This increase in political power provides the platform, audience and credibility to transmit their stance on guns and gun control on a larger scale than ever before. Pro-gun groups typically aim to protect the interests of dealers in a post-1996 environment[17] and suggest that the proliferation of guns would lead to less violent crime in Australian society.[18] These organisations are generally not supportive of gun control legislation or its enforcement. Thus, how dealers perceive the legitimacy of the gun laws is critical to understanding how they fulfil their role in compliance.

Australia's NFA is over 20 years old, yet it remains an important political issue in Australia and abroad. It appears that gun ownership has increased across Australia since 2015.[19] This increase is as high as 25% in some regional towns in New South Wales. At the same time, pro-gun political parties are using their increasing political power to relax some elements of the NFA. For example, in 2016, the Shooters and Fishers Party (who held the balance of power in the NSW parliament at the time) successfully lobbied for a relaxation of the restriction around the purchase and use of silencers for some weapons categories.[20] Gun control activists raise concerns that the ownership increase and relaxation of the NFA place more guns into communities across Australia and increase demand for monitoring compliance with the NFA by gun dealers and registry police. These trends reinforce the importance of understanding the position of gun dealers in relation to regulators and the gun laws they assist in enforcing.

The gun dealers' placement in the compliance process and the historically contentious relationship that they and the gun-owning community have had with lawmakers and law enforcement underscore the importance of examining how gun control works in Australia from the perspective of the gun dealers' themselves. This requires us as scholars to move out of our comfort zone and think of gun dealers as collaborators of gun control instead of those who singularly opposed to it. Most importantly, in learning how they approach their role, we can learn about how to collaborate with and bridge the divide between the public and the gun-owning community in achieving good quality and effective gun regulation.

Criminological Understandings of Compliance

Understanding why people comply with the law has received much attention from scholars of policing in the field of criminology. By using theoretical frames of legitimacy and procedural justice, compliance and cooperation with the law are understood to be a result of whether the law is perceived by individuals to be fair and just and that those who enforce it have the legal authority to do so.[21] Policing scholars suggest that in order to encourage compliance with the law, the legal system, including its actors, needs to foster attitudes of fairness and legitimacy in individuals whom they want to comply with.[22] What this means is that the way in which individuals experience the law through interactions with its actors, processes and institutions matters for how people feel about the law.[23] For our gun-owning community, what this means is that their experiences with gun control likely matter for how they feel about the law and therefore have implications for their willingness to cooperate with law enforcement and the compliance process itself. If we want to understand why Australia's gun control laws have such a high level of compliance despite initial resistance from the gun-owning community in 1996, then we need to acknowledge that resistance and attempt to understand how those who found those laws unpalatable have complied none the less.

Criminologists have long acknowledged the link between attitudes and behaviour in understanding why individuals choose to uphold the law or cooperate with law enforcement.[24] Belief that the law is legitimate is critical to understanding an individual's willingness to cooperate with the police.[25] Individuals with negative attitudes towards the law are less likely to obey the law and are less likely to have positive interactions with law enforcement.[26] Pioneered by the work of Tom Tyler,[27] legal *compliance* and cooperation are secured by fostering *attitudes* of legitimacy and fairness in legal actors and the legal system. According to Tyler, it is the *process* of experiencing the legal system and its actors that fosters compliance or disregard for the law. In the context of gun law compliance, attitudes towards the law influence the willingness to cooperate with police and comply with the law, and criminal justice outcomes for violations reinforce attitudes and perceptions of the law and its enforcers. If attitudes are critical for gaining compliance with the law, then understanding the attitudes of those who are central to its enforcement is an important element in understating the success or failure of Australia's gun laws.

Gun control laws, while seeking to keep firearms out of the hands of criminals, actually regulate law-abiding citizens with legal and legitimate use for firearms. To encourage compliance within the gun-owning community, "buy-in" from within the community is necessary for success and effectiveness. Scholars of regulatory practice note that regulations based on deterrence alone – the idea that penalties for noncompliance are what motivate compliance – are not enough to achieve buy-in from the community. Furthermore, those deterrence-based approaches should be a last resort for motivating people to obey the law and used only when more normative and cooperative strategies fail. More cooperative strategies are considered to be better at securing compliance because they are based on beliefs and identities that centre around civic duty and morality.[28] This is likely to be especially true for those who are subject to the laws they help to uphold. Given the role that gun dealers play, they have the potential to socialise and encourage compliance through collective shared interests, values and norms.[29]

Procedural justice frameworks from the field of criminology work well for understanding why people comply with criminal laws. However, these frameworks carry the assumption that all members of society agree with the basic moral principles of those laws. However, laws that regulate people's livelihoods, like gun laws, may need to be seen differently; these laws regulate socio-economic life – livelihoods that are generally accepted to be legitimate and necessary in society.[30] As a result, those who are active participants in that socioeconomic life are likely to have distinct views on how they are regulated as well as roles that can potentially reinforce or undermine those regulations. For gun dealers, who are both regulated and take an active role in regulations, a broader framework is required that recognises both the formal and informal roles they may play in compliance and how those roles help to achieve compliance.

Compliance Motivation Theory as a Way to Understand Compliance with Gun Laws

I began looking at ways to understand compliance behaviour that were broader than those that explained why people comply with the law from within criminology. In part because the frames that are typically used by criminology rest on the assumption that there is consensus that the behaviour to be regulated is criminal, and to broaden the scope of motivations to obey the law to include more normative motivations in addition to ones based on deterrence, I read work about the regulation of different kinds of livelihoods but found specific parallels with the work being done on understanding compliance with regulations in fishing communities.[31] Like gun control, fishing laws use criminal penalties to regulate behaviour that is generally acceptable yet requires regulation to respond to public demands to protect public interests (like conservation). Given that they regulate economic life, like gun control laws, fishing laws also draw resistance from within the fishing community as those laws attempt to place restrictions on their everyday activities. As a result, what regulations ask people to do is likely to conflict with the norms and values of the economic community being regulated.

Gezelius and Hauck[32] utilise *compliance motivation theory (CMT)* to study fishing regulations and understand how compliance is motivated by those who must adhere to the law. Their compliance framework makes room for deterrence-based regulatory models so common in criminological approaches, with those that account for the normative motivation generated by shared interests and collective morals. Furthermore, the benefit of this framework is that Gezelius and Hauck provide preconditions for compliance that help us understand how society and government can promote particular compliance motivations. As a result, not only does this framework lend itself to understanding why people comply with the law, even when those laws are unpalatable to those that are the targets of regulation, but also how governments might set the tone for promoting those motivations. I use the compliance motivation framework to examine the dual role of gun dealers as both enactors of regulations on the front line, as well as members of a collective where there may be an incentive to oppose the law.

CMT addresses three motivations for complying with regulations: deterrence, moral support for the law's content and legislator's authority. Each of these is seen as a reason why individuals comply with legislation that they might otherwise oppose. *Deterrence* is a rational motivation based on the understanding that individuals comply because they want to avoid the consequences of what might happen if they are caught breaking the rules. According to Gezelius and Hauck, this motivation only drives behaviour if people believe that a) law enforcement is actively enforcing the law and b) the risk of noncompliance being detected is relatively high. If the regulated community is constantly monitored by law enforcement, it heightens the perceived risk that noncompliance would be detected. It may also suggest that during times, periods or situations that are known to be in the blind spot of authorities, noncompliance might be higher. Therefore, if gun dealers are complying due to motivations of deterrence, then we would expect them to have knowledge or perception of law enforcement's presence and perceive the risk of being detected for noncompliance to be high. In order to motivate compliance via deterrence, the state needs to use regular enforcement mechanisms to surveil and monitor the regulated. *Enforcement* becomes the governable precondition that provides power to regulators to incentivise compliance.

There are good reasons to assume that deterrence is an important motivator for compliance for gun dealers and the gun-owning community in general. The NFA and the resulting state and territory legislation in Australia specify severe penalties for gun dealers who violate the law. Loss of a gun dealer's license for a period of up to 10 years would have considerable implications for a gun dealer's livelihood if caught for noncompliance, and monetary fines or jail time could be used as penalties for significant noncompliance. Furthermore, given that the very nature of gun dealer's everyday tasks involves communicating and interacting with law enforcement, it is likely that gun dealers are aware that their behaviour is being monitored closely. Examining to what extent deterrence motivations explain why gun dealers comply with the law at such high rates in Australia gives us important information about how to incentivise compliance.

Moral support for the law's content is a normative motivation that carries the assumption that when regulated communities agree with and support the aims and content of regulations, they are more likely to comply and they are more likely to communicate the moral importance of those regulations through their community and their networks. In this case, compliance is more easily achieved because those who are regulated already believe that the law is right and believe in what the laws are aiming to do. Therefore, people will comply with the law because they share support for the law in the form of both attitudes and behavioural norms. In addition, given that the aims of the law are shared collectively within the community, compliance can be reinforced with current community members and communicated and internalised by new members. To drive moral support for the law, the government can incentivise compliance via *empowerment*. Empowerment provides power to citizens when they are able to be assured that their rights are protected rather than violated by regulations. By giving people opportunities to participate as experts in creating and designing regulations, we can ensure that they can be assured that regulations are justified.

When the NFA was first proposed after the Port Arthur massacre in 1996, gun dealers, and the gun-owning community more broadly, were concerned about what those new laws would mean for them and their livelihoods. They resisted the laws because they felt that they had been unfairly targeted. This resistance may indicate that there was not widespread moral support for gun control within the gun-owning community at the time, much like what we have seen in the American context. However, the role of gun dealers in the compliance process and the apparent high levels of compliance may indicate that there is more support for what gun control was aiming to achieve than we first thought. Are gun dealers helping to implement gun regulations that they don't agree with? Or is support for the aims and content of the law driving their motivations to comply? These are the questions that sit at the centre of understanding how and why compliance is achieved, particularly where there is a history of resistance from within the regulated community.

Complying with the law due to a *legislator's authority* means that we comply not necessarily because we agree with the law but because we believe that breaking the law, any law, is wrong in and of itself. There are likely many laws that we might identify as those we don't agree with but comply with anyway if we subscribe to legislators' authority. For example, I don't agree with the criminalisation of marijuana. But I understand it is against the law. I don't use it and I don't allow it in my home because I am a law-abiding citizen. To break that law would be wrong, even though I don't believe this is behaviour that should be dealt with by the criminal justice system. Furthermore, that law-abiding identity is shared within my community, therefore reinforcing the importance of compliance through my interactions with other community members who feel the same way. In this case, we have been taught and socialised that we should follow the rules regardless of what the rules are. When we fail to comply, we risk judgement and consequences from our fellow community members and are reminded of what behaviour is "right" and what is expected of us. If we want to incentivise and encourage this subscription to the legislator's authority, then governments must provide an opportunity to develop a sense of community or commitment to the overarching goals of the state – they need to encourage conditions that make people want to participate in their civic duty as part of their *civic identity*. Civic identity as a governable precondition ensures that individuals are connected to something bigger than themselves, and they feel obligated to support the aims of the collective over their own individual interests.

A core issue for the gun debate in Australia in 1996, both in the media and in parliamentary debates that led up to the NFA's implementation, suggests that the notion of firearms bans and regulating gun owners violated the law-abiding identity of the gun-owning community.[33] However, we would expect, according to this framework, that despite their disagreement with gun control laws, their identities as law-biding citizens would motivate them to comply anyway. Are the identities of gun dealers as law-abiding citizens more important than the parts of the legislation they find unpalatable? Is this why their compliance rates appear to be high and gun control has been so successful in Australia? These questions about compliance are critical for understanding how to motivate compliance even in the face of community disagreement with what is being regulated.

The little scholarly work that does exist on the gun-owning community appears to suggest that gun owners in the USA, like those in Australia, see themselves as law-abiding citizens – citizens who uphold the constitution and protect the nation's interests.[34] Other scholars have suggested that while American gun owners see themselves as law-abiding citizens, the broader public sees them as people who oppose and disregard the law.[35]

While the CMT framework suggests three compliance motivations, Lipsky's[36] articulation of the challenges for street-level bureaucrats suggests that there may be specific barriers to these compliance motivations as a result of the difficulties and complexities experienced in their everyday compliance tasks. Existing work on the challenges of navigating the criminal justice system supports this idea.[37] When the law, the process of compliance or the system with which we must interact is difficult to understand, is overly complicated or adds additional and unnecessary burdens for us, the pressures we face undermine the legitimacy of the law and our support for its aims and content and provide an incentive to find ways to avoid those pressures. For gun dealers, as participants in the compliance process, if their tasks are fraught with difficulty, complexity and additional financial, social, or time burdens, this burden may make compliance difficult to achieve and undermine any existing motivations for compliance. Figure 1.1 shows the three compliance motivations and their governable preconditions as articulated by Gezelius and Hauk's[38] study on fishing communities. It also shows where administrative complexity and burden may produce disincentives or undermine compliance motivations, which will be explored in the chapters ahead.

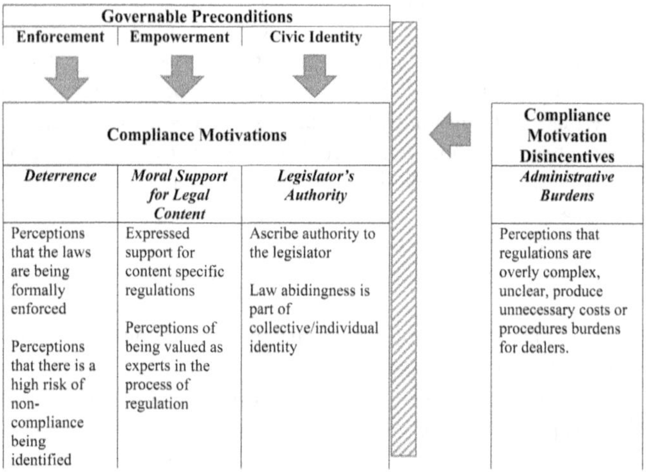

FIGURE 1.1 Compliance Motivation Framework

Source: See Fay (2022) in Endnote 10

The vast majority of gun control laws globally seek to decrease violence and gun-related crimes by regulating those who have legitimate reasons for firearm ownership. The benefit of the compliance motivation framework is that it uncovers the nuances and diversity in how the gun-owning community might feel or believe about the merits of gun control and how those beliefs can incentivise compliance rather than undermine it. Rather than thinking of members of the gun-owning community as subjects to be controlled, the CMT framework acknowledges the role of deterrence and underscores the more normative and informal ways they can support compliance with laws even when they don't like it. This then opens new opportunities to engage with the gun-owning community on matters of compliance, regulation and normative processes that facilitate responsible and reasonable uses of firearms. Gun dealers in Australia not only demonstrate that they do agree with the overarching aims of gun laws, but their strong identity as law-abiding citizens drives how they approach their compliance tasks and their interactions with the community. And while deterrence motivations also drive compliance, regulations that overly rely on formal enforcement and deterrence mechanisms are likely to miss opportunities to collaborate and find less taxing and more organic mechanisms to drive compliance.

Chapter Summary

Australia's reputation for swift gun control shares a number of similarities to other mass shootings that have had global impact. The media framing of the Port Arthur massacre shared similarities to the way in which the media has framed the Dunblane massacre and the Parkland, Florida, massacre. All of these share media frames that have drawn on the division between gun owners and the rest of the public amid the grief experienced in these tragedies. As a result, what we remember about the gun control debates back in 1996 and even newer ones today is that gun owners are resistant to gun laws despite cries from the public and law enforcement to tighten regulations or, in the case of the USA, create new legislation. Australia's experience of gun control is therefore not wholly unique but follows a distinctly common pattern that pits the gun-owning community against the rest of society in the framing of gun violence as a social problem.

Australia's response to the Port Arthur massacre put gun dealers at the centre of gun control compliance and implementation, placing a formal responsibility on them to participate in policy enactment via their everyday tasks in the gun dealing business. In addition, due to their standing in the community, they are also likely to take responsibility for more informal and normative tasks that communicate and socialise compliance behaviour. Understanding why gun control appears to be working in Australia requires an acknowledgement of the work that gun dealers do to participate in the compliance process. Without them, it would be more difficult for law enforcement to encourage compliance, given the resistance of the gun-owning community to the idea of tighter restrictions on legal and legitimate gun owners. As such, any exploration of how to achieve gun control effectively should consider the role that gun dealers play in the Australian context. A compliance motivation framework that incorporates the role of deterrence as well as more normative and identity-driven motivations not only helps us understand why people comply with gun laws but also provides ideas on how to engage the gun-owning community in the development of gun laws where they are most needed.

Notes

1 Thomson, S., Stancich, L., & Dickson, L. (1998). Gun control and Snowdrop. *Parliamentary Affairs*, *51*(3), 329+. https://link.gale.com/apps/doc/A21099997/AONE?u=anon~d540027c&sid=googleScholar&xid=5b813927
2 Prince Philip Angers Britons on Gun Control – *The New York Times* (nytimes.com)
3 https://www.buzzfeednews.com/article/buzzfeeduk/heres-a-powerful-letter-to-parkland-students-from-the?utm_source=dynamic&utm_campaign=bfsharecopy
4 Schildkraut, J., Gruenewald, J., Gilliam, M., & Novak, M. (2021). Framing mass shootings as a social problem: A comparison of ideologically and non-ideologically motivated attacks. *Aggression and Violent Behavior*, *60*, 101533.
5 Smadi, H., Obeidat, M., & Haider, A. S. (2022). Paratextual (re) framing of media coverage of Christchurch Mosque Shootings: A translation-oriented study. *Cogent Social Sciences*, *8*(1), 2029251.

6 Wondemaghen, M. (2014). Media construction of a school shooting as a social problem. *Journalism*, *15*(6), 696–712.
7 Wondemaghen, M. (2014). Media construction of a school shooting as a social problem. *Journalism*, *15*(6), 696–712.
8 https://www.resources.qld.gov.au/__data/assets/pdf_file/0010/1399510/17-257.pdf
9 https://www.police.qld.gov.au/weapon-licensing/what-are-weapons-categories
10 Fay, S. (2022). Gun dealer motivations for complying with the law: lessons from the Australian experience of gun control. *Sociological Perspectives*, *65*(1), 154–176.
11 Lipsky, M. (2010). *Street-level bureaucracy: Dilemmas of the individual in public service*. Russell Sage Foundation.
12 Lipsky, M. (2010). *Street-level bureaucracy: Dilemmas of the individual in public service*. Russell Sage Foundation.
13 Cook, P. J. & Goss, K. A. (2020). *The gun debate: What everyone needs to know®*. Oxford University Press.
14 2017 National Firearms Agreement | Attorney-General's Department
15 Cook, P. J. & Goss, K. A. (2020). *The gun debate: What everyone needs to know®*. Oxford University

Bricknell, S. (2012). Firearm trafficking and serious and organised crime gangs. https://www.aic.gov.au/sites/default/files/2020-05/rpp116.pdf

Altman, J. (2009). The hybrid economy and anthropological engagements with policy discourse: A brief reflection 1. *The Australian Journal of Anthropology*, *20*(3), 318–329.

16 Chapman, S., Alpers, P., Agho, K., & Jones, M. (2006). Australia's 1996 gun law reforms: faster falls in firearm deaths, firearm suicides, and a decade without mass shootings. *Injury Prevention*, *12*(6), 365–372.
17 Chapman, S. (2013). *Over our dead bodies: Port Arthur and Australia's fight for gun control*. Sydney University Press.
18 Lott, J. R. (2013). *More guns, less crime: Understanding crime and gun control laws*. University of Chicago Press.
19 Australian Crime Commission. (2015). *Organised Crime in Australia*. Commonwealth Government of Australia.

Senate Legal and Constitutional Affairs Committee. (2015). Ability of law enforcement authorities to eliminate gun-related violence in the community. Commonwealth Government of Australia.

Gorrey, M. (January 12, 2016). Gun ownership increase with more than 19,000 firearms in the ACT. *The Sydney Morning Herald*.

20 Robertson, J. (March 9, 2016). Gun control lobby raises alarm over silencers. *The Sydney Morning Herald*.
21 Sunshine, J., & Tyler, T. R. (2003). The role of procedural justice and legitimacy in shaping public support for policing. *Law & Society Review*, *37*(3), 513–548.
22 Mazerolle, L., Bennett, S., Davis, J., Sargeant, E., & Manning, M. (2013). Procedural justice and police legitimacy: A systematic review

of the research evidence. *Journal of Experimental Criminology*, 9, 245–274.

23 Papachristos, A. V., Meares, T. L., & Fagan, J. (2009). Why do criminals obey the law? The influence of legitimacy and social networks on active gun offenders. *The Influence of Legitimacy and Social Networks on Active Gun Offenders (January 12, 2009). Yale Law & Economics Research Paper*, (373), 09–199.

24 Mazerolle, L., Bennett, S., Davis, J., Sargeant, E., & Manning, M. (2013). Procedural justice and police legitimacy: A systematic review of the research evidence. *Journal of Experimental Criminology*, 9, 245–274.

25 Murphy, K., & Cherney, A. (2012). Understanding cooperation with police in a diverse society. *The British Journal of Criminology*, *52*(1), 181–201.

26 Papachritos, A. V., Meares, T. L., & Fagan, J. (2012). Why do criminals obey the law-the influence of legitimacy and social networks on active gun offenders. *Journal of Criminal Law & Criminology*, *102*, 397.

Tyler, T. R., & Fagan, J. (2008). Legitimacy and cooperation: Why do people help the police fight crime in their communities. *Ohio State Journal Of Criminal Law*, 6, 231.

Sunshine, J., & Tyler, T. R. (2003). The role of procedural justice and legitimacy in shaping public support for policing. *Law & Society Review*, *37*(3), 513–548.

27 Tyler, T. R. (1990). Justice, self-interest, and the legitimacy of legal and political authority.

28 Parker, Christine. 2006. The "compliance" trap: The moral message in responsive regulatory enforcement. *Law & Society Review*, *40*(3), 591–622.

May, Peter J. (2004). Compliance motivations: Affirmative and negative bases. *Law & Society Review*, *38*(1), 41–68.

Braithwaite, J. (2002). *Restorative justice & responsive regulation*. Oxford University press on demand.

29 Paternoster, R., & Simpson, S. (1996). Sanction threats and appeals to morality: Testing a rational choice model of corporate crime. *Law and Society Review*, 30(2), 549–583.

Parsons, T. (1968). The structure of social action/1 Marshall, Pareto, Durkheim." The structure of social action a study in social theory with special reference to a group of recent European writers.

Becker, Gary S. (1968). "Crime and punishment: An economic approach." In The economic dimensions of crime, pp. 13–68. Palgrave Macmillan.

30 See note vi

31 Gezelius, S. S., & Hauck, M. (2011). Toward a theory of compliance in state-regulated livelihoods: A comparative study of compliance motivations in developed and developing world fisheries. *Law & Society Review*, *45*(2), 435–470.

32 Gezelius, S. S., & Hauck, M. (2011). Toward a theory of compliance in state-regulated livelihoods: A comparative study of compliance motivations in developed and developing world fisheries. *Law & Society Review*, *45*(2), 435–470.
33 Bricknell, S. (2012). Firearm trafficking and serious and organised crime gangs. https://www.aic.gov.au/sites/default/files/2020-05/rpp116.pdf
34 Melzer, S. (2012). *Gun crusaders: The NRA's culture war*. NYU Press.
35 Cook, P. J., & Goss, K. A. (2020). *The gun debate: What everyone needs to know®*. Oxford University Press.
36 Lipsky, M. (2010). *Street-level bureaucracy: Dilemmas of the individual in public service*. Russell Sage Foundation.
37 Alm, J., Cherry, T., Jones, M., & McKee, M. (2010). Taxpayer information assistance services and tax compliance behavior. *Journal of Economic Psychology*, *31*(4), 577–586.

Feeley, M. M. (1979). *The process is the punishment: Handling cases in a lower criminal court*. Russell Sage Foundation.
38 Gezelius, S. S., & Hauck, M. (2011). Toward a theory of compliance in state-regulated livelihoods: A comparative study of compliance motivations in developed and developing world fisheries. *Law & Society Review*, *45*(2), 435–470.

2

FINDING COMMON GROUND BETWEEN THE GUN-OWNING COMMUNITY AND THE PUBLIC GUN CONTROL AGENDA

Vet them. Vet them as strongly as you want

On May 24, 2022, during the drafting of this chapter, an 18-year-old male entered an elementary school in Uvalde Texas, with an assault rifle and killed 19 children and two teachers, once again renewing calls for stricter gun control in the USA. Approximately two weeks after the shooting, actor Matthew McConaughey gave a press conference from the White House pleading for more prevention, more gun laws and more responsible gun ownership. The use of celebrities to motivate public and political support is not new. But this instance felt different. There were two things that stood out in McConaughey's message that represented a marked difference in the typical public discourse on gun control I'd previously witnessed in public conversation and media reactions about gun control in America. First, he wore his identity as a gun owner and recreational shooter on his sleeve, and second, he called out the lack of division between gun owners and the general public on the desire for gun laws. Towards the end of his speech, where he calls for "reasonable, practical and tactical regulation," he notes "we are not as divided as we are being told we are."[1] It was the first time I could recall a gun owner with this amount of public recognition and clout calling for gun control and drawing attention to what the majority of gun owners believed about the need for gun laws.

DOI: 10.4324/9781003271642-3

I wondered if this would be an important turning point that the USA needed in its public and political discourse on gun control; gun owners themselves calling for regulatory control, where in the past, it had been resisted on their behalf so vigorously by the NRA. Until this point, it felt that the voices of the vast majority of gun owners had been drowned out by the louder political ones of the NRA.

Links between Australia's gun lobby, political interests and a lack of support for gun laws have also been drawn in the Australian context. The debate in 1996 and beyond typically pitted the law-abiding gun owner and members of the public who are concerned about public safety and victims of gun violence against each other. It is easy for these debates to be co-opted by emotions surrounding death and violence, and therefore it is easy for the public to assume that these groups have competing interests. I assumed I would see these competing interests when I began this project. Instead, I saw more overlap in their views and attitudes towards gun control than I saw difference. I saw a lack of division between the general public and gun owners, much like the lack of division McConaughey described in his speech.

Outside of Australia, some might question whether it's surprising that gun dealers and owners in Australia support gun regulations. Australia's swift uptake of gun control in 1996 might suggest a lack of division in the first place. Therefore, perhaps there are many aspects of gun regulation that gun dealers support, which is an uninteresting finding for the Australian context. However, disagreement and divisive debate were not foreign to the discourse of gun control in 1996 in Australia, nor today when gun control laws are reviewed, revised and discussed. The assumption remains that gun owners and the public have competing interests when it comes to gun laws.

Empirical evidence suggests that McConaughey is right about the similarities in gun control views between the public and gun owners. Criminological and sociological research tells us that the average gun owner in the USA and abroad is likely much more moderate in their view of gun laws than what has been pushed by the NRA.[2] However, more moderate voices have typically been drowned out by a much louder, more well-financed and more politically connected gun lobby. McConaughey highlighted a more generous view of the average gun owner that might surprise many: they are not anti-gun control, they support reasonable gun laws and they don't see second amendment protections as mutually exclusive to preventative gun measures. As a non-gun owner and outsider to the gun-owning community, I too was surprised to find that gun dealers and owners in Australia share so much common ground with those who want to regulate guns in the interest of public safety. Gun owners and gun dealers are also mothers and fathers who want to protect their children from violence; some have personal connections to victims of violence, and they also have an interest in protecting their local communities more broadly.

This chapter highlights the overlaps between gun dealer views of gun laws and the global public cry for gun control. This overlap is crucial for productive public and political conversations about gun control in Australia and worldwide. For too long, productive discussion about gun control here in Australia, the USA and globally has centred on the differences between the interests of public safety and the gun-owning community. The findings from my work on gun control in Australia echo the message McConaughey so eloquently delivered in his White House speech and align with existing scholarly work on public perceptions of gun control, which suggests a possibility for a different approach to the gun control debate. One where there is substantial common ground on which to base good, effective and efficient gun control debate and policy. This chapter highlights this common ground in the hope that it can be used to generate a foundation for a more inclusive conversation about the need for and maintenance of good-quality gun regulation globally.

What Is Common Ground?

I've learned a lot about common ground from the gun dealers and owners that took part in my study. They were generous with their time and were willing to spend so much of their day talking to me and showing me what it was like to be a gun dealer in Australia. I had asked all of the gun dealers who had been in business during 1996, when the National Firearms Agreement (NFA) came into being, what they remembered about their feelings and perceptions of gun control at the time. Some were able to report what they witnessed in their parent's reactions who owned gun dealerships that have now been passed down to current business owners. I also asked them to reflect on how they feel about gun control now, 20 years later, and if their feelings have changed over time. I asked them to reflect on these things prior to asking them directly what elements of the NFA, and the state legislation that flows from it, they thought were good for crime prevention, safety and were otherwise considered to be a good idea. In part, and as an indication of my own prejudicial assumptions about this community, I assumed I'd get quip, politically safe answers to those direct questions. Instead, I received thoughtful reflections on the value that gun control has provided both the public and the gun-owning community. These dealers had clearly thought about and reflected long and hard on the question of how to control and regulate guns effectively. And, to my surprise, they had more in common with the public and their cry for safety and violence prevention than I had been socialised to believe. The division between the gun-owning community and the wider public appeared to be much smaller than I had anticipated.

The common ground I refer to in this manuscript is more than just policies where both the public and the gun-owning community agree. Shared and agreed-upon policies do provide a starting point and foundation for any policy debate that is controversial. For example, starting with one of the most widely agreed on policies in gun control – restricting firearm access to risky people – helps us understand where gun control has gotten traction early in North America. However, it is the motivations and values that underlie this support and agreement that I refer to as "common ground". Common ground represents the moral motivations and the identities regarding community and their relationship to firearms that are likely to be shared across the population. These values and identities represent even better places in which to embed hope for a more productive and collaborative conversation about gun control, whether it is developing controls that are new, revising controls already in place, or responding to incidents that shake our faith in the law, the government and our own safety.

This conceptualisation of common ground also helps gain insight into why Australia's gun control has been so successful and how more controversial and regulations can gain support and success even from those who find these policies most unpalatable.

Gun Dealers Are Businesspeople

I remember my very first interview on this project. It was the first time I realised how many hats gun dealers can wear. It was a small gun shop in Victoria that sold diving equipment as well as guns. One side of the store had wetsuits and flippers, the other side had rifles and ammunition. New to the world of shooting and completely outside of the world of deep-sea diving, I wondered what kinds of potential cross-overs of these sports there could be? None, as it turns out – although spear fishing might fall into that category, I supposed. I learned that many dealers diversify their businesses in order to increase revenue or simply stay afloat. As a result, gun dealers have many hats, even some that have nothing to do with firearms. As business owners, they seek to stabilise their businesses and support their livelihoods the same way that we do our own careers and livelihoods.

Approximately 70% of the gun dealers I spoke to had been in business for over 20 years. Their long-term experience in the industry provided detailed and rich information about how the industry has been changed and shaped by the Port Arthur massacre and the gun control regulations that followed. Many had inherited businesses from their fathers and grandfathers. Gun dealers often operated family businesses handed down through the generations. Some even still worked with fathers, sons and partners in the retail stores or ranges I visited. The family feel of many of these places was more common than not. These dealers talked about guns being part of their lives since they were young. They were taught and socialised into the gun-owning community at a young age. Their knowledge, expertise and passion for their sport, livelihood, or pastime were just as palpable. In talking to these gun dealers, who had been in business for so long, they articulated distrust of the government during the 1996 NFA implementation and gun debate but generally made peace with the regulations that followed. They understood why things had changed. The dealer below talked about how the introduction of the NFA in 1996 was political but was needed, and he has come to understand it as a good foundation for control despite its shortcomings.

> *There were some great laws created and still operate today. There could have been far better laws created at that time with a better process. But it's all to do with political gain, public opinion, all of those things. So the time wasn't on our side. It had to be done fairly quicky. A lot of people have still rued the day those laws came in. Unfortunately, those people have to realise that they're a minority, all of us have to coexist.*

Gun dealers who had come into the business of firearms retail more recently talked about what they remembered as young children watching the media coverage of the Port Arthur Massacre and the politicised gun debate that followed. However, these dealers were generally more detached from recalling any community angst from the 1996 gun regulation implementation in comparison to their older counterparts.

These newer gun dealers had businesses that tended to be larger in size and less likely to be filled with family members, but had a professional retail feel to them that underscored the legitimate livelihoods of hunting and shooting sports. Their expertise was just as palpable, but they were much more likely to embrace the regulations that permeate so much of Australian life. They were used to regulation – like so many of my own generation, the regulation of so many aspects of our life is commonplace and normal. Gun laws were seen as no different from the way in which we regulate driving, the sale of real estate or even working with children, and did not evoke the anger or feelings of negativity towards gun control debates of the past when regulations came into being.

> *In Australia today you need a licence to do about anything. You go online and you get a permit...you've got the social acceptance of the process. You've got the older generations that*

will never accept this process. Now this [current] generation, the spending demographic, between 22-35...so that bracket is used to getting licenses, is used to waiting for permits, is used to applying online to do recreational activities.

Common among both of these groups were the underlying drivers of being in business. Gun dealing was a legitimate business. It is their livelihood. Their views about regulation appeared to be driven by how best to run that business and support their livelihoods. While gun dealers who had been in business during 1996 had remarked that the gun regulations had become a deterrent for new gun owners and, for a time, had significantly decreased their business revenue, even these dealers had evolved to become successful and function within the system of regulation now in place. In short, they had gotten used to it, had learned to adapt to a new system of regulation and had even found new opportunities amid the changes the NFA had brought to the market.

For us, [the NFA] flipped the whole thing. So, we had some of these established companies, evacuated from the market, didn't know how to respond, wouldn't put capital in, couldn't invest, weren't nimble, weren't agile, weren't able to do anything, and we've gone 'okay, here our chance.' Movement created opportunity. And if that hadn't have happened, we never could have grown our business. We just couldn't have through normal efforts, we just never would have broken those really established companies down if there was no disruptive activity.

Younger and more recent gun dealers remarked that the gun laws had been good for business. Regulations in Australia have forced all firearms transactions to go through a licenced gun dealer's hand. This ensures their necessity in operating a gun dealer business as a result of their important role in regulation and compliance. Gun dealers are now critical for the gun-owning community to continue their shooting sports, hunting or employment. The gun laws had made them indispensable not only to regulators but also to their fellow gun owners and the broader gun-owning community.

As business owners, gun dealers also have a strong interest in keeping firearm ownership and sales directly contributing to their profits. The illegal market does not benefit them. It's in their interest to ensure that firearm purchases are done legitimately and legally. This point is an important flag for common ground with the public, which also has a vested interest in ensuring that black market or illegal firearms transactions are limited or erased altogether. Unless operating in the black market directly, licenced gun dealers have no interest in participating in the illegal sale of firearms. With the amount of oversight of gun dealers that occurs as part of the process of regulation, there is limited incentive to risk the legitimacy of their business, given the high risk of detection.

These underlying business motivations are also those that are often obscured or twisted in public discourse. Business motivations are often cited as reasons why they want to arm everyone or ignored as if regulation provides no benefit or opportunity at all. The reality is that gun control helps to ensure that firearms transactions are confined to those with the most knowledge and expertise of firearms. As a member of the public, that gives me quite a degree of confidence that these are the right people for this particular job. This is common ground. They share an interest in limiting illegal sales of firearms and forcing all firearms users to go through proper channels. While this motivation may be an economically rational one, and some may wonder whether their business is needed at all, this motivation to comply with and accept gun control legislation is one that could be used as a starting place for generating more collaboration between the gun-owning community and the public, policymakers and regulators.

Gun Dealers Are Members of the Firearms Owning Community

Gun dealers are members of the gun-owning community. Almost all of the gun owners interviewed were themselves involved in shooting sports, hunting, farming, or other legitimate firearms-related activities. They are members of the community they participate in regulating. From the perspective of law enforcement, this makes them insiders to the gun-owning community, as they have insight, understanding and knowledge about the community that the government seeks to regulate. As members of the firearms community and participants in the gun control compliance framework, gun dealers have the opportunity to see how regulation and law enforcement impact the community of which they are members. As a result, dealers are best placed to understand and communicate to the rest of the gun-owning community what regulations entail, how compliance is achieved and why it is necessary. This unique positioning naturally elevates gun dealers as community leaders able to both educate and socialise members into law-abiding gun owners. Their membership in the gun-owning community therefore becomes indispensable, as they act as gatekeepers capable of protecting the gun-owning community from irresponsible firearm use, undesirable membership and unintended surveillance from the government.

Gun dealers take their membership in the community and their role in protecting that community seriously. I have come across repeated examples of gun dealers participating in activities specifically designed to sustain and support the wellbeing of their community. In the summer of 2019, I travelled to Victoria in Australia's south to give a keynote speech at a sporting shooters event, where I learned about some of the activities that local dealers and association chapters were setting up to care for their community. One chapter president told me about a program where they were contributing more than 30 thousand dollars per year to ensure that mental health services reached farmers in remote areas where those health services were limited. These gun dealers had recognised the long-term stress that farmers were under in Australia due to drought and economic conditions and the impact on their livelihoods. Furthermore, they understood that suicides among farmers had been increasing and that farmers had higher suicide rates in comparison to the rest of the Australian population. These beliefs are reflected in current academic research on rural suicides in Australia, where firearms are most often the chosen method of suicide.[3] As leaders of the community, they wanted to contribute to preventing suicides, in part due to the recognition that farmers represent a large portion of their own community of firearms owners. About this initiative, he says:

> *We don't want people resorting to using their firearms for [suicide]. It's not good for them, not for their families and it's not good for the rest of us (gun owners).*

This dealer clearly demonstrated the underlying concern for the broader gun-owning community, which includes Australian farmers who often have high rates of suicide linked to the stress of farming in the wake of drought, flood and fire disasters in Australia and now post-pandemic economic strain.[4] It also demonstrates an understanding that when gun owners experience violence themselves, they recognise the potential impact on the gun-owning community more broadly.

As members of the gun-owning community, gun dealers often expressed sentiments that demonstrated their protectiveness of their community. This was particularly evident when they expressed frustration with members of their community who had behaved in ways they felt reflected poorly on them and the gun-owning community. Gun dealers routinely expressed disapproval of gun owners and even fellow dealers who were seen or perceived to be acting irresponsibly. In addition, they often spoke highly of gun dealers, whom they saw as acting professionally in the way they undertook their everyday tasks. Furthermore, it was clear they saw their role as one that was designed to help new and existing gun owners do the right thing and help them when they encountered problems. The dealer below reported that his clients often encounter errors in the licencing and registration system, and he talked about the ways in which they helped the client manage the relationship between the client and law enforcement.

> *"[in response to an upset client] I tell him 'look, just make note of your phone call [to law enforcement], make a note on your sheets, and just make your own notes.' I said because they're dealing with a couple of hundred thousand people as well. And you know, I know that their records aren't right."*

The dealer above provides a good example of the customer service nature of their business as it is connected to regulatory compliance tasks. In the example above, the gun dealer was describing some of the problems they have encountered with record-keeping with the state firearms registry administered by state police. He talks about how he advises customers on who to talk to and what records to keep to ensure they are doing the right thing. The helping behaviour described here was common among gun dealers. They saw themselves as leaders of the gun-owning community and sought to advise customers in ways that protected the community.

These underlying motivations to protect and preserve the gun-owning community are another example of common ground. Community preservation comes naturally to us as human beings. We seek to defend our communities in order to preserve them. While this includes responses to external threats like scrutiny and judgement from outsiders as well as risky undesirables, we also tend to respond to internal threats. These internal threats include existing members who act in ways that bring criticism to the community. This motivation to preserve and protect is both natural and important for all kinds of communities. As such, the gun dealers' desire to protect their community is not different from our own motivation to protect the communities we are also a part of.

After the Christchurch massacre, I had numerous conversations with members of the gun-owning community who were concerned about what another shooting incident might mean for the gun-owning community here in Australia. They voiced concern about being seen as violent and dangerous and wanted to know how they could better protect their own community from those who sought to use firearms irresponsibly. Some even sought my advice on putting out public statements to the media that would denounce the violence in New Zealand and voice support for victims and their families. While I had no doubt that they found the Christchurch massacre just as upsetting as I did, I also saw how their concern for the backlash they might experience in their own community was intertwined with their emotions.

The desire to protect the gun-owning community by addressing the risks of firearm use in suicide or violence and reducing the likelihood of outside judgement and scrutiny also coincides with the goals of the public and regulators; they also want the firearms community to use firearms responsibly. But it is the gun dealers' membership as insiders, their role as experts and leaders in that community, and their recognition that irresponsible behaviour on behalf of their members can harm their community, where we find common ground between gun owners, dealers and the public. All have a vested interest in responsible firearm use. This interest transcends whether they like the laws or not. Gun owners know that bad behaviour puts them, their livelihoods and their community at risk. This becomes motivation to comply with gun control laws. This motivation for compliance is not driven simply by a desire to avoid law enforcement intervention alone, but to avoid the damage to the reputation of the gun-owning community as legitimate law-abiding citizens.

Gun Dealers Support the Overall Aims of Gun Control

Gun dealers consistently expressed support for the overarching aims of the NFA and spoke positively about specific aspects of the gun control laws in their state. Dealers connected this support to basic morality about safety, preventing violence and keeping guns out of the hands of those who would use them irresponsibly against others or themselves. This moral support is consistent with the broader population, which wants to keep society safe from gun violence. Gun dealer attitudes towards the aims and purpose of the law demonstrate the common ground between the gun-owning community, the public and lawmakers, particularly around the issues that the public supports most. However, it wasn't just their professor's support for the content of gun laws that demonstrates this common ground, but the ways in which their support for gun laws is enacted by gun dealers in their everyday business practices.

Consistent with findings from other countries around the world, gun dealers in Australia supported the importance of background checks. Dealer's all agreed that there were people who were too risky to have access to firearms and that owners should be vetted to ensure that the community is protected. As the quote below demonstrates, this dealer expressed strong support for background checks and licencing requirements that ensured that those who got legal access to firearms were properly vetted.

> *We agree with licencing. We think it's a great idea. Vet the people, vet them as strongly as you want.*

The above quote is consistent with all gun dealers that I talked to, and many gun dealers believed that even back in 1996, most of the gun-owning community would have supported measures that ensured only those who were responsible law-abiding citizens had access to firearms. These claims appear to be substantiated by transcripts from Prime Minister John Howards interaction with the gun-owning community when the gun laws were most hotly debated in Australia. In conversation with the gun-owning community, many gun owners

> *In fact, had you stopped to talk to us you would have learned that the shooting organisations support 90% because that is the part that has been lifted from the Victorian legislation that has operated very well in this country for 10 years.*

Gun control regulations that aim to restrict access to risky people were not just provided because it's safer or more politically correct to do so. It was clear that gun dealers enacted these principles in their everyday business practices. I asked dealers if they had ever had customers come into their stores who they felt should not be allowed access to firearms and what they felt they can or should do with these potential customers. The following dealer articulates what most dealers felt about those who displayed signs of being a danger to themselves or others, or otherwise came to the shop under the influence of drugs or alcohol.

> *I have turned away people who have come here [to my shop] high or drunk. I would never sell to people like that. I've also turned away people who have asked question about firearms that made me think they were a danger to themselves. You never really know for sure, but I'd rather be safe than sorry.*

Dealers often indicated that there is legislation that guides their decision-making on selling to people who exhibit signs of being under the influence of drugs or alcohol, suggesting that they are duty-bound by law to prevent sales to risky people, but it also indicates that even if legal guidelines did not exist, dealers would still take care of who they do business with.

> *It is legislated that you can't sell to those people (without need, who are in distress or under the influence) but if it wasn't legislated, I still don't think it would be something that most dealers would do.*

It was clear that dealers felt a strong sense of duty and responsibility to only sell to safe and law-abiding people. It was also a source of frustration. Dealers felt as though they did not have the appropriate discretion to be able to turn people away from their stores if they had been approved and vetted by law enforcement. As dealers are not part of the vetting process itself, dealers felt as though they were in a difficult position when they thought that someone should not be sold a firearm. This difficult position where discretion is limited is explained by one Victorian dealer, who described an experience where he was uncomfortable selling firearms to an approved and licenced customer.

> *I've has a customer exhibit some disturbing, disturbing behaviour as he's going through the test and doing the process and you know well I can't not say you've been successful, because you've legitimately passed the test, there you are. Questioned it with firearms branch and "well you just let us know his name and we'll look into it".*

Approximately 60% of the dealers shared stories like the one above. These stories demonstrate that dealers are going above and beyond what they are legislated to do and demonstrate their commitment to the overarching aims of gun laws. Their support for vetting gun owners is supported by their willingness to ensure that firearms are only sold to those they believe are responsible and law-abiding citizens.

Vetting requirements were not the only gun control content dealers supported. Gun dealers also strongly agreed with the safety training requirements. Across Australia, one of the defining features of gun laws is the requirement for basic training in firearms. In 2016, when this project was getting started, I also required my research team to undertake the same safety training requirements as a new gun owner would. While I wanted to ensure that my research team knew how to safely handle firearms should they ever find themselves in a position to handle one, I also wanted to understand what safety training entailed. In the state of Queensland, safety training was a day-long course that was split into two parts: theory and practice. The theory portion of training involved a seminar where we learned about the law and gun owners' legal responsibilities when owning a firearm. It also covered safe storage requirements and ended in a multiple-choice test. The pass mark was 100%. You were not able to get any answers wrong. The practice portion involved learning how to handle a range of different firearms. On five different firearms (revolver, semi-automatic handgun, leave action rifle, bolt action rifle and break action shotgun), we were taught how to check whether the firearms were loaded, load them, clear them and fire them. We first practiced on blank-fire training firearms before we were taken to a range to pass a practical test under the supervision of an instructor for each of the five different firearms. At the conclusion, we were also provided information on shooting clubs we could join in order to find a community that would help further our education.

Gun dealers consistently raised the requirement of safety training as a benefit of Australia's gun laws. They believed they had made a difference. Gun dealers who also had experience working on or operating gun ranges were particularly complementary about the safety training requirements, as indicated by the dealer below.

> *The compulsory safety training, I think, has made a difference. After they started making people do that, there are much less incidents and mishaps with firearms, especially on the range.*

The dealer above believed these compulsory requirements had made a difference to safety, or the gun-owning community as well as the broader society, and demonstrates their moral support for the content of these gun laws. However, not only do gun dealers support these initiatives, they also believe that they have an important role to play in educating new customers about safety, particularly when it comes to new firearms owners. The dealers below articulate what many dealers expressed about their responsibility in interacting with customers.

> *We do our best, always when we're selling firearms to individuals, a new license holder, we talk to them about firearm safety. When they pick the firearm up we go through the firearm with them – safety, loading, unloading – always.*

Furthermore, dealers felt a strong desire to educate their customers, and this education had concerns about safety at its very core. The dealer below walked me through what he and his staff do with new firearms owners who purchase firearms in their store.

> *To the best of our ability we try and make sure that the person picking a firearm up is aware of the firearm, its operation and safety.*

The dealer above also walked me through the process of coming to the store to purchase a new firearm. In this *hypothetical* exercise,[5] I learned not only how to safely operate the firearm but also how to clean it and take care of it in order to minimise problems with the mechanical workings, my responsibilities to store it according to current regulations, and learned that the dealer would be happy for me to return to his store if I had questions about the firearm and its operation, use, or the laws. While this demonstration was helpful in showing me how gun dealers see their role as educators in spending time at retail shops across the country, I also had the ability to see this enacted by dealers in real time. Not only do dealers support the safety requirements of gun regulations, but they also make educating customers, especially new customers, a purposeful part of their everyday business activity.

Vetting requirements for gun owners and safety training and storage requirements are core components of Australia's gun laws, and these components are central to the public safety aims of gun laws. The support for vetting requirements and the active role in educating the public demonstrate the critical role that gun dealers play in keeping the community safe. I asked dealers whether they saw themselves having a broader role in public safety. Dealers like the one below recognised how important their position was in helping to contribute to the public safety goals that the NFA was trying to achieve.

> *Every dealer has a role in public safety... I believe dealers do play a crucial part in community safety because they're the people on the front line. They're selling ammunition, they're doing licence checks, they're the middle person in the supply chain. They're also responsible for safe storage in large numbers.*

Dealers also suggested that they wanted to be involved as much as possible in contributing to safer firearms ownership practices. One dealer from WA talked about wanting to have more opportunity to collaborate with law enforcement and contribute to initiatives that bolster responsible firearm use.

> *Wherever there is an avenue for us to be involved in public safety we're involved.*

These attitudes and views about the role dealers play in gun control compliance demonstrate that moral support for the laws is a central motivator for compliance with the law and that gun dealer business practices were built around ways that supported the central aims of the NFA. Their views and attitudes suggest that common ground exists between the gun-owning community and the public on the content of the law, particularly those that keep firearms out of the hands of risky people, and proper protocols on ensuring that privately owned firearms are stored safely to minimise misuse. Gun dealers share with the broader public their moral beliefs regarding firearm use and public safety. Furthermore, gun dealers are willing participants in the enactment of gun policies that are aimed at ensuring the public and gun owners are kept safe from irresponsible behaviour involving firearms and firearm-related accidents.

The support and commitment to implementing the law exhibited by gun dealers during my time with them offers a counter-narrative to what is most often found in media stereotypes of firearms owners and dealers. Thinking back to the time of the NFA's creation and implementation, media narratives framed dealers as those who were resistant to or uninterested in community safety when it came to firearm regulation. I have found that not only are dealers passionate about educating their customers and the public about firearms safety, they are also committed to doing what they can to fulfill the overarching aims of the NFA as leaders in their community. Given their role as front-line workers in gun control regulation, gun dealers are well placed to translate and reinforce the expectations of gun laws for firearms owners, not because the laws say they must, but because they believe in the goals of that law in protecting the public. As a result, gun dealers are perfectly placed to fill that educative role, given that they are the conduits with whom new or experienced gun owners must interact with.

Gun Dealers Are Law-Abiding Citizens

On June 16, 1996, Prime Minister John Howard addressed members of a pro-gun rally in the town of Sale, Victoria. He began that rally, acknowledging their concern that the new gun laws had hit hard at their collective identity as law-abiding citizens. In his speech, he said:

> *I want to Start my address to you today by saying at no stage in the weeks that have gone by since the decision taken by the Federal Government and the Police Ministers in that decision, at no stage have I sought to describe or categorise the attitude of people who enjoy shooting or people who are shooters as being in anyway criminal or un-Australian. I have not used language which has thought to label or smear you or other tens of thousands of law abiding citizens.*[6]
>
> *(Prime Minister John Howard, June 16, 1996)*

His remarks were in response to the reaction from farmers, shooters, hunters and other legal firearms owners who felt that the creation of gun laws had turned them from law-abiding citizens into criminals with the stroke of a pen. Approximately 70% of the gun dealers I talk to across Australia remember or were in business in 1996 when the gun laws were introduced. Twenty-two years later, gun dealers still balk at the way in which they were made to feel like they were criminals.

Over and over again, dealers in my study expressed their feelings that the 1996 gun laws made legitimate and law-abiding gun owners into criminals by outlawing specific firearms that had previously been legal. But it was the narrative that was built around the need to regulate legal firearms owners that gun dealers felt offended by their strong sense of identity as law-abiding citizens who used firearms within the bounds of law, safely and responsibly. In this case, detachment from the policy they enact is not possible for gun dealers, given that regulations target them as much as they target their clients. The dealer below expresses concern that legitimate gun owners had been blamed for the Port Arthur massacre and suggests that this narrative is still present more than 20 years after the incident.

> *Generally, shooters, the organization, legitimate people, had been blamed for the Port Arthur incident. They [shooters] felt victimized, and as it goes down the line, consistently demonized even to this day. It always is a negative connotation.*

The dealer above specifically refers to the way in which he felt as though legitimate shooters had become scapegoats in the wake of the port Arthur massacre and suggests that this connotation persists. This perception was a consistent worry for dun dealers, and it cut right to the centre of their angst about national gun control: that new regulations would immediately criminalise activities that they had lawfully engaged in for any number of years.

Gun dealers are law-abiding citizens. They have to be in order to be eligible for gun ownership and to be issued a gun dealer licence. But being law-abiding is more than just a box to check on a gun licence application or background check form. This is a core part of their identity, which resonated with every single gun dealer whom I have interviewed. The concept of being "law abiding" is so critical to the identity of the dealer that most flagged this early on in the interview – putting it on the table almost immediately as we sat down to talk. They see themselves as the safest members of society; they are the least criminal and subject to the most amount of surveillance possible. Current regulations across Australia would confirm that any prospective gun dealer or gun owner must pass a background check that includes criminal and mental health, and even medical history to ensure they are a fit and proper person to own a firearm or operate a licenced dealership. Furthermore, dealers are subject to inspections by law enforcement, which include any property and any firearm under their control, to ensure that they are compliant with regulations. Gun owners, more broadly, must also pass a background check in order to qualify as a fit and proper person and are subject to random inspections of their firearms in order to ensure they are stored safely. Few populations in Australia would experience this level of surveillance, and so it was easy to understand why they believed they were one of the safest groups of people in the country.

My observations in talking to dealers across the country are that being a law-abiding citizen is central to their identity. Dealers often made reference to the distinction between legal and illegal work related to firearms, but always in the context of reminding me that they are law-abiding citizens and in an attempt to correct what they feel is a public misunderstanding of their community. The dealer below reiterates the legality of their work and suggests that negative public perception is based on a misunderstanding of who they are as a collective.

> *We do get that people don't necessarily like us, but our product is legal, what we do is legal, and they don't necessarily like isn't me or our industry, but what they don't like is what they perceive it to be, which is quite often not the truth.*

Every single dealer or gun owner I talked to made a point to construct their own and a broader collective group of gun owners as legal and law-abiding citizens. By doing this, they clearly distinguish between themselves as safe and responsible gun owners and others who are irresponsible and illegal gun owners. Referring to themselves as "licenced people" was a common descriptor used by dealers that highlighted the link between being approved gun owners and those that comply with the law no matter what. The dealer below uses the term "licenced people" to describe the concern that licenced gun owners were treated by law enforcement as if they were criminals.

> *...if you get pulled up in your car [by the police] and they run your number, you come up, red flagged 'beware: a firearms owner'. We are in the crime portfolio. Licensed people.*

The reference to licenced people to underscore the law-abiding nature of gun owners and their activities did not appear to refer only to individual dealer identities. Dealers routinely referred to themselves as part of a collective by referring to "we" when answering questions about their experiences.

The dealer's identities as law-abiding citizens are important because they demonstrate what compliance theorists believe is a primary motivator for complying with and upholding the law: civic identity and a willingness to subscribe to the authority of the legislator. What this means is that those with a strong identity as law-abiding citizens are more likely to uphold the law even when they don't agree with the law's content. In Chapter 1, I defined legislative authority as the belief that upholding the law is more important than the content of the law itself. In other words, there is a moral obligation to obey the law, regardless of whether they agree with it. For gun dealers in Australia, their strong identity as law abiding citizens helps us understand why, even among the initial angst regarding new gun laws back in 1996, they comply with the law anyway.

While dealers generally supported the aims of the NFA, there was also plenty of evidence to suggest that dealers complied with regulations they didn't like, didn't enjoy, or didn't think were worthwhile. When dealers' expressed dissatisfaction with the implementation of regulations, they frequently commented that because this is *the law*, it had to be followed regardless of their views about its value. These instances suggest that dealers subscribe authority to the legislator and comply with regulations, even though they may find problems with their implementation. Dealers frequently expressed frustration with the gun control implementation (as opposed to content) and suggested that law enforcement had gone beyond the aims and intentions of the legislature to create regulations that didn't make sense or potentially created problems. The dealer below suggests that they often have customers who have been issued firearms licences and permits that they, the dealers, do not believe are fit and proper to own a firearm. When asked what they can do about these questionable customers, he says that the decision to issue firearms licences is made by the police only and that dealers are not in a position to use discretion and must follow the law, regulation, or law enforcement decision even when they don't agree with it.

> *We can't make that decision (to deny an application and not serve a customer), but we can also be held liable because they're offended or we've defamed them somehow.*

My travels across the country talking to gun dealers often left me thinking about the delicate balance gun dealers appeared to have to manage between their support for the law and frustration with some aspects of it. The dealer above highlights this balance well and speaks articulately about how their positions as gun dealers are often difficult to navigate. They had to make peace with aspects of the law or regulations they didn't like because it was their job to ensure that firearms sales complied with the law. These attitudes towards the law as something that must be obeyed no matter what indicates two commonly overlooked opportunities for working with the gun-owning community in order to achieve gun control creation and compliance. First, there is a solid foundation of willingness to obey laws simply because being law-abiding is critical to their identity. Second, the gun dealers' position as leaders in their community provides a unique opportunity for them to socialise others in the gun-owning community into moral and law-abiding expectations of behaviour. I argue that both of these are critical to the long-term success of gun control regulations.

Gun Dealers Are Agents of Informal Social Control

As members of their community who hold respect, authority and expertise, gun dealers are important enforcers of what criminologists call "informal social control." Informal social control refers to the way in which our behaviour is influenced by those around us. *Informal* social control is most often contrasted with *formal* social control, which most of us recognise as the formal institutions of society that intervene when we break the law, such as the police, courts and corrections components of the criminal justice system. Laws and regulations, like those that make up Australia's gun control policy, represent formal social control. These laws tell us what behaviour is expected and what formal control systems will do if we are found to break those laws.[7] Informal social control refers to the way in which normal and appropriate expectations of behaviour become internalised via our interactions with others, including our parents, teachers and peers. These people who play meaningful and important roles in our lives teach us what behaviour is expected and what behaviour is unacceptable. Starting from childhood, institutions such as the family, schools and even religion help us learn what normal and appropriate behaviour looks like. Informal social control relies on our need to be accepted and in good standing with those around us. This means that we behave appropriately or comply with the law because we want to avoid negative public reactions and disappointment from those most important to us.

While these more social punishments might seem less harsh than jail time or financial penalties, they are often considered to be just as influential. When we breach social norms or laws, there are important social consequences from parents, teachers, friends, or other members of our community. Those consequences when we are young may range from physical punishments (if you are from my era), time outs, or (god forbid) making your parents "think about your punishment." But the disappointment shown on our parents' faces is usually what sends the signal that we've crossed the line and jeopardised trust and good standing in our family circle. These informal processes are critical because they teach us about social norms and morality. This socialisation becomes internalised, and we come to accept, believe and enforce those social norms around us too. From childhood onwards, we are invested in what those closest to us think and feel about us, and being able to maintain trust, respect and affection influences our behaviour.

This process continues into adulthood. In our adolescence, we are concerned about what our friends think about us, which is one of the reasons why peer groups and their influence are so critical for understanding deviant and criminal behaviour.[8] As adults, we are concerned about losing our jobs, what our neighbours think of us, and our closest friends and family, even our children. These relationships help to condition our behaviour. We don't want to jeopardise these relationships by doing something deviant or criminal. Criminal behaviour would jeopardise their trust and respect, and possibly our inclusion and acceptance in those social groups. The risk to these important relationships is far more compelling than the threat of jail or formal punishment alone.

One of criminology's most long-standing research findings and theoretical principles is that informal social control is far more effective in motivating compliance than formal social control.[9] Why? Because we care more about what people in our own community think about us than about distant legal enforcers such as judges, the police and, by definition, gun control policymakers. Criminological theories, based on the assumption that informal social control is effective in motivating law-abiding behaviour, would suggest that if you want to ensure that gun owners comply with gun control regulations, having people inside the community who can socialise, influence and teach people what normal and responsible gun use looks like is critical. What that means is that if you want to effectively regulate the gun-owning community, getting that community to buy into those regulations and regulate itself is the best way to ensure people are complying with the law and, perhaps more importantly, operating firearms in a safe and responsible manner.

As leaders in the gun-owning community, gun dealers can and do act as informal social control enforcers, demonstrating and teaching what responsible and moral behaviour involving firearms looks like via their role in the gun control compliance process. As leaders who generally support the overarching aims of gun control and as law-abiding citizens who believe that obeying the law is important for their own and the group's identity, they have a vested interest in ensuring that new and existing members of the gun-owning community are upholding the values and beliefs of the broader community. Knowing that informal social control is far more effective for influencing compliance behaviour than formal social control, this makes leaders of the gun-owning community essential for bridging the divide between regulators and the regulated community.

As I spent time watching gun dealers go about their daily tasks in their retail shops, it became evident that their role in the compliance process is an understudied and even misunderstood component of what has made Australia's relationship with effective gun control successful. Despite what the public might think, this project revealed that there is far more common ground between gun dealers, the gun-owning community and the public/regulators when it comes to concern for safety than we often see in public discourse. This is important, primarily because our public discourse often focuses on difference rather than similarity. Differences as a starting point are often divisive, but similarity at least allows us to begin understanding that there is a common goal or begin with the common ground as a foundation for discussion and debate. Gun dealers in Australia, having a vested interest in their business, their community, holding support for the aims of gun control laws, and having a strong identity as law-abiding citizens, showcase where that common ground can be found for better and more productive conversations about gun control.

Are Australian Gun Dealers an Anomaly in Their Support of Gun Control?

I've often thought about why Australian gun dealers appear to be so different from existing narratives linking gun ownership and anti-gun control sentiment. I wondered if Australians have a higher tolerance for regulation or whether our culture is based more on collective values rather than individual ones. However, existing global research on what gun owners are willing to support regarding gun control policy is mixed and suggests that there is much less division between the gun-owning community and the public than we assume or we have been led to believe by media representations of the gun control debate. The research is mixed because it depends on how you ask the question about gun control and what kind of policy regarding gun control is being asked about. For example, asking people if they support widespread bans on specific firearms is likely to have different patterns from asking people whether they support safe storage policies. Gun control cannot be reduced to a singular policy. It can include any and all possibilities, ranging from bans on specific types of firearms to safety and storage requirements and anything in between. Gun owners may support some, all, or none of these. What more recent research is telling us is that the gun-owning community is not a homogenous group of anti-gun control advocates. Instead, there are nuances and distinctions within the gun-owning community that overlap with the rest of the public when it comes to gun control sentiment. In this sense, Australian gun dealers may not be as different from gun owners worldwide.

One of the most long-standing findings in the international research community suggests that gun ownership predicts attitudes towards gun control policies in general, helping to solidify the link between gun ownership and anti-gun control sentiment.[10] That is, those who own firearms are less likely to support forms of gun regulation and control. This suggests that gun owners are likely to have attitudes towards gun control policies that would protect their interests in hunting, shooting sports, self-defence, etc., without hindrance or interference from regulators. However, this kind of research has typically been based on research that compares non-gun owners with gun owners, which is good for understanding some of the distinctions between the gun-owning and non-gun-owning communities, but not good at helping us understand the diversity of attitudes within the gun-owning community itself. Furthermore, the majority of this research has been undertaken in the USA, which is not representative of other South Pacific, European, Asian, or even African countries in terms of how polarised or politicised gun control has become. While these studies are important, they often lead to the assumption that the gun-owning community is one homogenous group that thinks and feels the same about gun control no matter where they are around the world.

Studies that have focused on the views of gun owners specifically have done a better job of drawing out the nuances in attitudes and opinions towards gun control from within the community. Gun owners are usually supportive of controls that restrict access to firearms by those who might pose a risk to themselves or others. Those are people who are mentally ill, have a history of criminality or delinquency and those who are young are considered members of "risky groups" where gun access should be restricted.[11] These are also views shared by the population as a whole.[12] Underlying this support are the motivations that tap into our emotions of care and concern for the safety and wellbeing of others. That means gun owners too recognise the same potential risk to the community that the rest of the public does and typically want to protect the community from those who might use a firearm to harm others. This moral underlying motivation for restricting risky people from firearms is the common ground shared by the gun-owning and non-gun-owning populations. This finding is consistent globally, as it has been across gun dealers in Australia.[13]

Similarly, research has long linked gun ownership with conservative political views more broadly, reinforcing gun owners as a homogenous group politically.[14] Research that seeks to understand how guns have become so politicised suggests that gun owners who lean towards political conservativism and share common traits consistent with right-wing politics are less likely to support gun control policies. However, the assumption that all gun owners are politically right-leaning is also misleading. Research that looks at differences within the gun-owning community shows that gun owners are politically diverse just as they are diverse in their views about gun control, especially when you look outside of the USA.[15]

My experience with the gun-owning community in Australia suggests that the gun-owning community is just as politically diverse. In 2016, I attended the annual conference of the Sporting

Shooters Association of Australia as their keynote speaker. I sat at a table with SSAA representatives from all across the country. I listened to them talk about their families, their work, and about Australia's political climate. One of the things that surprised me most was how passionate many people are about the environment, especially after some of the recent floods and bushfires that have had devastating effects on wildlife across Australia. I also learned that SSAA had partnered with various government departments in the state of New South Wales to implement a code of ethics for sustainable and responsible hunting in order to maintain conservation efforts. That I was so surprised to find such passion for environmental issues (an issue typically aligned with left-wing politics in Australia) was another sign I'd be socialised to believe this group of gun owners were a homogenous group of right-wing voters. I certainly encountered conservative views on gun control and other social issues, but I also encountered just as many views aligned with liberal political stances. It was a reminder for me as a researcher that the gun-owning community is not one homogenous group of right-leaning gun owners who therefore abhor all forms of gun regulation.

In Australia, the links between political leaning and gun control support are different but still present, and public sentiment often assumes that gun owners are politically conservative, even though gun control was primarily spearheaded by a conservative government in 1996. However, we do see vehement and aggressive political dialogue regarding gun control in Australia. For example, one of Australia's more socially progressive parties, in strongly defending and promoting stricter gun control, appeared to make links between gun ownership and national terrorism threats, thus fusing labels of violence, risk and criminality with legal gun ownership in public debate. The emergence of smaller parties like the Shooters, Fishers and Farmers Party that hold influential seats in Australian state parliaments suggests that none of the dominant parties particularly resonate with the interests of gun owners in Australia. However, these interests also align strongly with people's livelihoods rather than a gun culture identity or wanting to use guns as self-defence, as we've seen in American arguments for retaining unfettered gun ownership. As such, linking views of gun ownership with right-wing conservatives not only diminishes the diversity within the gun-owning community but also prevents effective dialogue that is based on shared understandings of violence, safety and how to prevent irresponsible gun use, even if those shared understandings are small. Gun dealers in Australia have demonstrated that there is opportunity and possibility to capture the common ground that exists once you look beyond the typical political-driven narrative of the gun debate divide.

Chapter Summary

Public debates about gun control, here in Australia and particularly in North America, could have us believing that there is no common ground on which to base fruitful conversation about the regulation of guns. While Australia's relationship with guns, gun laws and gun rights is in some ways unique to the experience of debate in other places, especially the USA, we too find that the gun-owning community's concern for how regulation may impact their livelihoods, pastimes and even identity is an indication that they have no overlap with concerns about the dangers of irresponsible firearms use. In talking with gun dealers in Australia, I find that there is far more common ground than we realise. While there are specific policies that we can all agree on, background checks and limiting firearm access for risky people in the community who are most likely to harm themselves or others, what we do share are the values that underlie that support. Gun dealers care about the safety of their families, their community and a moral sense of what is right and wrong. This is what drives support for gun control laws. Furthermore, their identity as law-abiding citizens drives support for gun safety even deeper, perhaps even driving support for policies that have caused them concern.

Knowing that leaders in the gun-owning community share these views provides a foundation for a new kind of conversation. One that works towards a common goal in the regulation of firearms rather than one that appears to drive us apart. It's important to recognise that there are more similarities than we realise. With this knowledge in tow, it becomes easier to try to understand their concerns about gun control. Gun dealers in Australia had many concerns about gun laws in Australia. I found that I shared some of those concerns as a citizen worried about safety and violence and as a criminologist concerned about how to motivate legal compliance. In Chapter 3, I explore those concerns and why the general public should also share them.

Notes

1 You can watch McConaughey's White house Speech here: https://www.youtube.com/watch?v=nqx4wfnCD4w

2 Burton, A. L., Logan, M. W., Pickett, J. T., Cullen, F. T., Jonson, C. L., & Burton Jr, V. S. (2021). Gun owners and gun control: Shared status, divergent opinions. *Sociological Inquiry*, *91*(2), 347–366.

3 Kennedy, A., Adams, J., Dwyer, J., Rahman, M. A., & Brumby, S. (2020). Suicide in rural Australia: Are farming-related suicides different? *International Journal of Environmental Research and Public Health*, *17*(6), 2010.

4 Judd, F., Jackson, H., Fraser, C., Murray, G., Robins, G., & Komiti, A. (2006). Understanding suicide in Australian farmers. *Social Psychiatry & Psychiatric Epidemiology*, *41*(1): 1–10.

Berry, H., Hogan, A., Owen, J., Rickwood, D., & Fragar, L. (2011). Climate change and farmers' mental health: Risks and responses. *Asia-Pacific Journal of Public Health*, *23*(2) 119S–132S.

Kennedy, A., Adams, J., Dwyer, J., Rahman, M. A., & Brumby, S. (2020). Suicide in rural Australia: Are farming-related suicides different? *International Journal of Environmental Research and Public Health*, *17*(6), 2010.

5 At no point during this study, or since its conclusion, did I, or a member of my research team purchase a firearm.

6 https://pmtranscripts.pmc.gov.au/release/transcript-10030

7 Braithwaite, J. (1989). *Crime, shame and reintegration*. Cambridge University Press.

8 McGloin, J. M., & Thomas, K. J. (2019). Peer influence and delinquency. *Annual Review of Criminology*, 2, 241–264.

9 Chriss, J. J. (2022). Social control: An introduction. John Wiley & Sons.

10 Burton, A. L., Logan, M. W., Pickett, J. T., Cullen, F. T., Jonson, C. L., & Burton Jr, V. S. (2021). Gun owners and gun control: shared status, divergent opinions. *Sociological Inquiry*, *91*(2), 347–366.

11 Kruis, N. E., Wentling, R. L., Frye, T. S., & Rowland, N. J. (2021). Firearm ownership, defensive gun usage, and support for gun control: Does knowledge matter? *American journal of criminal justice*, 1–30.

12 Skeem, J., & Mulvey, E. (2020). What role does serious mental illness play in mass shootings, and how should we address it? *Criminology & Public Policy*, *19*(1), 85–108.

13 Celinska, K. (2007). Individualism and collectivism in America: The case of gun ownership and attitudes toward gun control. *Sociological Perspectives*, *50*(2), 229–247.
14 Burton, A. L., Logan, M. W., Pickett, J. T., Cullen, F. T., Jonson, C. L., & Burton Jr, V. S. (2021). Gun owners and gun control: shared status, divergent opinions. *Sociological Inquiry*, *91*(2), 347–366.
15 Burton, A. L., Logan, M. W., Pickett, J. T., Cullen, F. T., Jonson, C. L., & Burton Jr, V. S. (2021). Gun owners and gun control: shared status, divergent opinions. *Sociological Inquiry*, *91*(2), 347–366.

3

BARRIERS TO COLLABORATION AND EFFECTIVE GUN POLICY

The actual issue isn't the NFA, the issue isn't the Firearms Act.

The first set of interviews for the gun dealer project took place in the state of Victoria. My Research Assistant Emma and I had flown into Melbourne late at night and made our way out to the dealer shop just outside of town early the following morning. A typical Victorian winter morning is cold, frosty and, on this occasion, foggy. The dealer's shop was on a main street in town, shared with other retail outlets, cafes and restaurants. We noticed city employees setting up for work just outside the entrance of the dealer's shop. We didn't give it much thought, as it looked like they were doing concrete work on the footpath. We learned more about what these city workers were doing about halfway through our interview. The gun dealer brought our interview to an abrupt halt as he got up to talk to the city employees who had started to pour concrete. They were there to install cement bollards that would provide a barrier between the road and the front of the dealer's shop, and the dealer explained that the bollards were to prevent people from driving a truck or car into the front window of the dealer's shop in order to steal firearms. These "ram raids", as they are commonly referred to, had become a concern after several dealers had become victims of these crimes and firearms had been stolen in the process. The reason for the dealer's interruption to speak to the city employees is that he observed the bollards were being placed so far apart that a car or truck could still

DOI: 10.4324/9781003271642-4

pass between them, therefore preventing the bollards from fulfilling their main purpose. This incident I found indicative of the core and most common concerns that gun dealers reported about gun regulations – they are generally a good idea but implemented poorly.

The idea of the bollards to prevent ram raids and the risk of stolen firearms ending up in the hands of risky people is sound, and gun dealers often felt that many aspects of the gun laws were sound. As Chapter 2 demonstrates, gun dealers are generally supportive of the main aims of gun control to prevent gun crime and increase community safety. However, like the bollards in the story above – the implementation of which changed nothing to prevent a truck from ram raiding the property – gun dealers hold strong negative feelings and concerns about the way in which gun laws have been implemented. In the interviews of gun dealers across Australia, they were not shy in holding back many examples of where implementation had failed entirely, created unnecessary risks to safety, disregarded the expertise on firearms held by gun dealers, and made their everyday compliance tasks problematic and prone to error. Each one of these concerns has the potential to undermine the relationship between gun dealers and law enforcement, policymakers, the public, and run the risk of undermining gun laws altogether. This is, or should be, of great concern to all of us given that the success and effectiveness of gun regulation require the support of gun dealers formally and informally, and they can provide a unique and important perspective on how gun laws work on the ground.

In this chapter, I outline the primary concerns gun dealers raised about the gun laws in Australia. These findings were the ones that were the most surprising to me, not because I didn't think they had concerns about gun law implementation, but because their concerns about implementation brought into focus why gun dealers and the gun-owning community are so critical to gun control effectiveness, critical to community safety and highlighted the value of collaborating with a community that holds expertise in what is being regulated. Furthermore, research on how to gain compliance and support for policy suggests that addressing and acknowledging these concerns are likely to boost the efficacy of gun laws already in place and help to support the reduction in gun-related deaths and gun crime we have seen in Australia since the mid-80s. In Chapter 2, I framed the support of gun laws held by gun dealers as "common ground". Here, I frame the negative feelings towards gun laws as "barriers" because of the way in which they raise concerns about the primary goals of the NFA and undermine the collaborations necessary to ensure that gun laws remain effective in the long term. These barriers are not uncommon. The concerns that dealers raised about gun laws are primarily concerns that should be considered by anyone who wants smart, efficient, and effective gun laws in any context.

What Are "Barriers"?

During my interviews, I asked gun dealers a series of questions about what they would change about the gun laws in Australia, what could be improved, and what they disliked about Australia's gun control. At no time did a gun dealer suggest that getting rid of them altogether was preferable, and at no time did a gun dealer suggest that the North American argument about gun rights was appropriate for the Australian context. However, these conversations were the most impassioned, palpable with frustration and, at times, anger. But they were not frustrations and anger about the laws themselves, but about their implementation and the processes in place to enact them. Their concerns were many, and, for the most part, I found myself resonating with their concerns both as a member of society and as a criminologist. I saw that their frustrations represented potential threats to the effectiveness and efficiency of the gun control regulatory system when considering what criminological and legal research tells us about how to achieve compliance with the law. Their concerns highlighted the complexity of gun regulation, how frequently regulations are changed, and how challenging and tenuous the relationship is between gun dealers and regulators. When these concerns are unaddressed and unacknowledged, they can become barriers that run the risk of undermining effective gun control in Australia.

Barriers are more than just the concerns themselves. They are the underlying currents that chip away at the common ground that gun dealers share with the broader community. Barriers such as this matter not just because they are concerns raised by a large constituency of the gun-owning community who are directly affected by these regulations. Their concerns highlight important gaps in the law and, thus, risks to the community. They highlight misunderstandings about the use, availability and basic mechanics of firearms, and they highlight missed opportunities to capitalise on one of the most well-regulated and least criminal populations in the country. These barriers are important because they represent weaknesses in the construction and enactment of gun control regulations, and therefore opportunities for gun control policy and public support to be undermined.

I argue that the concerns raised in this chapter as barriers to effective gun policy are important risks to the performance of those regulations over time and risks that undermine the willingness to collaborate by gun dealers across the country. Gun dealers want more efficient, effective, and transparent implementation of the NFA's aims. They want to be collaborators, with their expertise utilised, respected and consulted when creating, revising and carrying out gun control policy. They want to be part of the solution, not the problem and are not assumed to be criminals putting society at risk. These concerns not only have implications for how to shift the broader cultural understanding of gun control and how to achieve it, but also represent the individual-level problems that consume the gun dealer's daily tasks. These barriers highlight where the implementation of gun regulation is putting society at risk rather than protecting it from gun violence.

In Chapter 1, I situated gun dealers as street-level bureaucrats who serve on the front lines of policy delivery and implantation. I found it helpful to borrow Lipsky's understanding of street-level bureaucrats in understanding the context of the concerns raised by gun dealers about the law. Their primary complaints about gun laws in Australia are directly related to the bureaucratic nature of their role. While compliance tasks take up the core components of a gun dealers' business, the bureaucratic components that accompany these tasks – complexity and number of forms, inconsistencies in processing and use of forms, navigating compliance tasks alongside law enforcement and learning to pivot their business to comply with each regulation change – were common concerns across gun dealers. They created confusion, unnecessary administrative burden and frustration for gun owners and dealers alike. These bureaucratic concerns and burdens are an important component of gun control implementation that helps us understand negative reactions and feelings about gun control among gun dealers and is an important factor in understanding how compliance might be best achieved when laws and regulations create debate and tension in public discourse. The barriers most critical to understanding the origins of gun dealer concerns about the law are considered here and include the way in which deterrence-based approaches dominate the interactions and relationships between gun dealers and law enforcement, the perceived lack of consultation and respect for their expertise in the regulatory process and the administrative burden gun dealers experience in carrying out their role in the compliance process. I argue that each of these concerns carries risks that undermine effective policy and support for gun control within the gun-owning community.

Deterrence as Enforcement's Primary Motivator

The concept of deterrence in criminology has a long and complex history. Deterrence, as defined in Chapter 1, refers to the way in which punishment and consequences for behaviour are designed to prevent people from deciding to violate the law. Western criminal justice systems are founded on principles of deterrence. Our system of law specifies punishments for specific legal violations to provide incentives to comply for individuals and society as a whole.[1] When individuals break the law, the punishment (fines, jail time, license suspensions, etc.), is designed to send a message to the individual not to break the law again. However, these punishments are also designed to send a symbolic message to the rest of society to reinforce what the expectations of behaviour are and incentivise compliance by warning what the consequences will be if we violate them.

Our system of regulating gun dealers and the gun-owning community is also founded on principles of deterrence; people will comply because they want to avoid the costs associated with non-compliance. Formal surveillance is necessary to complete this deterrent goal – a role that the firearms licencing branch of law enforcement provides to check that gun owners and dealers are complying with the law. For the gun-owning community, and especially gun dealers, the level of surveillance is relatively high. Inspections by police for gun dealers and legal gun owners, background checks for new licence holders and renewals are all examples of routine and regular surveillance by law enforcement to ensure that gun owners and dealers are complying with the law. When gun dealers and owners are found to be non-compliant, there are a range of consequences available: removal of firearms, suspension of licences for up to 10 years, monetary fines and possibly jail time. For dealers and many gun owners who use firearms as part of their employment, non-compliance means they put their livelihoods in jeopardy.

In order for deterrent methods to effectively influence behaviour, gun dealers must not only be aware that they are being watched but must also recognise what the consequences are for non-compliance. Findings from this study demonstrate that dealers are both aware of the level of surveillance they are under and aware of the consequences of non-compliance. Dealers also suggested that they believe there is a high possibility of being detected if they were not complying with the law, primarily because of the level of surveillance and the frequent interactions with law enforcement, which increase the odds of non-compliance detection. Theoretically, this means that deterrence is working – law enforcement's surveillance of gun dealers and gun owners appears to have a motivating effect when it comes to compliance with the law. In other words, deterrence is a motivator for compliance when it comes to understanding why gun dealers comply with gun laws.

Dealers consistently talk about the feeling of being constantly watched by law enforcement, indicating that they recognise that the gun laws are being enforced and that there is a high risk of any non-compliance being detected. When asked about whether they are aware of punishments being handed out to non-compliance dealers, the dealer below demonstrates that they perceive this threat vicariously through other dealers who have experienced such consequences, even when they have not experienced it themselves.

> *The threat is there, they've charge two dealers over the transport policy, they are going hard after another dealer at the moment for range compliance.*

This notion of *going hard* alludes to a perception of unfairness. This perception of unfairness is corroborated by other dealers, who believe that members of law enforcement are intent on finding problems simply to prosecute dealers.

> *There were a couple of officers from the [city], and all they wanted to do was find something wrong and prosecute you for it.*

Another dealer expresses using strategies of avoidance simply to minimise his interactions with police who he felt were treating them unfairly during formal surveillance processes, which led to negative emotional responses when working with police.

> *I try to minimize my interactions (with police) because I just get angry.*

These negative emotions were shared widely by 90% of dealers in the study. Their frustrations with feeling like the police were *out to get them* during times of surveillance were often expressed by dealers. And while gun dealers discuss their aim to comply because the costs of not complying are high, these frustrating and negative interactions undermine the possibility of a collaborative relationship with police. For one dealer, the manner in which surveillance is enacted by police undermines the value that gun dealers bring to the table as part of the compliance process.

> *The [police] just turn it into a nightmare. We are quite capable of logging into the system and doing it ourselves.*

This dealer refers to the frustration with the surveillance and partnership process itself. They are mandated to comply with the administrative responsibility, but at the same time, this dealer felt they were not trusted to do it without the police looking over their shoulder. These reactions and experiences of the deterrent model of motivating compliance become a barrier to effective gun control because they create an undercurrent of frustration and tension among gun dealers and therefore run the risk of undermining the belief that the law is legitimate.

Overall, dealers clearly indicated that they were motivated to comply with the law in order to avoid penalties and risks to their livelihood. Not only do they understand that there are substantial penalties for non-compliance, they recognise that the risk of detection is high. So why is the deterrent aim of the law considered a barrier here? First, deterrence alone is not enough to motivate compliance over the long term. Classical criminologists who develop a deterrence-based approach to crime control would suggest that compliance is likely to be undermined by overly harsh or unfair practices by law enforcement.[2] The gun dealers in this study share perceptions that the implementation of gun control regulations is often unfair, or too strict, or carries liabilities that unequally affect them and their livelihoods. Deterrence used as the primary motivator for the architecture and implementation of gun laws appears to undermine moral support for the law's content – a support that is generally shared between gun dealers and law makers. While this does not necessarily mean that deterrence-based approaches are not effective in motivating compliance behaviour, if this is the only motivator considered useful by policymakers, then there are missed opportunities to capitalise on the willingness of dealers to work with law enforcement. This risk becomes evident when dealers discuss the types of interactions they experience with law enforcement.

Gun Dealers, Law Enforcement and the Us versus Them Mentality

I recall the palpable tension between the gun dealer and law enforcement personnel throughout the day while on site during my first firearms audit. It could only be described as antagonistic. The gun dealer was angry and offended that he was being accused of being a criminal, and the law enforcement personnel were quite sure that this gun dealer was non-compliant and therefore a risk to society. While there were multiple legitimate violations found that day, in the end, there were few as serious as what I was told to expect. I specifically recall being told that the number of handguns on file for this gun dealer on the state registry could not possibly fit in the handgun safe on site. Police were concerned that the gun dealer had engaged in "cooking the books" to hide firearms or cover for those who should not have had them in their possession. As the audit got underway, there were multiple tense exchanges between firearms registry staff and the dealer. Snide comments, name calling, even threats of suicide by the dealer because of what the police were doing. From my observation as an outsider, it appeared to me that the gun dealers' antagonistic attitude only reinforced the officer's views that he was an irresponsible dealer willingly breaking the law. I recalled how much tension could have been reduced and cooperation encouraged by better relations between police and the dealer had those assumptions not been in play – especially since most of the violations were administrative in nature. Registry personnel told me multiple times that electronic record keeping would have made things much easier – but I wondered whether there was a real reluctance on behalf of the dealer to switch to computers given his age, the learning curve required for new technology, and the cost of making that kind of business investment. I had wondered if the administrative errors could have been used as an opportunity for education rather than an assumption of criminality. Especially because registry personnel knew this dealer and worked with him as a part of daily registry/firearms compliance activity, and an existing relationship was in place. I was left wondering how this working relationship became so tense and uncooperative.

Gun dealers in Australia work closely with law enforcement as a core part of their livelihoods and daily activities as gun dealers. While every sale and acquisition of a firearm must pass through a gun dealers' hands, each one of those sales or acquisitions must be accompanied by the appropriate approvals provided by the law enforcement weapons licencing branch in the state. This means that gun dealers must interact with law enforcement out of necessity. For example, if there are questions about checks to be made in regards to paperwork or approvals, gun dealers will call law enforcement to clarify before sales can be finalised. In addition, gun dealers are also subject to scrutiny by law enforcement as a natural part of gun control regulations. This means that gun dealers are inspected regularly and held to account for their role in selling firearms to the public. This scrutiny can take many forms but is most likely to involve physical inspection of the property and regular audits of the dealer's stock of firearms. As a result of these two types of interactions with regulators, police need gun dealers to cooperate with implementing gun control regulations and complying with them themselves. In order to understand the working relationship between dealers and law enforcement, I asked dealers about their experiences in interacting with law enforcement in order to understand how this cooperation comes about and what the challenges are for cooperation.

Overall, gun dealers reported very mixed feelings about their interactions with police. And none of the dealers expressed outright negative views about the police. Some dealers demonstrated how they had been able to develop good working relationships with law enforcement in their everyday activities. But there are types of law enforcement interactions that lend themselves to building these relationships more than others. *Local police* are officers that worked in the community across several typical policing capacities and were considered most amendable to building good working relationships. These were the police who responded when a firearms dealer made a report about theft, property damage, or needed someone removed from the store. These regular beat cops were able to interact with firearms dealers in person and in more diverse capacities rather than just as an auditor for a dealer's firearms stock to check compliance. "*We seem to have a pretty good relationship with local police*" one dealer articulated nicely what over 70% of the dealers in the study stated about regular everyday police. The local nature of their interactions and the opportunity to form a relationship based on those interactions increased the potential to form a trusting and cooperative relationship. Dealers appeared to form attitudes towards police based on individualised experiences with law enforcement rather than painting the police with a broad brush. The dealer below highlights this individualised nature of good and bad police experiences for dealers and their interactions with police:

> *The local people, it depends on who you get. Our local person at the moment is very, very good. But that can change overnight, and you can get a nightmare.*

Registry police, on the other hand, work with dealers at arm's length and primarily via phone or email. In fact, according to most dealers, registry police would rarely physically visit a dealer's place of business unless it was to audit firearms stock or because there was a suspected problem of compliance and an investigation was needed. As a result, dealers had fewer opportunities to develop collaborative relationships with registry police based on face-to-face interactions, even though they might have dealt with the same person each time over the phone or email. However, dealers still expressed their views of registry police based on the individuals they interacted with and attempted to form working relationships with law enforcement personal they interacted with at the state registry.

> *It seems to be that the people in there who are really helpful seem to get moved. Or when they understand how everything works, they seem to get moved. So you then go back through and you have to start again with, with people with new people in the registry office.*

Because perceptions of police were very much embedded in personal experience and face to face interactions with police, dealers saw potential collaboration and good working relationships in some individual police members and not in others. Even gun dealers who had opportunities to work with state registry police on a regular basis believed that a cooperative relationship was possible if they found the right individual. The dealer from Queensland below suggests that they had found a registry officer who understood their role as dealers and their position as a business owner.

> *In QLD, the two officers that are in there now are very receptive to a.) to business, and b.) and trying to help the needs, offering the service for what they're paid for.*

This dealer highlights the customer service nature of registry and dealer work, which requires an understanding of the primary purpose of police. According to the dealer above, registry police are there to aid and assist gun dealers and gun owners in the compliance process. Furthermore, not only did this dealer see the purpose of the firearms registry as providing a service to gun owners, just as they did as dealers. As a result, dealers often talked about the shared aims of police and dealers in fulfilling the aim of gun control regulations: maintaining the registry, and processing permits and licences. As both organisations served the gun-owning community, gun dealers saw that gun dealers and weapons licencing police were working towards a common cause. Despite this, dealers remained pragmatic about their interactions with police. Good relationships were seen as the result of relationships built over time with specific individuals inside law enforcement. These police personnel were described as respectful, good problem-solvers and collaborative.

Poor relationships between dealers and police were consistently described as problematic for three primary reasons. First, dealers felt the police treated them with suspicion. Second, dealers felt that police enabled problems with bureaucratic red tape in order to complete their everyday compliance tasks. Lastly, dealers felt that the police lacked respect for a gun dealer's expertise on the matter of firearms and firearm safety. These concerns were generally characteristic of the nature of the complaints gun dealers had about police and the overall tension that existed between gun dealers and the law enforcement personnel they were required to work alongside. As such, these concerns represent barriers because they directly challenge the ability for collaborative relationships to form between dealers and police. I argue that collaborative relationships are required to ensure the compliance process is operating as it should.

Dealers reported that they felt some police approached them as if they were criminals and felt that police were "out to get" them. Reports of this experience were often accompanied by comments that dealers felt the police should be working with them rather than against them. Like a self-fulfilling prophesy, these bad experiences with specific law enforcement individuals meant that dealers were more weary, more defensive and they described their interactions as being fraught with tension. The dealer below not only describes the "us versus them" mentality but specifically expresses the perception that police are not willing to work collaboratively with dealers.

> *It's definitely a huge anti-gun culture within licencing [branch of police], it's the culture of; we're the police and we're here to police the firearm dealers, not work with firearms dealers. It's definitely us vs them.*

"Us versus them" was a phrase that was often used by dealers when describing what bad interactions with police were like, even though they may have had plenty of good interactions with specific individuals at the local and registry level. The us versus them mentality described by dealers was one that was tense, and dealers felt that police were looking for errors and mistakes that could be used to punish dealers as opposed to working with them to sort out any errors in the record – most of which were perceived by dealers to be administrative or clerical in nature, honest mistakes that could be corrected by working together.

> *[Registry police] are always calling with questions. I try to help them out because you never know, one day we might need their help too. We are continually helping them find things.*

Dealers made sense of these interactions by relating them to the heavy administrative burden that was required for each firearm sale and acquisition. The multiple paper forms were described as prone to human error – having to write down by hand barrel numbers, firearm serial numbers, and ensure these were matched with registry records, which were also prone to clerical error.

The overlap between the administrative and bureaucratic burden of their everyday paperwork tasks, which required multiple paper copies for the purchase and sale of firearms, coalesced with the interactions with police because so many of those interactions were about the paperwork, problems with inaccurate records, missing paperwork, and different levels of competency in ensuring that paperwork was complete. A number of dealers described their frustrations as "mind boggling" given that police and dealers should be working towards the same goals.

> *My biggest issue in this industry, as a firearms dealer, there is a 'them and us' attitude. Licencing will not work with you... We're all working for the same end as far I'm concerned, and it's a very "them and us" attitude, it makes no sense.*

Dealers often reported that they found errors themselves in their everyday business tasks and sort to correct them by calling registry police. However, dealers expressed concern that even when they were proactive in attempting to resolve bureaucratic errors via phone, email or postal mail, errors were slow to be resolved. These left dealers feeling like they might be vulnerable to reprimand if errors were still on the books at the next police audit or inspection. The dealer below goes further to describe police as being willing to focus on mistakes that could be blamed on the dealer, despite the potential for human error in reporting by both dealers and police personnel.

> *There were a couple of officers from [city], and all they wanted to do was find something wrong and prosecute you for it... and I found that bizarre because anybody can make a mistake. An honest mistake, including them.*

Reports by the auditor general of firearms registration units in multiple states have documented these kinds of errors that exist in firearm registry records and claim they undermine the aims of the NFA. For example, in NSW, a review of the weapons licencing unit found that basic information about gun owners had not been updated for five years or more in the police registry and that police record-keeping technology was outdated and prone to error.[3] Similar findings have been found in reviews of Queensland[4] and Western Australian[5] weapons licencing units that are responsible for transferring records provided by dealers into the firearms registry. In a response to the NSW Firearms Audit Report, the state's Commissioner of Police acknowledges the co-regulatory model whereby police partner with the firearms-owning community to implement gun control.

> *...firearms regulation is co-regulatory in that the firearms industry – being approved clubs, dealers, ranges, and instructors – are invested with the responsibility to administer and oversight aspect of the Act and Regulation.*[6]

He then suggests that the report's findings unfairly blame the firearms registry for the errors and suggest those errors are a product of the co-regulatory model and work done by members of the gun industry by saying, "*The onus of compliance of these activities rest with those third parties rather than with the firearms Registry.*"[7]

In his response to the report, the NSW commissioner appears to simultaneously acknowledge the cooperative role gun dealers play in the compliance process and blame them for the errors in the system. This stance by the police seems to corroborate dealers expressed concern that they are seen as the problem despite the partnership model that the gun control compliance process requires.

Overall, this perceived us versus them mentality by dealers is an important barrier that requires consideration if dealers are designed to function as a primary port of call for the gun-owning community in the sale and acquisition of firearms. Furthermore, if gun control regulations effectiveness in whole or in part hinges on the dealer's cooperation with law enforcement in the process of compliance, there is a vested interest in ensuring the cooperative relationship between dealers and police is healthy and positive.

Underutilised Expertise and Lack of Voice

In sociology and criminology, agency and voice are important concepts for understanding social behaviour. When people in society don't feel like they can exercise their own agency or have the ability to voice their concerns and have them taken seriously, people tend to withdraw from society.[8] This could simply mean they choose not to participate in normal social rules – like complying with the law, or they rebel against their oppressors to make their voices and concerns louder. Either way, not feeling like you have a voice in your community or society undermines the perception that laws are legitimate and, likely, your willingness to cooperate with them.

Gun dealers are experts in their trade. They are one of only a few groups in society that have high-level practical, tactical, and historical knowledge about firearms and how to use them. To run a successful firearms dealership, a lack of expertise would likely end in business failure and potentially dire consequences for the community, along with implications for the success of regulatory compliance. These are the people we should want to be involved in any safety discussion about firearms. I can remember sitting in with a gun dealer and collector in Victoria who was so eager to share his knowledge. He showed us some of the firearms he had in his collection, talking through historical details on where they were first used or why a particular firearm was chosen for troops in World War 2. I hadn't appreciated that there was so much nuance, meaning and significance in firearms, or how they had been linked to Australian histories of farming, industrial development, or craftsmanship. There was passion in the way he was educating us. Across Australia, we saw this level of passion, knowledge and expertise reflecting in how gun dealers approached their work in the sale of firearms to the legal gun-owning community and in their role in regulatory compliance. However, gun dealers frequently expressed feelings that their expertise had been disregarded, along with any opportunity for voice and participation as leaders in the gun-owning community or participants in the compliance process.

The gun dealers in this study *all* reported that they felt like they had not been consulted appropriately based on their level of expertise when the NFA was constructed back in 1996. This dissatisfaction with how their expertise had been passed over has remained over the last 25 years and continues to be a frustration for gun dealers today. In 1996, a small advisory group from the gun industry was constructed to advise the government. This advisory group included people from the largest gun importer in Australia, members of gun enthusiast groups and a select few gun dealers. But even representatives of this group – members of the gun-owning community – felt that this type of consultation was in name only. They got to consult, but rarely did they see the fruits of their labour, their views or their expertise reflected in the policies that they consulted on. These dealers were willing to cooperate, to be part of the conversation about constructing national gun regulations and to provide valuable expertise on how to regulate guns safely. As the dealer below suggests, these offers to cooperate were often ignored, or they were not offered a seat at the table in these discussions at all.

> *I knew the process or lack of process [involved in the introduction of the NFA legislation]. Our senior people in our [organisation] went to Canberra, and desperately tried to have some consultation and were roundly refused. There was no consultation, for us to have any input into it, and we felt the NFA was presented in such a short space of time and there was a strong rumour that it had been prepared and been sitting there for quite some time and waiting for the opportunity to be laid on the table.*

As is alluded to in the comment above, those gun dealers who felt that the opportunity to hear from the gun-owning community and incorporate their expertise was missed or actively avoided felt as though there were ulterior motives for constructing gun regulations, feeding the fire of mistrust and suspicions between gun owners and the government. While there have been many conspiracy theories linking the Port Arthur massacre to the government for the purposes of getting gun control through, very few gun dealers raised this when talking about the 1996 event and legislation. But I wondered if this mistrust and lack of agency and voice might increase the risk of those conspiracy theories gaining traction in a community that feels like they have been marginalised. This mistrust remains an important part of how gun dealers make sense of how police interact with them and why they don't get proper opportunities for consultation. The gun dealer below specifically mentions the lack of trust between them and the police as a way to understand the lack of collaborative relationships.

> *That's probably why they [the police] won't consult with us, is because they have no trust in us or anything we say. Even though we've got a wealth of knowledge about the firearms industry.*

It is not that consultation opportunities have not been provided. But gun dealers reported feelings of marginalisation even when consultation was offered. Rather, they often suggested that their consultation opportunities were tokenistic rather than a serious attempt to find out what gun dealers might have to say. This significantly increased frustrations about the implementation of gun control across Australian states, as indicated by the following dealer.

> *Theirs is a consultative meeting where we're all supposed to discuss all this stuff (legislation and policy). There's no consultation, it's all just; this is the way it's going to be... we don't really want to go to the meetings, there's no point but we can't pull out because then the police will just say; oh well we've tried... so you're damned if you do, damned if you don't.*

The dealer above, in suggesting that there is a decrease in wanting to contribute to these consultative meetings, is indicative of the danger that perceived "lack of voice" has in undermining the collaborations needed between gun dealers and police. They want to withdraw from the process when they don't feel like their expertise is respected or wanted. This is problematic since gun dealers must help facilitate compliance with gun control regulation.

Several gun dealers in this study were also licenced to hold firearms collections and/or were involved in the curation of firearms for museums. These dealers raised concerns about police disregarding their expertise when it came to the handling of historical pieces in their collection. In Australia, gun collectors must be licenced, have to abide by certain rules in order to legally maintain their firearms collection and are subject to the same compliance inspections that other dealers are. Gun collectors must only keep non-operable firearms. This means that the firearms must be permanently made to be unable to fire a bullet ever again in order to remain in a collection. While many collectors expressed regret about how that process rendered their collections valueless, most understood why this was necessary. Study participants who were museum operators and firearms collectors also shared other dealer's perspectives in that they have found that cooperative relationships are linked to individuals only, but that their expertise is largely unacknowledged. Furthermore, they express substantial concern when police come to inspect the collections. One museum operator explicitly highlighted a lack of knowledge on behalf of police during a recent inspection of the museum site.

> *The local licencing people, there are a good and bad. But when you get a bad one of them, you're in for a bad day. There is a lack of knowledge, they wouldn't know a flint lock from a bolt action.*

Furthermore, museum operators suggested that police were destructive and exhibited a lack of care when handling experience and important firearms in their collection. These experiences made dealers feel like their stock or collections were at risk of being devalued when the police came to perform their part of the regulatory process.

> *We did have to get those police people to be careful with our firearms, they were very gung-ho about in trying to take screws out to get a look at serial numbers under grips. We had to stop them.*

These experiences appear to reinforce the dealers' perceptions that the police were not knowledgeable and did not respect the knowledge of the dealers. Firearms collectors understood this to be a lack of education, knowledge and understanding of firearms rather than wilful disregard, but it was evidently a source of tension that surrounded interaction with police, and dealers felt it was a direct rejection of their expertise and knowledge of the field. This again illustrates a tension based on a lack of respect and understanding between dealers and police and undermines the collaborative relationships that are possible, are needed and are wanted by dealers.

Collectors and museum operators also helped me understand the historical significance and meaning that they saw in firearms. In a piece for The Conversation that I wrote about gun control on the 20th anniversary of the Port Arthur massacre, I can recall the comments from those who read the piece regarding the photo chosen for the article by the editor. The photo was a large pile of firearms that had been collected and readied for destruction during the buyback period and a member of law enforcement sitting on top of that dome-shaped pile of guns. These commenters expressed angst for the loss of history in those piles of firearms. Their lament was not unlike the lamenting of historical losses expressed by dealers when talking about the buyback scheme. The dealer below demonstrates that there were promises to consolidate the historical pieces for collectors, but this never eventuated.

> *They were taking anything and everything. The buyback was meant to be for self-loading [firearms], but they were taking anything and everything, even flintlocks and stuff like that, that should never have gone into [the police]. They said they were going to talk to museums and other interested people, they didn't... And a lot of stuff got destroyed that way. Links between classic firearms have been lost, and they're gone for ever.*

Museum operators and collectors shared the same concerns about the lack of respect for their expertise and opportunities for serious consultation in relation to the buyback and in determining how to dispose of firearms that were handed in. Perceptions of mistrust were often linked to complaints about missed opportunities to be consulted by dealers and museum operators alike. Furthermore, along with those perceptions of mistrust and complaints of lack of voice, dealers often reported that they thought that policies created in the absence of their expertise did not properly reflect how firearms work, what they're used for or their historical value.

In this case, a lack of voice and respect for their expertise directly undermines support for the moral content of the law. For example, it was explained to me that varieties of the leaver action shotgun have a range of different purposes. While mostly used for hunting, one museum operator explained that variety in what you are hunting, at what distance and for what purpose may necessitate a particular kind of firearm. He went on to argue that when regulators assume all leaver action shotguns are the same, they run the risk of creating policies that may categorise leaver action shotguns improperly – and thus make them unattainable for people who may legitimately need them for hunting/farming, or force people to keep them as a collector's item and therefore render them inoperable and destroy any practical or financial value. When these kinds of regulations are made without the consultation of experts, it can create confusion, mistrust and come at a financial cost to dealers and collectors, who now must rush to comply with new regulations in order to stay compliant. As many gun dealers have pointed out, these consequences are not consistent with what they see as the spirit of the NFA. Instead, these regulatory decisions made with limited serious consultation with experts can create a barrier to effective gun control because they alienate gun dealers as experts from the process and undermine their perceptions of the legitimacy of the law and moral support for legal and regulatory content.

The frustration dealers felt in attempting to correct the records when errors were discovered, which they discussed in relation to their interactions with police, overlapped with the frustration they expressed when they found that police disregarded their expertise on firearms matters. Dealers often discussed their long history in the firearms business, and many of them had built careers around and/or were considered world and national leaders in sports shooting, hunting, and craftsmanship. One dealer explained that he had discovered that police were wrongly advising new gun owners on what firearm was suitable for the reason listed for legal ownership – police were recommending the use of particular firearms without understanding what the purpose of the firearms was or the nature of the firearm needed for the job at hand.

Overall, gun dealers felt they could contribute more to the process of compliance should they be given the authentic opportunity to share their expertise in firearms as well as their practical knowledge of the compliance process when interacting with the gun-owning community and the public. The absence of this ability to participate demonstrates that dealers feel they have been disempowered in their role. This disempowerment is dangerous if we think about how to motivate compliance. Without a seat at the table where their views are heard and their expertise is acknowledged, regulators put at risk the moral support for the law that gun dealers currently have. My concern as a criminologist is whether the support for the law currently held by the gun-owning community is sustainable if they feel they have been marginalised from the decision-making process which affect them in the most financial and practical ways. While sociologists and criminologists like myself see lack of voice as a larger structural problem in the way in which laws are constructed, dealers continued to link their concerns to the bureaucracy imposed on them as front-line workers in the compliance process.

The Administrative Burden of Gun Control Compliance

In Chapter 2, gun dealers talked about their support for the law and expressed sentiment that suggested complying with the law is important to their identity. In addition, they described themselves as willing to participate and take it on themselves to educate and serve the gun-owning community because they morally believe that responsible firearm use is critical. However, these dealers also overwhelmingly describe their day-to-day tasks as having practical difficulties that can make it hard to comply with gun control laws. Not only are regulations described as complex, but they reported that changes to regulations are often not well communicated by the state. Furthermore, the fundamental nature of the activities in which they must perform makes it increasingly difficult for dealers and gun owners to comply with regulations. I call these concerns with gun control an "administrative burden" because they all relate to the bureaucratic nature of the gun dealer's role and the bureaucratic process of compliance rather than the content of the laws themselves. These administrative burdens become potential barriers to good quality and effective gun control because they do not make it easy for people to comply, even when they intend to.

The complexity of the bureaucratic process was consistently raised as a major concern by gun dealers across Australia. The administrative paperwork was described as unmanageable and prone to error. Gun dealers felt that these errors made them vulnerable during law enforcement inspections, even though the errors were unintentional. The administrative burden became a financial strain on the business, challenging for new gun owners to navigate, and deterred people from wanting to engage with the compliance process.

Administrative burdens due to the complexity and amount of paperwork were seen by gun dealers as a financial strain on their business. Gun dealers across Australia would often lament the sheer amount of paperwork that consumed their daily tasks.

> *We're choked in paperwork. Can you imagine what it's doing to us financially?*

Another dealer talks about the amount of paperwork and the inconsistency in systems used to undertake their daily responsibilities in ensuring compliance with the law:

> *We have nine different forms I have to fill in every month, now those forms we do in hard copy, then our firearm returns we do electronically.*

These dealers are not complaining about the content of the law, but that the physical process of enacting policy is burdensome due to the volume of forms and the inconsistency of the methods by which they must complete them. Gun dealers also commented on how the complexity has become more burdensome over time since the initial implementation of gun laws in 1996 and the subsequent changes to legislation and regulations over time.

> *There was accountability prior to that [the NFA]. People say there was no accountability and there was. Every firearm that was sold needed to be recorded. Every firearm that moved*

> *through did as well. But now we're just recording everything in triplicate, and we have another register we record things in. We're just recording, recording and recording, and this is where mistakes are made.*

The dealer above explained that the NFA-based requirements to track and trace firearms have become unnecessarily bureaucratised and that prior to the Port Arthur massacre, gun dealers routinely were able to track and trace firearms without government intervention. His frustration with these newer ways of going about compliance with the law is not only a reflection of its complexity and volume, but also of the assumptions that gun dealers were irresponsible in not doing this prior to 1996.

I thought often about this idea that the current level of paperwork is overkill when there were processes to track and trace firearms in place prior to 1996. The counterargument is, of course, that what was used prior to 1996 wasn't working and that more detailed tracking would provide an extra level of assurance and safety. However, it was not the sheer amount of paperwork that gun dealers found unpalatable about their everyday compliance tasks. Rather, it was the error-prone nature inherent in this level of paperwork that was the cause of concern and put them, their clients and their businesses at risk.

My experience on the gun raid in 2014 was illustrative of the concerns being raised by dealers here about error-prone recording practices. The forms referred to by dealers that needed to be filled out each month required the reporting of firearm serial numbers, firearm types and other important features such as magazine capacity. To me, it appeared that even gun licencing staff were unable to identify a firearm serial number correctly.[9] I overheard law enforcement personnel talking about the errors being due to misinterpretation of handwriting. When dealers talked about the process being error-prone due to the number of forms and the handwritten nature of forms just for one firearm sale, I could see why they were concerned about the nature of bureaucracy; they were concerned that there were too many risks in the compliance process for themselves and for their clients, and this was perceived to be a threat to their livelihoods and their identity as law-abiding citizens. The dealer below talks about how the complexity of the compliance process is contributing financial pressure to his business, and this has implications for staffing.

> *I have serious concerns for my guy's employment. My staff's ongoing employment if it [the process] keeps getting more and more difficult, I'm going to have to lay staff off or cut hours back and not just because of a market downturn. It's because the process of complying is just too overwhelming.*

Financial pressures due to the complicated process of compliance were common concerns for dealers. And while complex gun control measures may have altered the gun ownership market, dealers attributed much of the financial pressure to the compliance process itself rather than any change in attitudes about the use of guns or a shift in the need for legitimate firearms such as farming, pest control or shooting sports. These perceptions indicate that the bureaucratic process developed to ensure compliance is burdensome for dealers to comply with, despite the fact that they otherwise have good intentions to comply. Some dealers have found ways to balance these burdens for themselves and their clients. For example, the dealer below suggests that in order to keep the business afloat, they provide a service to gun owners to help them navigate the licencing and registration process, which would otherwise be too complicated for prospective gun owners to navigate alone.

> *That's why we made the decision at our store, we do the application process for our clients, if I didn't do that we'd probably go broke – a lot of people would just go: 'this is too hard'.*

The link between the complexity of the licencing requirements and the wellbeing of the business is clear. Helping new gun owners with the application process is not required or expected of dealers under the current policy for any state, but dealers are increasingly taking on these tasks in order to help sustain business and continue to support legitimate firearms owners.

Gun dealers also held concerns about the ease of compliance given the subtle but important differences in regulations across the country. This was particularly visible in the state of Western Australia (WA), where their process for licencing and firearms purchases had very distinct financial implications for business. This state also had a range of regulations that, while they did not apply in other states, had flow-on effects for gun dealers in other states who did business across the country. While the NFA provides national guidelines on what gun control legislation should look like, each state has adopted and implemented these guidelines in their own way for their own jurisdiction. In most states and territories, firearms owners must apply for and get approval for a firearms licence prior to the purchase of a firearm. However, in WA, firearms owners select a firearm for purchase, then apply for their licence while gun dealers hold their purchased firearm until approval from law enforcement is given. This particular implementation of policy was unpopular among dealers in WA, primarily because it meant they were holding stock without knowing whether the applicant would eventually be approved for ownership and able to pick up the firearm that was purchased. Not only did this create financial uncertainty for dealers, but this waiting period between purchase, approval and retrieval of the firearm had implications for space and safe storage for gun dealers, as indicated by the dealer below.

> *We've been left with about half a million dollars' worth of stock we can't do anything with. We had we still have a decent supply of ex-military firearms, if we couldn't frate them around the country, that's half a million dollars in stock are there's not enough people in to absorb that. So for me, I've had many sleepless nights about it.*

Multiple dealers wished that regulations between states and territories aligned more easily. Their clients, as well as their business, were often impacted by having to navigate different systems of compliance in order to travel interstate for gun shows, shooting events or collectors exhibits. These administrative burdens had implications for the activities they undertook to support their livelihoods, as well as for disconnecting firearms owners from the broader gun dealing community and their activities.

Despite these burdens, dealers demonstrated ways in which they are complying with the law and making business work for them. At no time did a dealer in this study indicate that they had found loopholes they were exploiting in the law or that they were seeking ways to not comply with the law. So why is this a barrier to effective gun control and collaboration with policymakers and law enforcement? The problem with administrative burden is that when the process of complying is complex and difficult, rather than deterring people from gun ownership (which is what some may see as a sign of success in gun legislation), it potentially decreases legitimacy in the law and breeds disregard for the law. As such, the frustration surrounding administrative burden becomes a barrier that undermines motives to comply if the process of complying is made too difficult for dealers or gun owners to maintain, especially when gun ownership is core to their business or livelihood. While no dealer suggested that the administrative burden has led to noncompliance, their collective narrative demonstrates concerns for how they can sustain business under such pressure. As such, this kind of administrative burden felt by gun dealers feeds discontent with the nature of how gun policy is enacted, even when they may agree with its content.

This type of administrative burden is not new to the field of criminology. Malcolm Feeley's[10] work in understanding the efficiency and effectiveness of how courts operate rests on how difficult it can be to navigate the court system. Feeley was interested in why so many court clients in the lower court failed to avail themselves of the resources that are guaranteed by their due process rights and thus failed to appear for court dates. For Feeley, the reasons these noncompliance patterns occur are directly related to the difficulty and complexity of navigating the court process. In other words, court clients didn't understand how to comply, didn't know what was expected of them, or how to achieve it. The process itself was the barrier to compliance rather than any attitude towards the law, the courts or the judiciary.

Criminologists would argue that compliance with any regulation is increased and its aims are more effective when those regulations and their expectations are easy to understand and are well communicated to those who must follow it.[11] Noncompliance can occur consciously or unconsciously when individuals do not understand what is expected of them or how they should perform tasks efficiently to adhere to the law. Does the complexity of compliance and the administrative burden of gun control policy in Australia provide a possible incentive for noncompliance? There isn't any evidence of this kind of noncompliance in my study. But dealers raise an important question about the sustainability of the processes used to maintain and implement gun laws. The argument here is not that dealers or gun owners will consciously choose not to comply with the law, but that it is difficult to know how to comply when the system is so difficult to understand and follow. Noncompliance is a natural consequence of this kind of complex policy.

I've argued that dealers have demonstrated their moral agreement with much of the content of gun control laws and hold their identity as law-abiding citizens as a central motivator for compliance. The administrative burdens felt acutely by gun dealers become a barrier to collaboration with law enforcement and thus compliance, as they hold the potential to undermine the legitimacy of the laws and the regulations that gun dealers currently feel are important and they do support. The administrative burden is not just the complexity; it is the inconsistency, the volume and the impact it has on gun dealers' everyday business tasks that have the potential to wear down any support for the content of the law that is currently held. Undermining those perceptions of legitimacy is an important consideration for good quality gun policy because you need gun dealers to be able to continue to socialise new and current gun owners into having respect for those regulations as well as responsible gun users.

Compliance Fatigue

Gun dealers often expressed frustration and even outrage at new regulations they did not feel made sense. This sentiment was felt most strongly by dealers in WA, whose frustration with law enforcement was more palpable than that in other states. Dealers in WA talked about the frequency at which they experienced having to comply with new interpretations of the law and new regulations in which they did not understand their rationale.

My interviews with WA gun dealers occurred soon after new handgun storage regulations for dealers were implemented after an incident of theft from a gun dealers' inventory. Regulations included significant upgrades to the type and level of security their facilities provided for the storage of handguns in what dealers felt was a short period of time. The dealer below reported that these rapid regulation changes had a significant financial impact on their business.

> *In the last 12 months or so, there has been this sudden interpretation. It's not law. It's policy of pistol security. That's cost us over $35,000 so far which we will never recoup.*

Other WA dealers also criticised law enforcement for their lack of transparent communication, leaving them wondering why the regulations are needed or what they were designed to achieve. The dealer below expressed feelings of being duped while trying to comply as best as possible when it came to constructing handgun storage on their property.

> *The new handgun policy has cost us $40,000 odd dollars in a brand new building that they were aware was coming when they approved us. They didn't tell anyone, so it's cost us.*

The dealer's frustration appears reasonable, indicating that he could have financially planned for these changes had they been communicated at the time law enforcement was issuing approvals for his gun dealership. The fatigue of having to comply with frequently changing regulations dominated the sentiment of dealers across Australia, but most vehemently in the state of WA. These frequent regulatory changes were particularly burdensome in rural areas, which ran small but critical services to gun owners who were far from metropolitan areas. Rural dealers all reported having to make business decisions that reduced their inventory and business opportunities simply because it was too difficult to comply or they were unable to make the financial investment.

WA dealers provided another example of where sudden regulatory changes and a lack of communication provided additional strain on dealers that undermined the legitimacy and support for gun laws. After firearms were stolen from the postal service (along with other packages), regulators limited the transport of firearms to only two approved transport companies and required that all firearms packages be clearly marked as firearms during transport. While most gun dealers understood the need to rethink security to prevent such thefts, the narrowing of competition in transport companies increased the prices of transport, providing additional financial strain on every day business activity.

> *Almost overnight we were stopped from using transport. Australia Post came next. Two people were changes for using Australia Post and they didn't even know it at the time. We are not allowed to use Australia Post and yet our legislation says "post"...suddenly they said you can't send firearms in Australia Post. There is one or two trucking companies that will take it, then we suddenly we weren't allowed to send parts...not allowed to send magazine or any other items of a firearm by post.*

The dealer above talks of the frustration of constantly having to pivot business practices in order to comply quickly with regulation changes. He also suggests that these regulations were not communicated effectively to dealers, so people have been prosecuted for using incorrect transport carriers without knowing they were not in compliance with the law. Even though this regulation was implanted in WA, dealers in other states also indicated that it had implications for their businesses.

It was not just the ability to comply with fast-changing regulations that was problematic. Gun dealers in WA and in other states reported that the regulation to clearly mark packages as "FIREARMS" was impetuous. Dealers did not understand why drawing attention to particular packages as firearms during transport would provide any additional security; some even suggested it diminished security further by letting criminals know what packages have firearms in them.

> *I makes no sense to me why you'd label something that says 'firearms'. Why don't you just tell the criminals where to go?*

The frustration with the frequency of regulatory changes, the lack of communication about their reasons and rationale, combined with the knowledge that surveillance would be constant, made dealers feel like consequences for regulatory noncompliance were inevitable and that the effort required to comply was not sustainable.

Chapter Summary

If I am to think about the most dominant media frames of gun dealers and what they think of gun control, it would be easy to assume that gun dealers and the gun-owning community as a whole are unsupportive of gun control measures. Even here in Australia, where a right to bear arms is absent from constitutional and common law provisions. Gun dealers do have concerns and problems with the law; however, the nature of these concerns centres mostly around the administrative and bureaucratic nature of their compliance work, the conditions of the working relationships between themselves and law enforcement and perceptions that there has been little acknowledgement of their expertise and no consistent authentic consultation with them as a group. These concerns are notable not only because they dominated every interview of gun dealers across Australia, showing the consistent experiences and perceptions gun dealers report, but also because they reinforce earlier findings in this book that the vast majority of gun dealers not only see merit in gun control but morally support the overarching aims of gun control.

The deterrence-based approach to enforcement, while perhaps effective in ensuring dealers are complying with the law, is unlikely to be the best and most sustainable solution for achieving good-quality gun control. How do we know? Criminological research on the effectiveness of a deterrence-based approach has mixed results at best.[12] Most research finds that deterrence-based models often fail because they offer penalties that are too small to motivate compliance or so harsh that businesses cannot sustain activity once penalties have been applied. Both undermine the deterrent effect of the law.[13] Most legal scholars and criminologists would only recommend relying on these strict deterrence-based methods when more collaborative methods have failed.[14] Modern day deterrence perspectives clearly highlight the importance of the quality of the relationship between police and those they regulate to encourage cooperation. The deterrence-based approach adopted in Australia appears to sideline or ignore the willingness of dealers to cooperate and contribute to gun control creation and implementation and assumes they can only cooperate when provided deterrence-based incentives to do so. I understand why many people are comfortable with this approach when the stakes (like reducing gun violence) are high. However, as a criminologist, I'd much prefer people to comply with the law because they share the belief that those regulations are important for the safety of all.

Criminological theories that help us understand why people comply with the law indicate that tension between law enforcement personnel and the community undermines the potential for and quality of cooperation and, ultimately, law-abiding behaviour.[15] Therefore, undermining cooperation undermines motivations for compliance. It appears that there is a missed opportunity on behalf of the police as an organisation that holds the balance of legal power in this instance to perform their gun control regulatory duties in the spirit of collaboration with gun dealers. To sustain gun laws, the collaborative partnership between police and dealers must be prioritised in order to consolidate shared interests in public safety and simultaneously provide service to the gun-owning community.

In the case of Australian gun dealers, the lack of communication and transparency, the us versus them mentality between police and dealers, and the administrative burden involved in compliance are red flags for where our gun control policies are weak. They are weak due to their over-reliance on enforcement and missed opportunities to foster a more collaborative partnership with dealers that would increase legal legitimacy and moral support for the law. I would much prefer that people comply with the law because they see merit in its aims rather than simply out of fear of penalty. Dealers have indicated there is a foundation for building a strong and continued model of compliance based on those informal social control mechanisms, one in which they are partners with the construction of and implementation of gun control regulation. The concerns raised by dealers are barriers to effective gun control regulation because they highlight weaknesses in the law that carry risks to long-term compliance. The overwhelming burden that compliance tasks require, the fatigue that comes with navigating the complicated system of compliance, and the often tense relationships with law enforcement chip away at normative motivations for compliance; their moral support for the law's content and their identity as law-abiding citizens.

Research demonstrates that compliance is heightened when people understand how to comply, why they are complying, when they feel included in the construction of the law, and when the burden of compliance is not so high that failure is likely.[16] Regulators have an incentive to make the compliance process understandable and transparent. There are two benefits to this. First, you minimise the risk of noncompliance due to ignorance or lack of knowledge. Second, you enable gun dealers, who are on the front lines of gun sales and acquisitions, to be able to communicate the purpose of those regulations to the community they serve, which helps to socialise new members with the community on what is expected of them in regards to firearms-related behaviour and ownership.

When I think about what gun dealers have told me about their experiences with law enforcement, how they feel about their role in the compliance process, I see a pattern of perceived marginalisation and frustration in navigating a system where they feel as though the goal posts change too often. The notion of feeling excluded in the process of creating legislation, as well as being the target of legislation rather than its partners, is significant. The implications of feeling marginalised also carry implications for the success of effective gun control in the long term. In Chapter 4, I take a more detailed look at how gun dealers perceive themselves to be unfairly stigmatised and how that may impact their views of gun control and their willingness to participate in it.

Notes

1 Paternoster, R., & Bachman, R. (2012). Perceptual deterrence theory.
2 Young, D. B. (1983). Cesare Beccaria: utilitarian or retributivist? *Journal of Criminal Justice*, *11*(4), 317–326.

3 New South Wales Firearms Regulation Audit https://www.audit.nsw.gov.au/our-work/reports/firearms-regulation
4 Performance Audit: regulating Firearms. https://www.qao.qld.gov.au/sites/default/files/2020-11/Regulating%20firearms%20%28Report%208%E2%80%942020%E2%80%9321%29_1.pdf
5 Firearms Controls WA. https://audit.wa.gov.au/reports-and-publications/reports/firearm-controls/
6 https://www.audit.nsw.gov.au/sites/default/files/pdf-downloads/Firearms%20regulation%20final%20report.pdf Page 25.
7 See endnote vi
8 Rosenbaum, D. P., & McCarty, W. P. (2017). Organizational justice and officer "buy in" in American policing. *Policing: An International Journal of Police Strategies & Management*, *40*(1), 71–85.
9 The serial number is a unique number assigned to each individual firearm.
10 Feeley, M. M. (1979). *The process is the punishment: Handling cases in a lower criminal court*. Russell Sage Foundation.
11 Lignier, P., Evans, C., & Tran-Nam, B. (2014). Tangled up in tape: The continuing tax compliance plight of the small and medium enterprise business sector. In *Australian Tax Forum*.
12 Pratt, T. C., Cullen, F. T., Blevins, K. R., Daigle, L. E., & Madensen, T. D. (2006). The empirical status of deterrence theory: A meta-analysis.
13 Parker, C. (2006). The "compliance" trap: The moral message in responsive regulatory enforcement. *Law & Society Review*, *40*(3), 591–622.
14 Braithwaite, J. (2002). *Restorative justice & responsive regulation*. Oxford University press on demand.
15 Mazerolle, L., Antrobus, E., Bennett, S., & Tyler, T. R. (2013). Shaping citizen perceptions of police legitimacy: A randomized field trial of procedural justice. *Criminology*, *51*(1), 33–63.
16 Gezelius, S. S., & Hauck, M. (2011). Toward a theory of compliance in state-regulated livelihoods: A comparative study of compliance motivations in developed and developing world fisheries. *Law & Society Review*, *45*(2), 435–470.

4

STIGMATISATION AND THE GUN DEALER

with Amy Templar, The University of Queensland

In 1996, you were a leper if you were a gun dealer.

I vividly recall the very first question I received from the audience at a keynote speech I gave at the Sporting Shooters Association of Australia (SSAA) Annual General Meeting. I had been invited to share my research on the approach to gun control as an outsider with no links and no insider information with the gun-owning community. I could see one particular attendee just waiting for me to finish my talk so he could ask his question. As soon as he was able, his hand sprang into the air, and he asked, almost yelling "*I just want you to tell me. Why do they hate us so much?!*". I hadn't expected that question, and while I answered it the best way I could, his question has remained with me as my research has evolved. In my answer, I drew on my criminological knowledge of stigma and stereotypes – the same kind of research that talks about the dangers of stigma and stereotypes that drive racial discrimination in the justice system. I said that people fear what they don't understand, and we are often socialised to believe or draw on harmful or singular stereotypes to understand things that are new to us. My answer seemed to pacify him for the moment. But it didn't pacify me. There was part of me that was trying to get my head around how this relatively privileged, predominantly white, and male community could feel so marginalised. Based on what we know of the experiences of marginalised populations

DOI: 10.4324/9781003271642-5

when they interact with the justice system, the experience of these gun owners should be much less problematic. After all, they would likely have access to resources, agency and social capital that would help them navigate the justice system more easily. My research findings suggest that this is not how gun dealers and owners feel. They believe they are hated and villainised by society and regulators simply because they own a firearm. My exploration of how gun dealers experience and perceive stigma became an important piece of the puzzle in understanding their positionality towards law enforcement, regulators and the law. I argue that their perceptions of being stigmatised are important to understand if we are interested in getting the gun-owning community to collaborate with policymakers on gun control.

Criminologists have a long history of examining the link between stigmatisation and its effect on legal outcomes, public discourse and crime. Stigma refers to a negative label or stereotype that is applied to a group in society. In turn, this label comes to reflect how they are understood by society and even how they understand themselves. For example, social scientists have a long history of documenting the stigma experienced by those experiencing mental illness. Negative stereotypes such as "dangerous", "unpredictable, "incompetent", or "crazy" may be some of the ways those individuals are seen. The research on stigma acknowledges that these negative labels have come to dominate the way in which these people are understood.[1] These labels continue to overshadow how we see their identity, often obscuring other, more positive parts of their identity.

In the throes of gun control implementation after the Port Arthur Massacre in 1996, then Prime Minister John Howard addressed a rally attended by members of the gun-owning community in Sale, Victoria, in June 1996. He did so wearing a bulletproof vest. This incident alone was powerful in linking the labels of "danger", "irresponsibility", "violent" and "criminal" to the gun-owning community represented at that rally and across Australia. The rally, which was emblematic of the gun-owning communities' anger about the sudden change in laws and sudden restrictions on their livelihoods or legal activities, was described as ugly by reporters. Feelings that they were being blamed for the actions of a criminal didn't sit well with farmers, sporting shooters, hunters, collectors, or gun dealers. Howard's decision to wear a vest was considered an overreaction, one that offended the community's sense of identity as law-abiding citizens. They were angry, and while they did disagree with how the government was handling the implementation of gun control, it was the assumption that they too were dangerous criminals that appeared to deepen division between the gun-owning community, the government and the public. While I suspect that creating these negative stereotypes of the gun-owning community was not the intention of the Prime Minister, the incident legitimised those labels and reinforced division at a time when people were reeling from the largest mass shooting Australia had ever seen. Later, Prime Minster Howard spoke publicly about his regret for following the advice of his advisors to wear the vest on that day. He said he never felt his life was in danger and acknowledged that the group he spoke to that day was not violent.[2]

Despite John Howard's regret, the link between those narratives of danger and violence and the gun-owning community has been hard to shake. Gun dealers report that this negative narrative has continued and has had important implications for their business and their social lives. In this chapter, I outline why stigma is so important to understand, even in communities that are relatively privileged. Though studies on stigma are numerous, this is the first study to systematically capture these kinds of experiences for gun dealers and consider the implications for the gun control debate. This is significant given that gun dealers in Australia are typically white, male and middle to upper class – all characteristics of social privilege that are typically known to offer advantages in the legal system and society as a whole rather than against them. Regardless, perceived stigmatisation may undermine moral support for gun control, collaboration and policymakers; these things are needed to sustain the success of the Australian gun control model. This chapter highlights the importance of understanding how the social cleavages between being viewed as pro or anti-gun control have implications for how gun control laws are enforced. I argue that stigmatisation carries potential danger for noncompliance with gun control laws in the gun-owning community, particularly for new members of that community, and the public. Effective gun control should consider the important implications that stigmatisation of an entire community has on crime, violence and gun control effectiveness.

What Is Stigma?

The study of stigma in the field of criminology has a long history. In short, stigma is defined as the set of negative beliefs about someone's identity and character that are used to exclude them from full acceptance and participation in society.[3] Typically, someone becomes stigmatised when they fail to meet society's standard of "normal" or acceptable behaviour. The other way that stigmatisation can occur is when certain characteristics or attributes are intertwined with unacceptable behaviours. Negative labels become applied to or attached to particular groups because their behaviour or traits go against the grain of society. For example, stigma studies help us understand why people suffering from mental health often feel excluded from the rest of society – their behaviour is considered abnormal. In the field of criminology, we use the concept of stigma to help us understand what kinds of discrimination certain groups face when interacting with police, judges, juries and probation officers. The concept of stigma also allows us to trace how individual differences are transformed into deficiencies relating to an entire group through the medium of stereotypical narratives. Through this lens, people are divided into two categories – those who belong and who are worthy and those who aren't. Those falling into the latter category can be treated differently because of their diminutive status. In short, the concept of stigma demonstrates how deviations in our behaviour from the social norm can become labelled negatively by others.

The concept of stigma aligns closely with criminological and sociological theories about labelling. But these theories are really about power – who has it and who doesn't. Labelling theorists believe that when a negative label is applied to an individual, that label is reinforced by others in society to the point where the stigmatised individual comes to believe that the label is true. This leads to that negative behaviour being reproduced in the

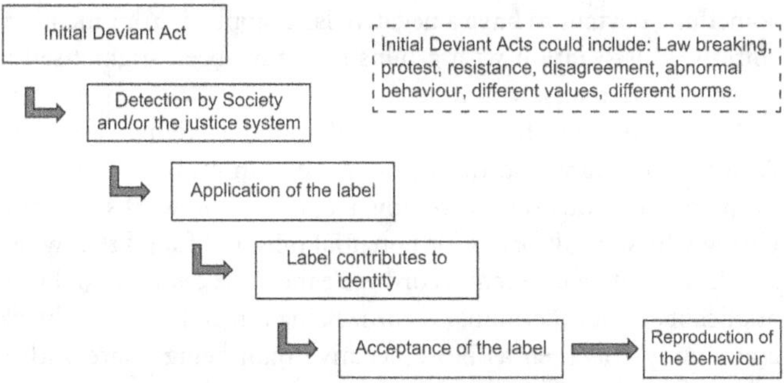

FIGURE 4.1 Stigmatisation as a Part of the Labelling Process

individual as the negative label becomes internalised and then accepted (Figure 4.1). This is the idea of a self-fulfilling prophecy. Where power becomes relevant is when we attempt to understand what labels are applied, who gets to apply them and what behaviours are seen as violating social norms. When the Prime Minister of Australia publicly wears a bullet-proof vest to a rally of law-abiding gun dealers, his relative power sends a message to the rest of society about that group. They are dangerous, risky and troublesome.

Stigma research in criminology has often focused on the stigma that occurs once someone has been in contact with the criminal justice system. For example, we know that after incarceration, the stigma of being a criminal influences an individual's ability to find employment,[4,5] reconnect with children who are in the child welfare system,[6] and even navigate daily life tasks such as gaining housing without being seen through the lens of an incarcerated felon.[7] The label of criminal becomes a master status that dictates how others in society interact with this individual.[8] Research has also shown that you don't need something as significant as a firsthand experience of being arrested or incarcerated to become stigmatised.[9] People can be stigmatised by their association with or membership in a group that has had negative stereotypes developed through isolated incidents and/or structural disadvantage over time. What that means is, you don't have to have done something deviant to have a negative label applied. Your membership in or association with groups that have been stigmatised is enough to stigmatise you too.

Sociologist Devah Pager's[10] work on the stigmatisation of African Americans and those who have been incarcerated is one of the best demonstrations of how stigmatisation works. In comparing who got call-backs for potential jobs, she found that white applicants with a criminal record were more successful than black applicants with no criminal record. Being a member of the black community was seen as more negative than being white with a criminal history. This illustrates the way in which negative stereotypes can be pervasive in society and attached to group membership even when members have not engaged in bad or deviant behaviour. Rather, this is about things like structural disadvantage in society and the legacy of slavery, which has forged particular kinds of negative labels for particular group characteristics. These groups may experience higher levels of deviance due to their structural disadvantage, but the label "criminal" has become fused to their identity as members of a particular ethnic group.[11]

According to sociologists, stigma can be applied to anyone, but those with relative social power (money, status and authority), are better able to avoid or manage those negative labels so that they don't become part of their identity and outsiders don't come to know them as members of a stigmatised group. Politicians, community leaders and even celebrities can and often do engage in deviant behaviour and can be members of a historically stigmatised group, but scholars would argue that their relative privilege acts as a protective factor, minimising the likelihood that the negative label gets applied or internalised.[12] Power and privilege help to mitigate the effects of negative labels. For this reason, the speech made by actor Matthew McConoughey at the White House after the Uvalde Texas school shooting is influential because he is using his power and privilege to de-couple the link between the gun-owning community and the perceptions that they are anti-gun control, anti-community safety and dangerous.

The Prime Minister's attendance at a rally wearing a bulletproof vest was likely significant in reinforcing the growing feeling within the gun-owning community that they were being unfairly labelled as criminals and dangerous because of the Prime Minister's authoritative power. This likely would have been less impactful on society and on the gun dealers themselves if a random, unknown person had come to the rally wearing one. It would have been easy to see that as a silly antic or the act of a lone troublemaker. Power and how people see your power matter. When someone with authority and power makes those links, not only are those links evident to the individuals who have to wear those negative labels, but the public also sees those links and uses them to understand those who are members of that stigmatised group.

The gun-owning community in Australia is primarily white, male and not living below the poverty line (it's expensive to maintain legal gun ownership in Australia) – all of which are characteristics of social privilege, and so they should be able to navigate or avoid any stigma. As I started to think about this assertion that gun owners feel stigmatised by society, I wondered in what ways they experience stigmatisation and how that impacts their behaviour. In this chapter, I explore the ways in which gun dealers talk about the assumptions people make about them as gun dealers, gun owners and members of the gun-owning community as a whole.

The Gun Dealers' Experience of Stigma

So far in the academic literature, firearms owners' experiences of negative labelling and stigma have been anecdotal. In my interviews with dealers, I asked them if they had personally experienced any negative backlash as a result of their business or participation in shooting sports/activities in order to understand those anecdotal reports of stigma. Gun dealers talked about their own experiences and the experiences of their employees and colleagues, demonstrating that their own experiences and vicarious experiences reinforced the perception that they were among the outcasts of society. For older dealers, the Port Arthur massacre and the legislation that followed were a lens through which they came to understand why society has stigmatised them. Not only did they talk about their experiences of negative backlash, they talked about how it impacted them and their businesses, and I began to see links between these perceptions and the types of interactions they had with regulators and law enforcement.

In Chapter 3, I described the administrative and financial burdens and costs as a result of the nature of the practicalities of compliance. However, when gun dealers talk about their experience of backlash from the community as a result of their business, they are talking about the social costs that have come with gun control for the gun-owning community. Social costs include the unintended consequences of political discourse, media framing and public reaction as part of the social discourse on gun control in Australia. In order to better understand what the social costs gun dealers must endure even as critical members of the gun control process, we sought to understand how and what they describe as experiences of negative backlash or stereotypes and how they come to make sense of those stereotypes.

We asked dealers if they had ever experienced negative reactions from others because of their business or involvement with the gun industry. We found that firearms dealers who lived through the legislative changes in 1996 linked their negative experiences specifically to the implementation of the NFA, when gun control was a distinct part of social discourse and debate. One dealer specifically recalls the feeling of being an outsider in the aftermath of the Port Arthur massacre and the discourse between legislators and the gun-owning community.

> *In 1996, you were a leper if you were a gun dealer.*

Another gun dealer reported feeling as if the public blamed the gun-owning community for enabling and facilitating the incident at Port Arthur just by being a legal firearms owner and member of the shooting community.

> *Generally, shooters, the organisations, legitimate people, had been blamed for the Port Arthur incident, they felt victimised, and as it goes down the line, consistently demonised even to this day. It's always a negative connotation.*

The above dealer makes a point of drawing attention to the absurdity of this blame given that the gun-owning community consisted of *legitimate* gun owners, highlighting the law-abiding nature of community members. The irritation and anger felt by gun dealers in regards to feeling blamed for the Port Arthur incident is not about blame in and of itself, but because it cuts directly into their identity as law-abiding citizens – an identity that they hold dear. Another dealer acknowledges the difficulties of having to reorient their business to the new mode of regulation in 1996 but suggests that public perceptions made this transition even more challenging for gun dealers during this time.

> [During the buyback] *We saw it quite a bit, it was pretty stressful, very stressful. It hurt the businesses because of the public perceived idea of us and the media didn't help.*

Dealers often talked about media perceptions as part of their negative experience, and like the dealer above, they saw meaning in the way that public perception made their jobs harder. Dealers who experienced negative reactions from others because of their link to the firearms industry also reported receiving hate mail to their business, graffiti on advertisements or business frontage, negative comments from members of the public who walk past their store, and even messages on social media.

> *There was one person [on social media] that would regularly go on rants, accusing people of being murderers and rah rah rah rah. If there was a firearm on their Facebook picture, or this one family had an image I think it was a deer. Well you're an evil person, by killing people you shouldn't be alive anymore.*

The above dealer points out that even tangential links to the community can attract ire from the public. In the example he provided, a deer symbol, which is widely used in the hunting community and in hunting logos, has been subsequently used to link hunting and legitimate firearms activities to murder. Dealers typically understand that the negative reactions they receive are based on a misperception about firearms and the legal use and ownership of firearms. The dealer below links stigmatisation he has experienced to perceptions the public has about crime involving firearms and the illegal use of firearms more broadly:

> *If you go to a place and get asked what you do, and you say you sell guns for a living, the first thing they think of is what they saw in the media: mass shootings, America, all that negative stuff. They go down that thought trail, that that's you... We do get that people don't necessarily like us, but our product is legal, what we do is legal, what they don't necessarily like isn't me or our industry, but what they don't like is what they perceive it to be, which is quite often not the truth.*

This dealer taps into a broader connection to the global perspectives of gun owners that is most often linked to a uniquely American experience of gun violence. The gun dealer above believes that the Australian public views gun dealers in Australia as an extension of the American discourse on gun control. He further went on to explain that people are often surprised that he is not a member of the American NRA and holds different views on what has dominated the global discourse on gun control. So strong are these conflations between the NRA and firearms owners in Australia that in the aftermath of the Christchurch massacre in 2019, one shooting organisation in Queensland asked my advice on how to best formulate a public statement that would distance themselves from the NRA as much as possible. In this instance, the Australian-based group of shooters wanted to make a statement that would clearly reject the use of violence and promote the Australian firearms laws they believed would have prevented this tragic loss of life.

Though misperceptions may help to explain why the discourse around gun control in Australia has led to the stigmatisation of legal firearms owners, dealers also indicated that there are real consequences as a result of this misperception. Some dealers reported that they felt that the label of being a gun owner meant that they were treated with suspicion and mistrust. The dealer below talked specifically about feeling targeted by police because he was a licenced firearms owner, even though he had never violated the law:

> *...if you get pulled up in your car* [by the police] *and they run your number, you come up, red flagged "beware: a firearm owner". We are in the crime portfolio, licensed people.*

The above perspective suggests that, at least in the minds of gun owners, they are not only seeing their membership in the gun-owning community clearly linked to negative labels of dangerousness and violence but are also having interactions that reinforce feeling stigmatised. And importantly, these links were felt in interactions with others in positions of power, including the police. In thinking about the us vs. them mentality that gun dealers reported about their interactions with police as part of their daily work in the compliance process, I wondered how much that feeling of being viewed as dangerous and violent contributed to those more difficult interactions. I wondered if the perceived stigma had implications for the kinds of interactions that were needed to sustain high levels of compliance and collaboration between dealers and the police.

Dealers who had been in the firearms industry for a shorter period of time (in the last 5–10 years) indicated that they too often felt others were suspicious of them and that they were under attack as a result of their profession, even though they had come into this industry long after the 1996 implementation that forged mistrust between the firearms community and regulators. This suggests that perceived stigma, while it may be a common narrative within the firearms community, is not only isolated to those who lived through the legislative process after the Port Arthur massacre. Newer and younger dealers also talked about feeling as though they needed to be guarded in who they revealed their identity as gun owners to.

> *My guys, don't put stickers on their car, ok?...*

Another dealer suggests that firearms owners have learned where it is safe to reveal that part of their identity and where it is not. In observing his younger employees, this dealer notes that even the most vocal and proud firearms owners sense themselves in groups outside the firearms community.

> *I've got people who are very vocal, but you put them in a group of people they don't know very well, or a larger group of people from different demographics and everything else, they probably will never ever mention they enjoy shooting or anything like that.*

However, these younger or newer dealers also indicated that they thought there was much less negative backlash than there had been in previous years, particularly around the time of the NFA's first implementation. Some argued that generational change meant that new firearms owners and the public were socialised to accept the tight regulation of gun owners, while others believed that Australia's reputation as a gun control poster child had assuaged fears in the Australian community. The dealer below suggests that the improvement in public perception is due to this socialisation,

> *I think that we're probably more accepted now than, maybe 20 years ago, because I think people would have now had the opportunity to say, 'all right, well, that was put in place in 1996', and from 96 to now we've had 20 years, and there hasn't been a mass shooting.*

While there is some sense that gun dealers perceive that the stigma of being a gun owner has lessened since 1996, the narrative and perception that they are linked to labels of danger, violence, risk and criminality have become an intergenerational way of understating their position in society – passed down from older members of the community to newer ones. This is also a collective narrative. Gun dealers talk about how their community has experienced negative stereotypes as much as they talk about their own experiences. Scholars in sociology and criminology have long written about the dangers of stigma, in particular about how perceiving that you are stigmatised has consequences for future behaviour. While I did not observe or hear anything that demonstrated that experiencing negative backlash caused dealers to break the law, ignore the law, or find loopholes in the law, I sensed a desperation that I can only imagine would be exhausting. I wondered what could be learned from prior work on the consequences of experiencing stigma that could contribute to building a better and more collaborative relationship between gun dealers and the public, given the common ground that is shared. I also wondered if the stigma they claim to manage as part of their interactions with police and the public resulted in the same kind of disadvantaged outcomes as we have seen for other stigmatised and marginalised groups in society.

Stigma, the Gun Owner and the Justice System

Whether or not the negative label applied is true or not is irrelevant to what scholars believe the consequences of stigma are. In other words, the way in which we manage rule-breaking and deviance should be done in order to minimise stigma and avoid negative labels being accepted, enhanced and augmented. Feeling stigmatised has ramifications for a person's willingness to cooperate and comply, while alienating the communities that are vital parts of the process simply doesn't do any good for anyone. Learning about how gun owners feel stigmatised left me in a state of discomfort. How can I argue that these primarily white, male, middle to upper class members of society are disadvantaged? I wanted to understand whether the stigma of being a firearms owner was more powerful than the other elements of their identity that would normally be seen as protective factors for negative stereotypes, jarring treatment by police and harsh outcomes from the justice system as a whole. I wondered how judges and magistrates view their gun ownership status and how they determine who gets to hold a licence when it is in dispute. Do gun dealers and owners experience this kind of stigmatisation in the same way that other marginalised members of society do? I turned to state administrative justice systems where gun owners can appeal decisions and restrictions on their licence.

This new study allowed us to explore judicial decisions on licence revocations and violations of the law by legal gun owners.

These cases would allow us to see the kinds of individuals that are captured by the law as well as the ones that voluntarily seek out court intervention to mediate disputes between the licensee and law enforcement on decisions about licence conditions, renewals, or approvals. These voluntary entrants into the justice system were important because they would allow us to see those who willingly came to the justice system as well as provide an avenue to explore the role of privilege in courtroom interactions.

Analysis and examination of over 250 cases across three states in Australia led to two core findings. First, judges did often point out or use firearm ownership to justify decisions that adversely affected gun owners. However, we also found that legal decisions in these cases would have likely remained unchanged even if status as a firearms owner was not mentioned. Second, we found that the traditional markers of privilege worked in favour of gun dealers, leading to better outcomes and often overriding more serious behaviours of concern. Firearm owners were stigmatised because of their status as firearm owners, but they are also privileged. What we found was that there was a distinction between experiencing stigma and being subjected to the full consequences of stigma for firearm owners. Their privilege was a protective factor that mitigated some of the consequences of stigma. Firearm owners were taken to the cliff edge of stigma but not kicked off it. Here, we provide two cases that illustrate these findings.

The Case of Carrying a Concealed Firearm for Security

Alex[13] has had a licence to possess and use a handgun (category H) in connection with his business as a gun dealer and pawn broker. His licence was granted under the category of "security guard," which is one of the eight genuine reasons for firearms ownership in Australia. As a pawn broker, he qualified for this kind of licence as he must transport and guard large amounts of cash and valuables, such as jewelry. This licence provided approval for him to carry a concealed weapon as a component of his duties for security cash and valuables. The conditions of this licence, which he had held for over 10 years without violation or incident, read as follows:

> *This license authorizes the licensee to have possession of and use of one (1) category H weapon registered to this license in connection with the security or valuables or other high-risk items or substances held or transported by the licensee in the course of the licensee's occupation as specified herein. The licensee is only to carry the firearm while performing security duties of a nature that necessitate or warrant the carriage of such firearm. The weapons is to remain in secure storage unless otherwise authorized, justified or excused by law.*
>
> *(Emphasis added)*

When Alex needed to renew his licence, he applied using the appropriate channels but found that the approving officer had changed the conditions of his licence. The new licence conditions read as follows:

> *The license authorizes the licensee to have possession of and use of one (1) category H weapon registered to this license, for the 'specific purpose' only. Only one (1) category H weapon with a calibre of no less that .22 and no more than .40 may be registered to this license at any one time. The licensee may have physical possession of the weapon only when the duties being performed reasonably necessitate the physical possession of the weapon. The licensee must record details in the security guards register as per section 126A (1) of the Weapons Act 1990, on each occasion where there is a need to physically possess and/or use the weapon. The weapon is to remain in secure storage unless otherwise authorized, justified or excused by law.*
>
> *(Emphasis added)*

Alex was concerned about the specific purpose clause in this new condition, which read:

> *The 'specific condition' is the protection whilst transporting cash and valuables in connection with the licensees' occupation*

> *as the principle or employee of [business name] and for no other reason. The license remains in force only whist the licensee is the principle or employee of the business [business name].*
>
> *(Emphasis added)*

Alex, in appealing this decision to his state court, argued that limiting the licence to transporting only was impractical given his business, and he did not understand why he was no longer able to carry a concealed firearm while acting as a security guard. Alex had no problem complying with the new condition to log each use of the weapon in the security guard register. But he was concerned that the limitation to only using firearms while transporting cash, valuables and high-risk items would be limiting. Alex cited concerns that his business was in a high-crime area of the city, that he had prior experience of serious assault while conducting his business, and that he had well over $500,000 of cash, valuables and firearms in his store. He argued that being able to carry a concealed weapon was in his and his store's best interests.

The judge rested their decision primarily on two legal provisions in the Weapons Act: one that prioritises public safety, and a second that considers what other non-firearm security measures can be taken. The Act suggests that permission to carry a concealed weapon should only be granted when there are no other environmental controls that help to provide additional security. In issuing the decision, the judge notes Alex's clear record and history of being a responsible firearms owner and that his store has substantial security measures in place. The judge also claims that by virtue of being a firearms owner, he could find himself in a position where he might shoot or threaten to shoot offenders who threaten his business or himself and may encourage potential offenders to be armed if he is armed himself. The judge believed this may lead to a shootout where the public may be at risk. By doing this, the judge links his status as a firearms owner to danger, violence and a risk to public safety, thereby stigmatising him despite Alex upholding the behaviour consistent with responsible and legal firearms ownership and his clean record. The magistrate affirms the licence approvers' decision to impose the new conditions and justifies this decision by saying that the need to protect himself and the business does not outweigh the risks to public safety.

Our analysis illuminated the link between status as a firearms owner and links to dangerousness, violence and risk to the community. This evidence supports firearms dealers' claims that they are seen as problematic and a risk to the community and may be stigmatised as a result of their firearms ownership. However, we also found that in this case, and in other similar cases, the judge would likely have reached the same decision even without referring to this kind of risk as a result of firearms ownership; the outcome would have remained the same even if the negative associations of being a firearms owner were not used to justify the outcome. We conclude that while there is evidence that stigma is in play, it did not likely alter the outcome in this case given that the legal provisions would have given the judge sufficient discretion to impose these conditions by considering the security measures in place in the store environment, rendering the use of a concealed firearm unnecessary while located at the store.

We thought a lot about how the public would react to this case. We hypothesise that the public would be relieved that the judge has limited the use of concealed weapons by balancing risks with public safety. While there is limited research evidence on how the public views concealed carry laws since the NFA was implemented, we would expect that the public's view of tight and strong gun control would lead to support for the judge's decision in this case. We also considered how gun dealers would react. I suspect they would understand the legal provisions. But I also think they would view limiting a law-abiding and responsible firearms owner as an insult to the law-abiding nature of their identity and recoil at the link made by the judge between firearms ownership as a gun dealer and public danger. This case is an excellent example of the complicated nature of balancing public safety and legal firearm use. On the one hand, we may find comfort in the limitations placed on legal firearms ownership, and on the other hand, we can see how individual firearms owners may feel that this is an affront to who they are as people and leaders in their field.

The Case of the Illegal "Marine Parts" Shipped to a Fake Name

Korey has recently had his gun licence revoked. He has had a long and decorated career as a police officer, as evidenced by his numerous awards and commendations for service. His track record as a volunteer for the community was also noted by the judge in the case summary. As a result of his police career, Korey has experienced a number of experiences that have led to a diagnosis of post-traumatic stress syndrome (PTSD). As a police officer, Korey has extensive experience with firearms. And he has an employment history of delivering weapons training courses for the police. He is, by definition, an expert in firearms and firearms use. As a side business, Korey engages in feral animal hunting and makes plaques for police and army events that include molds of weapons.

Korey came to the attention of the police when customs intercepted parcels to be delivered to Korey's home address but to a fake name. These parcels contained parts belonging to an M16 military assault rifle that had been labelled as "marine parts" on the customs forms. This incident initiated a search of Korey's property, where they found a number of violations of the Weapons Act, including inappropriate storage of firearms and possessions of weapons he was not supposed to have. An internal investigation into his conduct by his employer did not result in any misconduct charges being filed due to a lack of evidence and the recommendation that it would not be in the public interest to pursue these charges. Korey retired from the police just after this, following a mental health crisis.

Despite this, Korey still had to face criminal prosecution. He pleaded guilty to all charges where he received a nominal punishment (not recorded in the judgement), and no conviction was recorded against his name. Even though no conviction was recorded, which would have immediately disqualified him from holding a firearms licence, the state weapons licencing unit still revoked his licence, claiming that it was no longer in the public interest and that Korey was no longer a fit and proper person to own a firearm.

Korey appealed this decision, allowing a judge to reconsider whether Korey could retain his firearms licence. In making this decision, the judge was required to consider the offenses that led to the licence revocation, his character, background, mental state and past behaviour in determining whether Korey is a fit and proper person. The judge, in their decision, draws attention to Korey's exemplary career as a police officer, his volunteer work with the community and the fact that he pled guilty to all charges. The charges represent clear violations of the law and are not disputed.

The judge pointed out that it is likely that Korey would have received approval to import those parts had he followed the proper procedure, noting that Korey testified that he was simply trying to save the time it would have taken to gain approvals through the current compliance process. He also noted that Korey's motives were not criminal and that his importation of these restricted weapons parts, and thus illegally obtaining controlled weapons were a result of his passion for collecting firearms.

> *I accept from reading the transcript of [Korey's] answers to the directed interview that was not sinister and the possession of these items was connected only with his passion for collecting firearms and parts.*

In his evidence, the state weapons inspector details the nature of the legal violations but mitigates them, claiming that they were not a concern because the vast majority of the firearms were stored appropriately. However, the judge also reiterated that, as part of the investigation into these violations, Korey had lied about the whereabouts of a firearm and thrown the illegal parts into a river to get rid of the evidence.

In the hearing, Korey's treating psychiatrist detailed the nature and extent of Korey's mental illness and the link to his activities with firearms. The doctor stated that the underlying PTSD resulted in feral animal hunting, and the making of plaques was a way of reliving stress for Korey. In that testimony, the psychiatrist also offered an explanation of why Korey lied to the police and attempted to conceal evidence.

> *I do think that [Korey's] difficulty in restraining his impulsivity and impatience might be analogist to someone who has post traumatic stress disorder and for example drinks alcohol*

impulsively. I think it's a rapid way of apparently alleviating distress which over rides regular good judgement and on the evidence of [Korey] himself, and his wife, his engagement in firearms related activities took the form of a destruction or a diversion from his emotional distress which I think he had trouble restraining because it was one of the few means of managing his internal distress.

The psychiatrist further testified that rehabilitation and recovery from PTSD would be facilitated by allowing Korey to continue to engage in firearms activities and suggested that he was not an individual who poses a risk to the community.

In arriving at his decision, the judge singled out a number of components in determining Korey as a fit and proper person. He relied on the initial judgement, where no conviction was recorded on Korey's record due to his employment as a decorated police officer. The judge also accepted the psychiatrist's testimony that continued engagement in firearms-related activities would help in supporting Korey's PTSD treatment. Korey's character witnesses were two decorated members of the armed forces and a city mayor, who attested to his professional conduct and described him as an upstanding citizen. The judge reinstated Korey's weapons licence.

In our analysis of this case, we highlight the markers of privilege that are evident in the case notes. Korey is an educated police officer and has high levels of connections to the police, armed forces and city leaders (Mayor). Despite his illegal behaviour, efforts to lie to the police, and conceal evidence, his violations are framed by the investigators themselves as "not a major concern". His mental health, while characterised as leading to impulsivity and deception, is used to frame his deception to investigators as a coping mechanism analogous to the abuse of alcohol. Yet, it is accepted that in his case, continuing firearms activities should be seen as part of the treatment plan for his mental health crisis.

We do not attempt to comment on or provide an opinion on whether shooting activities are good or bad for mental health. However, we find it interesting that in this case, acute mental illness is the accepted explanation for deceptive and illegal behaviour, and yet mental illness is in part the reason for an outcome in favour of the defendant. This is particularly interesting given that the one aspect of gun control that is most widely agreed upon here in Australia and globally is the limitation of firearms possession for those experiencing mental illness and distress. It appears in certain cases that one's privilege can even outweigh concerns that are part of our common ground.

The data from the gun dealers project clearly demonstrates that gun dealers and gun owners feel as though they have been negatively labelled as troublesome, dangerous and problematic members of society as a result of their firearms ownership. The gun violations study does suggest that the stigmatisation of firearms and firearms ownership is real – being a firearms owner is often linked to labels of dangerousness and violence even when it is recognised that the firearms owner themselves have a track record of being law-abiding citizens. However, we also found that while these stigmas may exist for the gun owner, they appear to be mitigated in court outcomes by one's relative privilege. In other words, we would not predict that any stigma related to being a firearms owner would result in unfair outcomes in court in the same way that we see for individuals from other marginalised and stigmatised groups.

Why Is Perceived Stigma So Important to Consider?

In early 2021, I sat at the back of the room during one of my PhD students' presentations on perceptions of gun control by gun owners in Australia. I wish I had sat somewhere else. A senior academic sitting near me, repeatedly mumbled and mocked the presentation saying, "*Why should I care what gun owners think?*" followed by comments that he better not anger me because of my connection to firearms. I thought this was an odd position for two reasons. First, it isn't normal for senior academics to heckle first-year PhD students in their first public presentation. Second, it was strange to me that a social scientist couldn't grasp the importance of understanding why it might be wise to consider the perceptions of a large group of constituents in society who are directly impacted by the policies on gun control. The continued commentary has increasingly made me angry, primarily in defense of my student, and it has had a long-lasting impact on the way that I interact with some of my colleagues. While I have certainly felt stigmatised by virtue of my research on gun control, and I suspect my graduate students have felt this too, this reflection has been helpful to think through the potential implications that perceived stigma has on our everyday interactions, behaviours and attitudes.

Where the research on stigma has been most useful and what the evidence primarily highlights when considering the impact of stigma is on the dangers of isolating groups or individuals from society.[14] Research suggests that stigmatised groups in society often feel disenfranchised or cut off from full social participation, treated as second-class citizens or outsiders to the broader community. Gun dealer reports of negative stereotypes demonstrate these same feelings. In Chapter 3, gun dealers reported that one of their primary concerns is that they are not consulted on matters of gun regulation despite their expertise, experience and being most directly impacted by these gun laws. They feel this disenfranchisement. Coupled with feelings of being stigmatised, it's not difficult to imagine how this might impact their support for gun control laws now or in the future. Research tells us that feeling disenfranchised potentially undermines people's feelings about the legitimacy of laws as well as the people who are enforcing them.

We have also learned that experiencing stigma or perceiving that you are stigmatised can have a dramatic effect on individuals. When we approach interactions with others with the belief that they think something negative about us, it has implications for how we respond to others, how we feel about our interactions with others and how we might approach others in the future. Labelling theorists argue that those interactions may lead to embracing and enacting behaviours consistent with those negative labels,[15] but scholars have also discovered that stigmatisation could lead to the separation of individuals or the group as a whole from the rest of society.[16]

In general, research demonstrates that those who face stigmatisation have poorer health and wellbeing outcomes and higher levels of psychological distress.[17] This is especially the case when the stigmas are internalised and concealable – individuals can and do go to lengths to hide the parts of themselves that are stigmatised by others.[18] Other scholars have found that when it comes to firearms owners in particular, they conform to these general research findings in that they appear more comfortable being honest and open about gun ownership with family, friends and others with whom they have developed relationships with.[19]

Scholars in the USA have acknowledged that gun collectives and gun-owning communities are required to address the stigma that has become attached to firearms and associated with violence and risk. One example from this research found that when individuals who are part of these collectives are forced to manage this stigma, it results in normalising firearms while minimising their dangerousness and juxtaposing firearms alongside other more innocuous items.[20] They also found that gun collectives use privacy and secrecy to help manage the stigma associated with firearms ownership. One example is gun collectives adopting practices such as being "cash only" vendors where no credit card information or electronic record of sale is made. This would make the tracking and tracing of firearm sales difficult to maintain and therefore have implications for public safety.

If we are interested in developing, creating and convincing people that gun control is good, then stigmatising those who hold leadership roles in the gun-owning community undermines these efforts. Another arena where the stigmatisation of gun ownership can be seen is in the public's reactions to firearm owners' critiques, disagreement, or discontentment about aspects of gun control regulations and the process of enacting them. We can see it clearly in the way in which conversations between leaders of the gun-owning community and the public typically come about. What we see are gun owners attempting to shake off the stigma of criminality and realign their identity as law-abiding citizens – an identity that they hold dear. The continued experience of stigma runs the risk of withdrawing from society and social discussions of gun control. In practice, this could mean that gun dealers no longer work to socialise community members into moral agreement with the laws or, in extreme cases, work explicitly against the laws as a form of protest, whether it is conscious or unconscious.

The gun dealers' experience of stigma is therefore important to consider if you are interested in good quality and effective gun control, especially as that control relies on their collaboration and investment.

The Gun Dealer Project and the project on judicial decisions of weapons act violations in Australia have provided an avenue to explore in what ways gun dealers feel stigmatised and whether that stigma helps explain outcomes of court cases. None of these projects allow us to determine if stigma is influencing behaviour and attitudes. That is research for a future researcher and/or a future project. However, in looking at the interplay between stigma and privilege in this community, my collaborators and students have tried to think through the implications of perceiving oneself as stigmatised for gun control, compliance with gun control and interactions with regulators and the public.

Stigma May Undermine Common Ground

In this book, common ground represents the substantial overlap in motivations, morals and values that are the foundations for our thoughts and beliefs about gun control policy. Remembering and building upon this common ground offers a refreshing way to approach policy debates and public discussions about gun control more broadly in place of the more divisive conversation we have come to know. I use the concept of "common ground" to showcase the drivers and motivations that gun dealers have in how they approach their business and their role in the gun control compliance process; they support the content of gun control laws; they also want to protect victims from gun violence; they want to protect their community from the stigmatisation that has become linked to firearms in society; and they believe that being a law-abiding citizen is not only important, but it is a core part of their identity.

When I think about the overall messages that gun dealers are sending when they talk about feeling stigmatised, attacked, or vilified, it is an account of being misunderstood. Although they feel as though they have been marginalised and used as a scapegoat for crime problems, it was clear to me that they also felt the weight of serious gun violence more heavily than the general public or others not directly affected by those crimes. Early on in my interviews, I met a dealer who talked viscerally about how he felt after a customer who had all of the necessary approvals and permissions from law enforcement purchased a gun from his shop and later went on to use that gun to shoot two other people. I could see the pain in his face. When this is juxtaposed with the attacks reported by gun dealers in this study, I have wondered how continued stigmatisation and a general misunderstanding of who gun owners are and what they support (at least from their perspective) might impact their willingness to collaborate and socialise others in the community about what responsible gun ownership and compliance look like. While that might sound like an indictment of gun dealers, it is hard to ignore the evidence from sociologists and criminologists about the consequences for society when we stigmatise individuals and groups regardless of whether or not those negative labels are true.

The common ground shared by gun dealers with the public and regulators demonstrates the potential for positive collaboration and a partnership aimed at maintaining compliance with gun control. This would create a foundation for not only helping to uphold community safety but also providing a pathway to socialise firearms owners into willing participants in responsible and legal gun ownership. Research suggests that experiencing stigma may undermine this common ground and therefore make this kind of partnership and collaboration much harder. Where research suggests that stigmatisation can result in adopting strategies of secrecy and normalisation and resulting psychological distress, these strategies, should they be adopted, move gun owners away from collaboration and weaken the common ground already in place.

We are already seeing research that indicates that gun owners are pulling back from sharing their identities as gun owners. Researchers have found that gun owners are increasingly not filling out our survey questions about gun ownership, leading to an increase in non-response on social surveys and impacting the representation of survey respondents. Theorists who study stigma view this as a consequence of recognising that it is better to hide their firearms ownership identity from others.

Recent research has demonstrated that the stigma management strategies of gun owners lend themselves to in-group bonding – those who feel the shared burden of stigma and the unfairness that comes with that stigmatised experience – bind together to create their own sense of norms and values. In the USA, researchers have already demonstrated that shared stigma not only leads to the normalisation of violence as a way to downplay the social reactions to their profession but can also lead to the development of a new set of practices for the exchange of goods that circumvent the law. This indicates that the strategies of stigma management may chip away at the strong moral support for the law over time as well as the shared seriousness of gun-related violence that is currently shared by gun dealers in Australia.

Does this mean that those who experience stigma will suddenly engage in illegal activities in the gun market? No. Nor have I seen any evidence of this in the Australian context. However, as a criminologist, I'm left wondering how easy it might be to manage social stigma within their community when, no matter how hard they try or no matter how much they want to maintain their legal firearms trade, it makes a limited difference in the eyes of regulators and the broader community.

Similarly, I've often wondered if the social stigmatisation experienced by gun dealers and owners slowly chips away at their moral support for the content of gun control laws. In Chapter 2, I outline how moral support for the law is not only a motive for gun dealers to comply but also to participate in the regulatory implementation of gun control. Despite this, gun dealers are conscious of the social stigma attached to their role and their livelihoods. This social "othering" marginalises those who are most able to leverage informal social control within the group. Instead of being part of the wider public, their experience of negative stereotypes and being perceived as dangerous enablers of violence may decrease feelings of empowerment as role models for their community and therefore decrease moral support for the law. Social stigma and the application of negative labels and stereotypes are social processes that reduce the power of groups and their members. This undermines the empowerment that is needed to solidify moral support for the law and motivate compliance.

Without gun dealers' compliance, gun control would cease to be as effective as it is today with their cooperation and motivation for safety and responsible gun use. Gun dealers have a strong sense of civic identity. Before they are gun owners and dealers, they are law-abiding citizens. Undermining this identity undermines their motivation to uphold the law, even when they don't agree with it.

Stigma May Enhance the Barriers

While stigma may undermine positive working relationships between the gun-owning community, the public and law enforcement, it also works to enhance the barriers that already exist in these regulatory relationships. Stigma works to drive people away from each other. Those who see the stigma naturally avoid the problematic stigmatised group, assuming that the negative stereotypes about them are true – often unconsciously – and those who are stigmatised retreat from those who see the stigmatised behaviour.[21] When I think about the barriers to effective gun control that I articulated in Chapter 3, it is difficult for me not to see where stigma could be playing a role. Acting on a negative stereotype and experiencing (or expecting to experience) a negative stereotype changes the way we interact with people around us.

Labelling theory scholar David Rosenhan wrote about one of his experiences while researching the stigma associated with mental illness, which is illustrative of the pervasiveness that stigma has on our interactions with others.[22] In one study, he and members of his research team checked themselves into a mental hospital with pseudo-complaints of hearing voices and vague mental illness symptoms. Once admitted, he and the other participants ceased to complain of the symptoms and were instructed to act normally. Instead of seeing that there was in fact nothing wrong with them and that their mental illness symptoms had eased, Rosenhan found that he continued to be labelled as mentally ill by hospital staff. His normal behaviour was explained away in place of the label of mentally ill – all his normal behaviours were reframed to fit the mentally ill description. The learning from this study demonstrated how, once labelled, labels are very hard to shift. Even though he was a professional, white and male, some stigmas even permeate the parts of our identity associated with privilege.

In Chapter 3, I described what I saw to be barriers that pose a risk to effective gun control based on Australia's experience. The administrative burden on dealers from heavily bureaucratic controls, the financial impact of having to comply with regulations that change regularly, the "us versus them" mentality experienced by dealers when interacting with local and registry police, and the lack of agency and respect for their expertise have led to the marginalisation of their role in policymaking. These are all problems that have been identified in the context of Australia's gun control framework, and I argue they could pose a threat to effective gun control in the long term. The impact that this stigmatisation has on individuals and the gun-owning community enhances this threat and further risks deepening the fissures that already exist between the public, law enforcement and the gun-owning community.

When dealers indicate that they feel marginalised and left out of the process of policymaking despite their expertise and willingness, they make sense of this by suggesting it is because they are stigmatised as gun owners. From the perspective of the gun dealer, they can't find any other reasons why they would be left out of the consultation process, given their expertise and the fatc that they themselves are responsible for implementing and upholding those policies. Their perception of stigmatisation is how they make sense of this. Do negative stereotypes about gun dealers being dangerous, irresponsible, or enablers of gun violence feed into this lack of inclusion? I'm not sure, but the gun dealers believe that that is so.

The perception that gun owners have become stigmatised is part of the explanation as to why gun dealers do not feel they have received an authentic seat at the table. They feel that they have been marginalised and alienated from the process. Research tells us that this kind of lack of agency and voice can lead to a range of consequences for both individual gun owners and the gun-owning community. Not only may they retreat inward to protect themselves from this stigma, moving them further away from public engagement, but it likely has implications for their interactions with regulators.

Research has demonstrated that experiencing stigma or expecting to experience stigma can inflame the *us versus them* mentality when it comes to interacting with others. A group of US researchers studying gun ownership in America found that when gun owners experience stigmatisation, they bond over that shared experience of being deemed an outsider by the rest of society. They found that this in-group bonding contributes to an us versus them mentality in how they react to and interact with non-gun owners, intensifying the wedge between the stigmatised community and the public.[23]

This finding from stigma research is not surprising. Humans have a tendency to regress towards those with shared experiences. These are the people who "get us" when society doesn't or/and might be even more important if we perceive ourselves to be on the fringe of society – that support is important.[24] We see evidence of this in most groups that have experienced some form of social stigma. These are the people who stand together with others to fight against injustice or withdraw from the society that has labelled them as outsiders.

The concern in relation to gun control is that the experience of stigma can become burdensome and may aggravate the us versus them mentality that gun dealers describe in their interactions with police. In addition, given that they expressed feelings that they could not shift the negative stereotypes of being a gun dealer or gun owner, there is a danger that that burden may become too much to carry. I wonder if that burden has implications for their continued willingness to cooperate.

Gun dealers routinely report that their business can be overburdensome when attempting to undertake the often changing and often confusing administrative responsibilities that are required for every sale and acquisition of a firearm. Many dealers had commented on the time burden, the financial burden and even the legal burden they endure when errors inevitably occur. While no gun dealer admitted to cutting corners, there are signs of where this has happened. Court cases against dealers demonstrate the ways in which business practices can be influenced by administrative burdens. Korey, from the earlier case, chose to import firearm parts illegally because it would be quicker, easier and less burdensome than going through the proper channels.

The administrative burden was the primary complaint gun dealers had about their work and the gun control regulations in Australia. The financial and practical implications of these burdens have already forced gun dealers to rethink their business practices, and some have even had to make tough decisions about keeping their employees or going out of business altogether. Marginalising the gun-owning community through the social process of stigmatisation undermines effective gun control. Gun dealers want to collaborate, and their livelihoods provide an incentive to prioritise safety above all else. But the constant feeling of being stigmatised would suggest that their support and willingness to collaborate could be jeopardised. Research would predict that the more shared experiences this group has in navigating negative stereotypes, the more likely they are to see the laws as illegitimate, unfair and problematic. Even if this doesn't lead them to willfully disregard the law, it still produces less effective gun control measures and more burdensome regulation of guns for society as a whole.

Chapter Summary

"That's just a victim mentality" is the phrase that was once said by someone responding to my findings that gun dealers have felt attacked and stigmatised as a result of their profession and connection with firearms. "They have guns! They are dangerous" is another. I understand why people think this. Particularly in the American context, where the needless bloodshed as a result of gun violence is hard to forget, especially when we see small children as victims in places where they should feel safest. However, I doubt the vast majority of gun dealers that I have met in the process of this research want to be blamed for gun violence, especially when they do care about the safety of their clients, their families and their friends as much as we do.

Whether the negative labels gun dealers feel have been applied to them are accurate or not, the application of those labels arises from interactions with others and has implications for future interactions. The media, politics and the public have come to view people attached to firearms as an extension of the danger and risk that firearms pose. It is important to remember that stigmatisation is about what society imposes on individuals and groups, not something inherent to the individuals who are part of the gun-owning community. As outsiders in the gun-owning community, we have the power to invite them to a more inclusive conversation about how to prevent violence. In the field of criminology, crime prevention is about community. The possibilities for ameliorating the negative labels attached to law-abiding and responsible gun owners and simultaneously reinforcing responsible and law-abiding use of firearms likely lie in the strength of the firearms community itself.

Notes

1 Pescosolido, B. A. (2013). The public stigma of mental illness: what do we think; what do we know; what can we prove? *Journal of Health and Social Behavior*, *54*(1), 1–21.
2 https://www.news.com.au/finance/work/leaders/john-howards-biggest-regret-in-his-11-years-as-prime-minister/news-story/06b3f2f50e9aa47586f155f2ac601ce0
3 Goffman, E. (2009). *Stigma: Notes on the management of spoiled identity*. Simon and schuster.
4 Pager, D. (2003). The mark of a criminal record. *American Journal of Sociology*, *108*(5), 937–975.
5 Sugie, N. F., Zatz, N. D., & Augustine, D. (2020). Employer aversion to criminal records: An experimental study of mechanisms. *Criminology*, *58*(1), 5–34.
6 Fay-Ramirez, S. (2016). Therapeutic practice through restorative justice: Managing stigma in family treatment court. *QUT Law Review*, *16*, 50.
7 Furst, R. T., & Evans, D. N. (2017). Renting apartments to felons: Variations in real estate agent decisions due to stigma. *Deviant Behavior*, *38*(6), 698–708.
8 Stiles, B. L., & Kaplan, H. B. (1996). Stigma, deviance, and negative social sanctions. *Social Science Quarterly*, 685–696.
9 Pryor, J. B., Reeder, G. D., & Monroe, A. E. (2012). The infection of bad company: stigma by association. *Journal of Personality and Social Psychology*, *102*(2), 224.
10 Pager, D. (2003). The mark of a criminal record. *American Journal of Sociology*, *108*(5), 937–975.
11 Decker, S. H., Ortiz, N., Spohn, C., & Hedberg, E. (2015). Criminal stigma, race, and ethnicity: The consequences of imprisonment for employment. *Journal of Criminal Justice*, *43*(2), 108–121.

12 Crenshaw, K. W. (2017). *On intersectionality: Essential writings*. The New Press.
13 Names have been changed to protect the identities of the parties.
14 Blithe, S. J., & Lanterman, J. (2017). Camouflaged collectives: Managing stigma and identity at gun events. *Studies in Social Justice*, *11*(1), 113–135.
15 Restivo, E., & Lanier, M. M. (2015). Measuring the contextual effects and mitigating factors of theory. *Justice Quarterly*, *32*(1), 116–141.
16 Braithwaite, J. (1989). *Crime, shame and reintegration*. Cambridge University Press.
17 Hill, T. D., Dowd-Arrow, B., Burdette, A. M., & Warner, T. D. (2020). Gun ownership and life satisfaction in the United States. *Social Science Quarterly*, *101*(5), 2121–2136.
18 Quinn, D. M., & Earnshaw, V. A. (2013). Concealable stigmatized identities and psychological well-being. *Social and Personality Psychology Compass*, *7*(1), 40–51.
19 Wallace, L. N. (2017). Concealed ownership: Americans' perceived comfort sharing gun ownership status with others. *Sociological Spectrum*, *37*(5), 267–281.
20 Blithe, S. J., & Lanterman, J. (2017). Camouflaged collectives: Managing stigma and identity at gun events. *Studies in Social Justice*, *11*(1), 113–135.
21 Blithe, S. J., & Lanterman, J. (2017). Camouflaged collectives: Managing stigma and identity at gun events. *Studies in Social Justice*, *11*(1), 113–135.
22 Rosenhan, D. L. (1973). On being sane in insane places. *Science*, *179*(4070), 250–258.
23 Blithe, S. J., & Lanterman, J. (2017). Camouflaged collectives: Managing stigma and identity at gun events. *Studies in Social Justice*, *11*(1), 113–135.
24 Bradshaw, D., & Muldoon, O. T. (2020). Shared experiences and the social cure in the context of a stigmatized identity. *British Journal of Social Psychology*, *59*(1), 209–226.

5

HARNESSING THE BENEFITS OF THE GUN-OWNING COMMUNITY

> *It's a very small industry in that regard. And you do try and look after each other, you know, if somebody doesn't have something and you've got it, you go help them out.*

The town of Wieambilla is approximately 300 km west of Brisbane. A rural town in a region primarily used for coal seam gas harvesting, the population of Wiambilla was 78 at the 2021 Australian Census.[1] Informally, I've also come to know through contacts in both farming and shooting communities that the area is also well known for people who live off the grid, and while there may be no record of these residents of Wieambilla, there are likely others that call this rural town home. On December 12, 2022, this tiny town made national headlines when a routine police welfare check ended with two police officers, aged 26 and 29, and a 58-year-old neighbour to the Wieambilla property being shot dead.

Four police officers had been dispatched to the Wieambilla property to look for a man reported missing eight days before. The missing man was at the property with his brother and sister-in-law. As police officers approached the home, they were shot at in what was described as a "hail of bullets" and "executed in cold blood" by Queensland Police spokespersons.[2] Two police officers died at the scene, while two sheltered from the gunfire and awaited police support teams. To coax one of the officers out of hiding, the inhabitants started a grass fire. Likely seeing the flames and hearing the gunshots, a neighbour came to investigate. He was also shot and died on the scene.

DOI: 10.4324/9781003271642-6

The standoff continued for six hours, with the perpetrators posting a video online indicating that they were intentionally planning to ambush and kill police officers. Dressed in combat gear and armed with what was described as a "stockpile of weapons," a 45-year-old woman, a 46-year-old man and his 47-year-old brother were eventually shot by police, bringing the incident to a close. In the house after the incident, more was learned about the perpetrators and their possible motivations. Online footprints of the group revealed that they may have been radicalised towards Christian right-wing fundamentalism, government mistrust and a range of other conspiracy theories. Debate about whether this could be classed as a case of domestic terrorism dominated media coverage.

Public and government reactions to this tragedy were strong. Amidst the grief of losing two young police officers and a concerned citizen, people wanted answers to their questions to help them understand how this could have happened. How and why did these people have access to weapons and ammunition? Why didn't the police know that they may have been armed? Why were the police so underprepared for this interaction? One of the perpetrators was a licenced gun owner from a different state. He was able to legally purchase ammunition even though his licence had been cancelled by New South Wales state police because this information wasn't available to gun dealers selling ammunition in the state of Queensland. It is unclear whether Queensland police had access to this information. As the QLD public and police community grieved, police leadership in QLD offered explanations for some of the questions people had been asking. In particular, it was argued that the police did not have sufficient intelligence to prepare them for what was awaiting them on that property. This explanation highlights an important problem for police and a missed opportunity to recognise the power of community and how we can harness its benefits.

I was asked for my reaction as a criminologist and a gun researcher in the aftermath of the Wieambilla incident, primarily in response to the call for stricter gun laws. I called for collaboration with gun dealers. I thought it would be important to know what they think and what could have been done better. Gun dealers and members of the gun-owning community were hesitant to speak about this incident, some suggesting that they felt it would be used as another opportunity to make gun owners scapegoats for violence. Others argued that this incident was a good example of problems they had been experiencing for years: inability to share information between gun dealers, police and across police jurisdictions, as well as the practical difficulties of operating businesses in rural areas with limited internet coverage. As a result of these limitations, there would be no way for QLD gun dealers to know that they were selling ammunition to someone whose licence had been revoked in a different state.

I thought a lot about this incident in the context of what gun dealers had been telling me: they want to collaborate but don't feel they are welcome; they don't want to sell to risky people but feel they have limited discretion once someone has been issued a licence by police; and they want to ensure that the members of their community use firearms safely and responsibly. Furthermore, they actively try to contribute to responsible firearm ownership via their roles as gun dealers and leaders of their community. Theories of how to motivate people to comply with the law and behave according to community expectations largely rest on community dynamics, structure and relationships. I wondered if the public, policymakers and even criminologists have underestimated the potential benefits of the gun-owning community in their explanations of gun control effectiveness and policy creation.

Communities and neighbourhoods have been the focus of my research across my career, and while I did not set out to study communities and guns together, I have found it hard to ignore the community dynamics that run through the findings of this research, the mechanisms of the theoretical frameworks I have used in this book to understand compliance motivations, and the possible pathways that might lead to better and more effective gun control. In this chapter, I map the findings from gun dealers in the context of what criminologists have learned about communities and their ability to prevent or enable crime – not as a foregone conclusion but as a way to consider a new perspective on engaging and collaborating with the gun-owning community. More specifically, I outline where the benefits of this community can be harnessed to prevent violence, what the positive elements of the community look like, and where we need greater understanding of this kind of community and how they can benefit society.

Why Are Communities So Important?

Social Scientists have found that communities and community dynamics are important for understanding behaviour, including behaviour related to crime and deviance. Characteristics of communities can help us understand how to encourage people to behave lawfully, how to reintegrate people after they have made deviant or criminal choices and how to help socialise people into understanding what appropriate behaviour looks like. In addition, community dynamics have helped us increase our understanding of where crime and deviance happen, how people learn criminal behaviour and what community characteristics we could use to predict higher or lower rates of lawful behaviour. Community and the characteristics of a community are important to consider if we are interested in preventing or eliminating crime, including gun violence and the unlawful use of firearms.

Communities are those whose members share common interests, values and norms. Our neighbourhoods are communities, but not just because we share common space. Neighbourhoods are also places where we form important relationships with our neighbours; we share values and beliefs about what is important in our neighbourhoods; and we share expectations about how we should behave. But our physical neighbourhoods are not the only form that communities can take. Likely, we are members of many different communities, all based on shared activities and interests, such as work, religion, school and hobbies. Our communities may take form in a physical location, like a gun club, or even online via Facebook groups and chat rooms.

Like most sporting groups, gun dealers and shooters form part of a community. Gun-owning communities share common interests and identities, such as hunting and sports shooting. Gun-owning communities formed along these interests also operate mutually beneficial kinships that provide resources, support and help to their members, which helps to foster and support a sense of belonging. Shared experiences may also include negative ones, like the shared experience of being stigmatised. In this sense, communities that centre around legal firearms use are not dissimilar to those based on other types of communities, such as neighbourhoods, sporting communities and religious communities.

I have found that gun-owning communities can take many different forms, but those that are the most common are those that are formed around firearms training, competition, hunting and collecting. There are over 30 different sports shooting clubs in the Brisbane QLD metropolitan area alone, each with a shooting specialty (such as clay target shooting), a shared organisation (such as the University of Queensland Rifle Club). Each of these operates as their own communities and offers mentoring, support and activities for members, therefore each representing an opportunity to socialise members into what responsible gun ownership and use should look like. My exposure to these communities is limited to the time I have spent as a researcher visiting clubs and gun ranges and as a teacher, whereby I take students to gun clubs to interact with their members. I always left with the perception that these communities are often close-knit, work together on a range of different projects, and care deeply about firearms use as a craft or sport to be respected. If we consider what sociologists have learned about the characteristics of communities and how they contribute to socialising people into responsible citizens, then it makes sense to consider what gun-owning communities might have to offer in encouraging compliance with gun laws or socialising acceptance and belief in the aims of gun laws.

Communities, Crime and Deviance

Since the 1920s, criminologists and sociologists have observed the important link between communities and crime. Burgess was one of the first to observe cities as ecological organisms that change with time.[3] Shaw and McKay found that particular community characteristics were correlated with higher levels of deviant or criminal behaviour.[4] Eighty years on, criminologists still study the community- crime link and have learned even more about how communities and the people within them help to prevent or encourage crime. The reason these approaches to deviant behaviour are so critical is that they put individual behaviour in the context of their environment, allowing us to recognise that law-abiding behaviour and law-breaking behaviour are influenced by an individual's social and physical environment.

Early criminologists focused on neighbourhoods within urban cities, but scholars increasingly recognise the diversity of the communities that we are a part of. Social Disorganisation Theory is the most prominent theoretical perspective that links community characteristics to crime. Based on Chicago school criminologists Shaw and McKay's[5] study of juvenile delinquents in the city of Chicago, they observed that the neighbourhoods that had the highest levels of juvenile delinquency were those that had high levels of poverty, high levels of ethnic heterogeneity (multiple different ethnic groups living in the one neighbourhood) and high levels of residential instability (people moving in and out of the neighbourhood and not staying there). What this meant was that juvenile delinquency occurred most frequently in the places that had the most disadvantages, the largest numbers of new immigrants to the country and people who did not plan to stay in the neighbourhood long term. Shaw and McKay's observation that these characteristics were highly associated with crime gave criminologists a critical starting place for understanding that criminal behaviour was connected to the physical and social environment. While Shaw and McKay were not able to untangle exactly why these characteristics produced crime, they suspected that it had something to do with weak social control or weak relationships within the community that prevented socialising people into law-abiding behaviour. In other words, these communities did not have the capacity to use informal social control – the same kind described in Chapter 2 – to encourage lawful behaviour. They were likely too strapped for resources and had limited connections to each other in the community for informal social control to be effective.

Criminologists proposed that poverty increases crime because of the relative inequality and high levels of unemployment, immigrant concentration increased crime because they experienced higher levels of inequality and unemployment than others and being new to the host country brought their own norms, language and culture (not because immigrants were committing crime), and residential instability meant that people move into neighbourhoods only seeking temporary stays before they can move to a more desirable area of town. As a result, these crime-prone neighbourhoods were filled with residents who did not take time to invest in relationships with each other or in the physical space of their home because they weren't planning on being there long, people who could not talk to each other due to language barriers or differences in cultural values and those who were either too busy looking for work or employed across multiple low-wage jobs to be able to make ends meet. These conditions don't make for the kinds of relationships in the community where people have influence over the behaviour of others. Instead, individuals in these communities were somewhat isolated or developed alternative norms.

Modern-day criminologists have continued to investigate the Social Disorganisation approach to try to understand why the physical or structural characteristics of neighbourhoods are linked to crime and deviant behaviour. Harvard University sociologist Robert Sampson discovered that the link between Shaw and McKay's structural characteristics and crime can be explained by something called "collective efficacy."[6] Collective efficacy can most simply be defined as the *willingness of people in the community to intervene* when they see problematic behaviour or events. For example, upon seeing school-aged children hanging out in the street during school hours, a community high in collective efficacy would have members who would either report that to the parents of those children, report it to the school or directly intervene and tell those kids to get back to where they should be. A community with low collective efficacy lacks people who would intervene in those and other situations, which allows those behaviours to continue unfettered.

Sampson's work helped to refine our understanding of what Shaw and McKay's "weak social ties" actually mean for communities. It's not about how well-connected people are in their communities, but whether there are shared values and norms and whether there is a shared collective belief that problems should be solved via intervention for the good of the community. We call this community trait "collective efficacy" or the willingness of community members to intervene when problems in the community arise. Even when people don't know their neighbourhoods well, when residents share similar values and a sense that something should be done, people are more likely to act: remind kids to get back to school, pick up after people or call the police when things go wrong.

Neighbourhood physical characteristics revealed more about the interpersonal relationships in the community than first believed. Sampson's work confirmed the findings of early criminologists that suggest that the physical characteristics of these crime-prone areas were important in understanding the kinds of relationships within the neighbourhood. Physical characteristics that were seen to be important were things like properties with unkempt or overgrown yards, graffiti and garbage left on the street, children hanging out in the street when they should be in school. Why were these physical traits seen as so illuminating? Because if the adults in the neighbourhood shared the values, norms and expectations about their community, they would intervene in those problems when they occur such as ensuring that children know where they are supposed to be, reporting problems to authorities, or directly attempting to respond. In other words, the shared expectations between community members were too weak to influence behaviour or motivate behavioural change. The physical traits were telling of the values, norms and expectations for behaviour of the people within those communities.

Collective efficacy is comprised of two components: social cohesion and informal social control. Social cohesion is the sense of connectedness and belonging shared among community members. Informal social control is the willingness of community members to intervene when problems arise in the community. This means that individuals within the community share a common sense of willingness to act or do something when a member behaves in a way that is problematic. The notion of collective efficacy is important because it highlights the importance of relationships within the community. Even though people might not know each other well, the sense of a shared community identity, shared norms and shared values drives cohesion among group members. This helps to keep law-breaking behaviour low.

How Do Communities Encourage Compliance with the Law?

The concept of collective efficacy has become a consistent component in how we understand neighbourhoods and even other forms of communities to influence the behaviour of those within. While criminologists have documented the crime-fighting benefits of collective efficacy in the USA,[7] Australia,[8] the UK,[9] and Europe,[10] other scholars have found that collective efficacy can bring other benefits to community members. For example, scholars have found that communities with a healthy sense of collective efficacy exhibit lower levels of obesity,[11] higher levels of group performance[12] and even acceptance of new behaviours to reduce the effects of climate change.[13] These benefits are due to a community's sense of shared norms and willingness to work towards a common goal.

Of course, our communities in the 21st century are far more diverse than simply the place and location that we live in. We are members of and participate in employment and professional communities, religious communities, recreational communities such as football clubs, book clubs and shooting clubs. As our online participation has increased, especially since the COIVID-19 pandemic, our involvement in online communities has increased as we find new avenues for social support when we have been challenged for physical contact.[14] Social media such as Facebook, Instagram, twitter and reddit have facilitated communities where people join due to shared interests and values. Community has meaning and value beyond just the sharing of physical space.

Communities, in whatever form, are important because they are a place of socialisation. We learn by experience, reinforcement, punishment and imitation how to behave, what values we internalise and what attitudes to formulate by participating in our communities and interacting with other members of our communities. Criminologists have multiple different approaches to understanding behaviour, be they criminal or law-abiding, but most of them are linked to how we are socialised by those around us. Communities play an important role in that socialisation process.

We can learn a lot about how communities, no matter where they are located, benefit the common good from what we understand about crime and deviance and the role of community documented by criminologists since the 1940s. And while there has been no study to my knowledge that examines the crime-fighting abilities of the gun community specifically, the explanations of how and why people become law-abiding or deviant likely apply to these communities as much as they apply to our schools, families and neighbourhoods.

Learning theorists believe that behaviour (criminal or non-criminal) is learned through traditional mechanisms of learning. Classical and operant conditioning take centre stage in understanding why people perform the behaviours they do. Behaviour that is rewarded is repeated, and behaviour that is corrected or punished is reduced.[15] Irresponsible firearms owners and the criminal use of firearms would be explained by exploring how a person learned those techniques, who they learned them from and how those irresponsible or criminal behaviours were rewarded rather than corrected by the community. Healthy gun-owning communities would be those that demonstrate a strong commitment to safety and responsible behaviour rules and expectations performed by community leaders and taught to younger and new members of the community. Violations of those expectations would be responded to swiftly, to respond directly to the violator and to reinforce to other community members what behavioural expectations are. This socialisation process through mechanisms of learning occurs in the context of our most important community groups – family, school and other communities that provide mentorship, belonging and a sense of identity.

Social control theorists (or bonding theorists) aren't necessarily interested in why people become criminals, but why people don't. They believe that what keeps people from engaging in deviant or criminal behaviour are the close *attachments* or bonds we have with important members of our community – parents, teachers and mentors. In addition, our involvement in conventional law-abiding and pro-social activities, our *commitment* to socially agreed upon goals such as "being a law-abiding citizen" and our *belief* in the underlying values that we have internalised from those in our most influential communities are all factors that pull us away from criminal and deviant behaviour. These attachments to and involvement in conventional norms, activities and people are found in the communities we participate in. If the leaders and members of gun clubs and other shooting clubs demonstrate commitment to values of law abidingness and responsibility, then they too can have an important impact on ensuring new and continuing members are socialised in legal compliance and responsible behaviour.

Where gun dealers in Australia have demonstrated a strong attachment to their law-abiding identity, an undertaking of how these communities work and how they benefit the greater good will provide insight into if and how gun-owning communities in Australia might provide benefit to normalising and socialising young hunters and sporting shooters to a similar identity. Their moral support for gun laws is likely to trickle down to other members of the community because their enforcement and participation in the gun control compliance process contribute to the socialisation of other gun owners who they interact with in their day to day business practices. We might predict that participating in this community naturally reinforces those strong identities, values and norms that are central to the acceptance and compliance of gun control laws. While there are limited empirical insights into whether gun communities espouse these healthy community traits that contribute to socialisation towards compliance, insights from Australian gun dealers help to provide an understanding of what the gun community looks like, how it functions and how it is contributing to gun control compliance in Australia.

Community Created via Gun Control Law

Throughout this book, I have referred to legal gun owners and dealers as a community. In actuality, there are many communities within. Not unlike sporting groups, book clubs and religious organisations, these are people who come together because they share a love for recreational shooting, collecting or firearms-related employment in some way, shape or form. My interactions with these communities have left the impression they are close-knit, meet regularly, discuss issues facing shooting sports and talk about gun regulation. These communities have members that share identities based on shared activities, shared values and operate mutually beneficial kinships that provide resources, support and help to their members, which fosters and reinforces a sense of belonging. My observations of gun-owning communities in Australia are not dissimilar to those that others have observed in other types of communities, such as neighbourhoods, sporting communities and religious communities where identities are shared.

Many of these shooting communities have been part of Australia's history since World War 1. For example, the Queensland Rifle Association (QRA) was formed in 1861 at a time of rapid social change in Australia. The State of Queensland had not long gained independence from the British. British forces were recalling their legions from the region, leaving the colonies feeling vulnerable with limited options for military protection. Sports shooting clubs like the QRA provided opportunities to build volunteer armies, and sports shooting provided an opportunity to hone the volunteer's skills. The Queensland Defense Act of 1884 specifically set out the conditions for which rifle clubs could support Australia's defense by relying on volunteer members from sports shooting clubs.[16] But these sports shooting clubs also provided opportunities to build networks and social connections, reinforce a service ethic in the community and thus play an important role in the colonies in building a sense of normalcy and community after the British had left.[17] In these ways, sports shooting clubs not only have a history of community and community building but also have been structurally supported by the law.

In part, one of the greatest strengths of the Australian legal framework on gun control is the way in which it has made community central to the implementation of gun control law. The National Firearms Agreement and its implementation across the states and territories include two stipulations that help to create community even if it was not there before. First, as articulated in Chapter 1, to qualify for a handgun licence, you must participate in a minimum number of competition shoots per year. And shooting clubs are responsible for ensuring that members participate as articulated in the law.

Section 36. (a) Sports shooters must have a valid membership with an approved club.
Subsection iii. Clubs must endorse a member's application to acquire a handgun. In endorsing the application, clubs should:

1 *Confirm that the licensee has adequate storage arrangements in place*
2 *Specify for which competition shooting disciple the handgun is required*[18]

Competition shoots are managed and regulated by gun clubs and organisations in various locations, each of which forms a community of people who come together due to their interest in recreational shooting. What this means is that even the most cynical handgun owner, who is just fulfilling the requirements in order to keep his handgun licence valid, is forced to interact with their local firearms-owning community. Each of those interactions is an opportunity for values and norm alignment, the correction of irresponsible behaviour and reinforcing the law-abiding identity inherent in how gun owners see themselves. As a result, members, staff, volunteers and officers all play a role in socialising law-abiding behaviour and communicating expectations of behaviour. Breaching these community expectations would jeopardise that community and therefore, members are much more likely to step in when they see or hear or suspect someone may be breaching those norms. Breaching those expectations would therefore likely have consequences for an individual's ability to continue gun ownership.

The second example in the legislation is in regard to connection to land for recreational hunting. Recreational hunters, in order to qualify for a licence, must provide written consent from a property owner that they have permission to hunt on their land.

Section 15. Recreational Shooters/Hunters

a *Recreational shooters/hunters must produce proof of permission from a landowner.*[19]

Recreational hunting is often species-based and revolves around particular times of the year that are optimal for the sport. Property owners often have multiple hunters using their property for hunting, which automatically creates opportunities for community via shared space, shared recreation and shared values around recreation. Even if hunting is not performed in groups, hunters typically know each other and have a good sense of what issues face them as a group. The ability for informal social control and socialisation of expectations of behaviour is high because breaching those expectations puts permission to hunt on land in jeopardy. This helps to reinforce the expectations that come with membership and participation in the hunting community.

This highlights how the gun-owning community is central to the success and efficacy of Australia's gun control law. Without it and the people who act as leaders in the gun-owning community, like dealers, compliance with the law is impossible. The laws rest on the members of the gun-owning community to participate with each other and set the standard of law-abiding behaviour. As a result, there is a legally structured foundation for the role that the gun-owning community and communities can play in understanding how to achieve compliance.

Community Created via Friend and Family Networks

Gun-owning communities tend to recruit members from existing connections within the community. I often asked gun dealers about whether their main clientele were people new to shooting or existing clients who had been part of the community for a long time. The most common answer was that it was both. From the gun dealer's perspective, most new shooters come to shooting because of their connection to a shooter that already exists in their own family. In fact, the family nature of shooting events, especially at gun clubs, was a prominent way gun dealers framed the nature of their communities.

> *I've had girls come in here and get into shooting because their old man shoots, and she's in her 20s now and like, she used*

to remember when she was a kid and she used to go shooting and you know enjoying that father daughter time but now she works and he's getting older and they've just drifted apart and there's just no common ground between them anymore, as to you know, talking about anything. So, she's gone and bought a gun to go shooting with her dad, so that's daddy-daughter time and that's something that we're seeing more and more of.

This perspective was also part of how gun dealers helped to explain the rapidly growing number of women shooters in Australia. Over the last 10 years, gun membership data shows that women are Australia's fastest growing category of shooters. This is evident not only in the increase in female participants but also in the increasing number of women leaders in the shooting industry, as well as in the number of events that are targeted towards women shooters. Gun dealers believed that the vast majority of these members joined because they were seeing other family members participate – namely fathers, brothers and partners. What has typically been a masculine and male-dominated sport appears to be rapidly changing, even if their pathway into the sport is via male family connections.

Many gun dealers also spoke about how legal shooting was something that was enjoyed with their kids and provided an opportunity to help their kids learn responsibility, resilience and skills.

And it's that same thing with a firearm [as teaching them teaching them other morals], you know, you hold it in a certain way, you don't point at a people … and I say to my kids, you can take back words, you can apologize for punching someone or hitting someone. You cannot take back a bullet. Once it's done, it's done. So if you handle firearms with that mindset, and it becomes second nature, you don't point them at people you don't treat them bad. It's not a joke. It's this is something that has the potential to not only take someone's life but ruin yours. You've got to respect that.

Recreational gun events are often dominated by families. Even small children. The presence of young children is a possible driver of the strong sense of safety and respect for proper protocol that I often find when visiting ranges and shooting events. The family nature of both recruitment and members of gun-owning communities also presents an important potential opportunity to benefit from the socialisation processes and interactions that are happening in these spaces.

One dealer pointed out that one of the reasons why women might be increasing so rapidly is because their kids are participating in shooting sports. In most jurisdictions, children under the age of 18 can participate in shooting sports, but only when they have supervision from a parent. While not always necessary, this often means that parents become licenced shooters in order to assist their children in participating in shooting sports.

> *I've got three boys. They started doing clay target shooting. I needed a license to be able to carry the gun to take them to things. So you'll find we've got a lot of women, mums like me, that come in with kids because they have got to have a license also.*

Part of that socialisation process is driven by opportunities to mentor younger shooters in these communities. Just like the coaching and mentorship that we see as normal in other sports, shooting sports require mentorship, training, coaching as well as active club membership and participation. Dealers often talked about school programs that allowed them to share firearms knowledge with young people, one even suggesting that these mentoring programs helped to lay a foundation for responsible behaviour.

> *We've got a lot of school participation around here, which is a great thing. So that's educating children at a young age before they are perceived as an adult and they ride off into the big wide world to get license for driving, license for shooting, and responsible consumption of alcohol. Al of those restrictions. It gives them a grounding. So they're not the... the dick head element is not as bad as it is with most kids that haven't had the coaching and the guidance.*

Dealers also suggested that their role in coaching and mentoring went beyond those who were engaging in shooting sports to those who were around other legal firearms owners. One dealer discussed the importance of teaching people who were around shooters but not shooters themselves the basic safety protocols of using a firearm in order to prevent irresponsible use and safety.

> *...even if a kid's not touching a firearm, if they're near someone who has a firearm, you've got to say to them 'you see that firearm? You never touch it. Right? And then notice when that person picks it up, they never point it any anyone. Observe what's going on.' And so even if they're not touching it, you're coaching them. You're training them, you're talking to them about it. That's all about safety.*

As a result, dealers talked about participation in the shooting community as a place to learn responsibility, especially around firearms. A place that was family-friendly, opened to newcomers and a place that demystified the firearm in order to ensure it was properly understood. These functions of the gun-owning community, as described by dealers, suggest that the shared values and norms about responsible law-abiding behaviour had an active opportunity to be passed down to young people and new firearms owners from within the community through the interactions between members while participating in community activities.

Social Cohesion and Collective Efficacy

In early 2020, My research assistant and I were invited to participate in a women's shooting event in Queensland's north. The event was designed to celebrate women shooters, recruit new women shooters to shooting communities and raise money for a foundation dedicated to breast cancer research in Australia. It was the last trip we made on this project before the COVID pandemic forced us into lockdown. The event began with a cocktail-style event in a gun shop with food, drink and an auction to raise money for charity. We heard from women shooters in the field who talked about their experience of being a woman in a traditionally male-dominated sport and why more women would and should be welcome to join them. The second day included a number of shooting events that ranged from air pistol target shooting to long-distance rifle shooting and handgun target shooting. My research assistant and I had some familiarity with sports shooting as a result of our research but had never participated in this range of shooting sports. Each shooting event had about 20 women participating, and there were enough volunteers and instructors for each person to learn about technique, skill and be encouraged when they were nervous or apprehensive. Regardless of performance, we were congratulated and encouraged to give things another go, especially when our target shooting wasn't particularly accurate. It was hard not to immediately feel like a member of the community. Even in the kitchen, where morning tea was served by volunteers, the comradery and inclusivity of conversation felt by those of us who were new left us feeling the warmth and positivity of the community. We could see the helpful behaviour in action during these events. Volunteers and club staff knew each other, supported each other and looked out for each other. But this did not detract at all from the willingness to intervene when things went wrong.

There are clear rules communicated to you when you enter a gun range. 1. Listen to the range officer at all times; 2. Do not point your firearm at anything other than the target. EVER; 3. Do not move the firearm away from the firing bench. On the air pistol range that day, a woman standing at the target, ready to shoot, saw or heard a friend of hers arrive at the range. She turned her body and pointed the fully loaded air pistol at her friend in jest. My assistant and I were at the back of the room, having already had our turn on the range, watching on in horror. But range officers were quick to intervene. They swiftly asked her to put the pistol down and leave the range. Their effort did two things: immediately removed the potential threat to the group and sent a clear message to the group that violations of those range rules would not be tolerated. The jovial and friendly nature of the day did not change the importance of safety. I don't know what happened to that woman once she left the range and was followed out by a staff member. I saw her later at another event, where she was once again allowed to participate. Her demeanor was more serious and behaviour more in line with what we expected from us as shooting participants. While I never directly observed what happened to her between being removed from the air rifle range and appearing at the handgun range later in the day, the change in attitude seriously led me to assume she'd had a serious chat with the range officers about what behaviour is and is not going to be tolerated.

Whether driven by their own moral compass, a utilitarian sense of protection of their own community, or both, gun dealers and other gun community leaders like range officers regularly discussed instances where they felt it was necessary to intervene when community members or guests in the community did not behave responsibly or according to group norms and expectations. Some of this intervention may be motivated by legal mechanisms, such as when regulations require range officers to report and maintain a register of range users and range incidents. The intervention and willingness to intervene may be driven by rational motives to avoid penalties. Penalties aside, cohesive communities tend to have individuals who are willing to intervene when the good of the community is in jeopardy. Gun dealers have provided examples of their willingness to do this over and over.

In Chapter 2, I described the ways in which gun dealers attempt to prevent problems by educating customers on matters of safety, handling and the law when they engage with clients in the course of business. Each of these examples demonstrates ways in which gun dealers attempt to socalise new and existing members of the gun-owning community about the social and legal expectations of owning and handing legal firearms. Through observations of gun dealers and learning about their everyday interactions via their own accounts, it appears that many of the elements that encompass the idea of collective efficacy are alive and well in the gun-owning community. Gun dealers routinely described situations of mutual exchange and helping behaviour that demonstrated a sense of social cohesion within the community, as well as an ongoing willingness to intervene for the good of the community.

Gun dealers are perfectly placed to be able to utilise their expertise, their position in the compliance process and their face-to-face link with the community to recognise when things go wrong. This is what makes their role so critical. Their capability for intervention can not only aid law enforcement in detecting problems in the licencing approval process and responding to problematic behaviour, but it can also aid the gun-owning community in being able to communicate those important expectations of behaviour that need to be upheld. Dealers often described incidents that demonstrated their willingness to intervene. While they often talked about instances where they felt they needed to query information with the police when they felt that additional checks by the police were necessary to ensure they were only selling to responsible people, they often felt that once a licence had been issued, the decision to sell was out of their hands. However, this did not appear to stop gun dealers from intervening directly when they suspect problematic behaviour in the process of interacting with clients. This demonstrates that they are willing and able to respond to violations of compliance informally in the community in order to reinforce the norms and values of compliance and reeducate members of the community about what is expected of them. The dealer below details one instance in which he found a customer illegally holstering a firearm when the customer came into the shop.

> *We had a guy come in and he was looking for gun oil.*[20] *I asked him, 'what do you want to use it on?'. Well he's pulled up his jumper and pulled a pistol out of a holster. He said, 'I want to use one of these' and I've just nearly died. Anyway, we've gone 'Mate you can't do that.' He says 'oh I've got a license'. We said, you can't do that. So we sold him the oil. When he was out the door we called the police.*

But the willingness to intervene by communicating concerns to police is coupled with the cohesive nature of the community as seen in the way in which gun dealers regularly attempt to help each other, the police and the public navigate gun regulations. The dealer below discusses the way in which they think about cooperation between his own dealership and others despite being competitors.

> *It's a very small industry in that regard. And you do try and look after each other, you know, if somebody doesn't have something and you've got it, you go help them out. I've got*

I've actually got a relative who's got a gun shop. So you've got to look after each other. Yes, it's competitive. But we're a little isolated in WA[21] in terms of, I guess, we're not here to cut each other's throats to make money. If you're an idiot you'll do it, but you're never going to last.

In part, the cooperative nature is due to the small size of the gun-dealing community. Another dealer talked about how he and his employees have worked for multiple dealers in the state and that employees sharing across dealers in a region was common in the industry. This means that dealers have connections between gun shops and dealers, which help to ensure dense network ties among the gun dealing community. This is a key component that supports the capacity for informal social control and thus increases a community's potential for collective efficacy.

Despite the "us vs. them" mentality that dealers often used to describe their relationship with police, dealers also talked about instances where they were helping police with law enforcement tasks related to gun control compliance. One dealer talked about how he and other dealers were often helping police fill gaps in knowledge and information, especially in regard to the registration process used to track and trace the sale and acquisition of firearms across the country. While the registration process can be quite complicated, with multiple forms to capture information about sellers, buyers and firearm descriptors, dealers often reported that registries had errors or were often incomplete. Given that dealers are the point of contact for that information, police often call them to ask for information that they have not yet been able to capture or that they need to correct on the law enforcement end of the process. He said, "*we're continually helping them find things.*" He said that the nature of the dynamic process of registering firearms necessitates cooperation and a willingness to provide the police with information. In one example, he explains how he needed to explain to law enforcement staff that old firearms that dated back to World War 1 often did not have serial numbers, which often became a point of confusion at the point of registration and auditing. While the registration process has the concept of unique serial number tracking for every firearm, he knew that his expertise as a firearms dealer meant that he would need to help police ensure that these firearms were properly registered, thereby avoiding problems with the efficacy of the registration process.

> *Various firearms have been registered by date stamps, by model numbers. And that buggers up the whole system. I was asked by weapons [police licensing unit] one day. She said 'this is registered as 1901. Oh! We've got a lot of those'. Yeah, we are continually helping them find things.*

Helping behaviour described by gun dealers also suggested that they often help to ensure that the gun-owning community can navigate the gun control registration system in order to stay compliant. While I have previously described how the complicated system of licencing and registration can be difficult to navigate for gun owners and dealers who have had to take on assisting clients with this process, their assistance does not end with navigating the application system alone. Dealers often described situations where existing clients would call to ask advice on how to get records corrected with the law enforcement firms branch. In response, dealers often said they helped clients, potential clients and long-standing members of the community navigate gun control regulations in order to ensure everything was above board. In the example below, the dealer said that one of his clients had been trying to get an error on the registry corrected with law enforcement. The client had discovered that the serial number on the registry document was incorrect. The client had found it difficult to iron out the error despite having multiple phone calls with the firearms police. The dealer helped the client create a document of what had been done to correct the problem in order to prevent problems in the future.

> *I tell him 'Look, just make a note of your phone call. Make a note on your sheets. And just take your own notes with it.... because they're dealing with a couple of hundred thousand people as well. And, you know, I know that their records aren't Right. So a lot of private individuals, private shooters, not so much dealers have that problem all the time.*

In helping this client navigate this error with the law enforcement record, the dealers also help to smooth over the relationship between their client and police by proving and explaining why law enforcement is not properly responding to the request. Incidents like these were common in gun dealer narratives about the issues faced by the gun-owning community. What is evident is how gun dealers respond to these problems by helping clients, helping police and helping each other. In doing so, these examples demonstrate the capacity that gun dealers have as leaders in their community to ensure that compliance with gun regulations is maintained.

The Dark Side of Cohesive Communities

Typically, social cohesion and close-knit ties are considered positive attributes of communities that help to keep everyone moving towards common goals and help to exert informal social control to keep deviant or criminal behaviour low. However, other scholars have found that close-knit communities can also have a dark side in that they can enable and reward bad behaviour, allowing it to continue unfettered. In these cases, scholars have argued that the goals of these kinds of unhealthy close-knit communities are different from those of broader society.[22] In other words, some communities may promote deviant behaviour as opposed to discouraging it.

What is it about these communities that has implications for the promotion of deviant and non-compliant behaviour that distinguishes them from the productive effects social cohesion and collective efficacy have elsewhere? Social structure is likely the first aspect that criminologists would link to these poorer outcomes. Communities that suffer from structural disadvantage, continuous turnover of members are those that are likely to increase an individual's exposure to deviant or criminal norms, values and beliefs. Communities that operate to protect the community identity at all costs may also explain why some close-knit and cohesive communities enable crime and deviance. And communities that are exclusively cut off from broader society may also develop their own values and norms that do not align with broader social expectations, such as complying with the law.

Scholars in Australia have found that rural communities that are close-knit and cohesive often tolerate particular crimes by community members.[23] One study in New South Wales found that less than half of property crimes experienced in the community were reported by police. The reasons given as to why property crimes were not reported included beliefs that the police were not interested in solving those crimes and were ineffective in responding to victim concerns and that there was often pressure not to report in order to protect community members. This study concluded that these attitudes likely lead to the facilitation of more crime rather than less. The idea that the cohesiveness of communities may work to protect offenders who are members of that community from detection and allow crime and deviance to continue is not limited to rural communities. These dynamics have been observed and underscore our understanding of why victims and bystanders choose not to report deviance and crime in other kinds of communities, such as sexual abuse crimes that have gone unreported in tight-knit religious communities,[24] why crimes like sexual harassment[25] or fraud are not reported[26] are not reported in workplaces.

Community membership is important for our survival. The communities that we belong to provide resources and connections for finding jobs, help when we need it, a sense of belonging and identity and a place where we can safely interact with people who share the same values and beliefs as we do. The behaviours of community members, especially in a tight-knit community, are likely to be seen as a reflection of the community itself. Other members may feel the need to work in ways to protect the reputation of the community and thus conceal deviant behaviour rather than responding to correct it. In these instances, criminals are protected, and crime continues to be hidden from law enforcement.

The community dynamics of gun collectives have received limited attention from scholars. However, research from the USA would suggest that when gun communities are forced to manage a stigmatised identity, the shared stigma bonds members together. Community events become places where discourse on firearm use, the problems and dissatisfaction with law and policy reinforce each other.[27] Under these conditions, beliefs and values that run counter to the aims of gun control can develop and take hold in a community. Ultimately, this could lead to practices of non-compliance and even the normalisation of violence within these communities.[28] In Australia, how much of a danger the stigmatisation currently felt by the gun-owning community poses to their current value alignment – which supports the aims of the NFA, is unknown. However, Australian gun-owning communities appear to continue to provide opportunities to engage with the broader public and demonstrate their commitment to important social values. These opportunities are signs that the gun-owning community is not generally in danger of endorsing behaviour that runs counter to the aims of gun control.

Interacting with the Gun-Owning Community in Australia

For the last four years, I've taken my third-year criminology class to the Queensland Rifle Association's (QRA) gun range for an activity. The activity is linked to a policy exercise where students have to apply criminological theories to evaluate and make recommendations on specific components of the NFA. The trip consists of a tour of the QRA museum, where they learn about the community that QRA has built, a Q and A session with firearms instructors where they learn about the law and can ask questions about regulations, and in recent years, some time on the range with instructors learning to shoot with qualified instructors.

For most of my students, this is the first time they have seen a firearm up close, let alone touched, handled and shot one. Many are excited, and most express hesitation and nervousness about the field trip in the days prior. What I love most about this experience is that they get to interact with the QRA volunteers and staff and get first-hand experience of what the QRA community feels like. I ask students to write a short reflective piece leading up to the event and ask them to consider how they feel about it and what their concerns are. This is where most students convey their nervousness, and some convey fear. Of course, the event is optional; students don't have to attend if they don't want to. But most show up on that day. At the end, they walk away excited and surprised at how much they enjoyed the experience, how much they enjoyed talking with QRA staff and how much the staff helped them feel at ease, safe and encouraged to try something new. Some students have taken up sports shooting as a result of this activity.[29] These students get to experience the benefits of this community via the mentoring they receive on the range, the openness of ideas, discussion and debate about perceptions of firearms that are shared. They also get a greater understanding of what the QRA community's purpose has been historically and how it is currently important for understanding how to regulate their activities. As criminologists in training, they get to embed their evaluations and recommendations on firearms policy in contact with the community that those evaluations are designed to impact most.

Firearms clubs and organisations across Australia publicly advertise their mission and goals as those that uphold safety and inclusive firearms activities that are friendly and family-orientated. For example, the QRA prides itself on being "place to belong", somewhere that is open to all ages, genders and sporting abilities.[30] Their values are those that espouse diversity and inclusion, accountability and integrity.[31] You'll find similar values and goals at other shooting clubs and organisations, such as the SSAA which also includes a code of conduct on their homepage, which draws attention to the importance of following gun laws and regulations and upholding the values of environmental conservation.[32]

Sports shooting clubs like the QRA and SSAA also encourage non-members to engage with them by providing opportunities for participation, which serves to demystify legal firearms use and encourage new members. Events and activities like these offer mentoring and coaching around sports shooting in a fun environment. These events often couple a barbeque lunch with time on the range. Range staff help people learn the basics of firearm handling, breathing techniques for steadying your movement and gaining focus while preparing to shoot at the target and how to do so safely. These events demonstrate a willingness to open up their activities and members to outsiders, allowing for opportunities to learn about and interact with members. These activities prevent these communities from being closed off from outsiders, and thus the likelihood that they can withdraw from broader society, which may put them at risk for the unhealthy kind of close knit that some scholars have warned about.

Gun organisations in Australia also provide services that benefit the broader community. Farmers in Australia often suffer financially due to the extreme weather conditions that have significant implications for their livelihoods. Pest control on farms is an important component of keeping livestock and crops safe and viable. Some firearms communities have been working to help support the farming community by offering their licenced and registered shooters for free as those that can help control common pests like rabbits, kangaroos and feral animals. These shooters are licenced, insured and provide these services at no cost to farmers who are already feeling the pinch of rising living costs and threats to their livelihoods. Licenced shooters who are members of these organisations are also recruited for programs that are designed to prioritise environmental conservation via the hunting of feral animals. These activities not only demonstrate that the gun-owning community is available and willing to interact with the broader community, but they also demonstrate their commitment to broadly accepted goals such as support for the Australian farming community and commitment to the conservation of our natural environment and wildlife. These activities not only demonstrate the intrinsic benefit of the gun-owning community, but also the alignment of the values and goals that overlap with those of the border public.

Wieambilla Revisited

What struck me as disappointing about the incident at Wieambilla in Queensland is the missed opportunity to gain intelligence from the community. Community members are the ones that reported the abandoned truck, handed in the firearms found within it and responded to the scene when something appeared to be wrong. Members of the community likely knew who was on the property and what they were doing, even if they didn't know them well. If these perpetrators were active in the gun-owning community, I would even wager that gun dealers in the area suspected something was not quite right. The community holds much knowledge, but if the police are unable or unwilling to recognise the value of that knowledge or be willing to engage with community members to help solve problems, then police will frequently miss important intelligence and their ability to enforce the laws will also carry the added risk of not having all the information necessary to keep themselves and the community safe. The capacity for informal social control as a way to identify and respond to problems and potentially problematic people is located within the community.

What police knew and didn't know going into the Wieambilla property is expected to be the focus of the QLD Coroner's inquiry into the incident in 2023. While much of that line of questioning I expect will focus on the sharing of information between two police jurisdictions, why police either don't have capacity or don't prioritise information from community members may also be important to consider. Media coverage of the investigation has found that one of the perpetrators purchased ammunition in QLD with a NSW firearms licence. That licence had already been suspended, but the suspension had not yet been served and gun dealers are not able to check records outside of the state in which they operate.[33] While those pose limitations for police and gun dealers to find and share information, good informal collaborative relationships with members of the community, including gun dealers, may have led to an increased amount of knowledge going into that property at the time.

Of course, my assertion is speculative. However, criminologists have pointed out that informal social control is far more effective than formal control. Informal social control relies on insider knowledge, has the capacity for action from within the community and has the potential to gather and share information with law enforcement who are not regulars in that community. Building relationships with communities is important so that knowledge, intelligence and problems-solving can be most effective. Informal social control gains strength in community relationships.

I answered many media requests in the weeks after this incident and all asked me the same thing – how should the gun laws be tightened. It's a difficult question to answer immediately after the aftermath of an event such as this because we know very little about the circumstances of the firearms used and whether they were or were not licenced to own them. I shut down this line of questioning until we had more facts on which to rest our assumption about the effectiveness of the gun laws. What I wanted to know first was whether the police sought to gain information from the community before going in. A few months on, what I suspect might have been more helpful is the ability for gun dealers to have more information about potential clients at the tip of their fingers. They are much better placed to be able to identify problems and potential risks. Police need to remember that these communities want to help and share the same goals to protect the broader community.

Chapter Summary

Community dynamics are important if we want to understand patterns of crime, who participates in crime and how to prevent it. Healthy communities that are high in collective efficacy are best placed to informally respond to problems. They are better able to identify problems and seek resolution before risks turn into incidents and often before the police can respond. While some close-knit communities turn inwards shutting themselves off from the rest of society and fostering their own values that may not align with legal requirements, it appears that the potential to harness the benefits of the gun-owning community is core to understanding why gun control compliance is high in Australia. These communities engage and welcome outsiders, are strong in their family and friendship networks and regularly engage in mutual exchange, helping each other when in need in their day-to-day interactions with each other, their clients and the police. Most importantly, the gun-owning communities appear to align member expectations with the law and set expectations for what responsible, safe and legal gun ownership looks like.

Gun regulations in Australia offer a starting point to create communities and embed their importance and purpose in the law. By ensuring that legal gun ownership is linked to gun communities, it ensures current and future possibilities for collaboration and socialisation. In addition, gun-owning communities routinely seek to contribute to a broader society, demonstrating their commitment to common social goals such as environmental conservation and farmer assistance. These are communities that want to interact with broader society despite feeling as though they have been made scapegoats for illegal firearms use and associated violence. Greater understanding of and collaboration with gun-owning communities is likely an excellent place to foster better relations and support for policy, enforcement and understanding why people comply with laws that often feel unfair and unpalatable.

Notes

1 https://abs.gov.au/census/find-census-data/quickstats/2021/SAL33072
2 https://www.theguardian.com/australia-news/2022/dec/13/queensland-wieambilla-shooting-timeline-what-we-know-so-far-nathaniel-and-gareth-train-six-killed-qld-police-officers-rachel-mccrow-matthew-arnold
3 Burgess, E. W. (2008). *The growth of the city: an introduction to a research project* (pp. 71–78). Springer US.
4 Shaw, C. R., & McKay, H. D. (1942). Juvenile delinquency and urban areas.
5 See 4.
6 Sampson, R. J., Raudenbush, S. W., & Earls, F. (1997). Neighborhoods and violent crime: A multilevel study of collective efficacy. *Science*, *277*(5328), 918–924.
7 Sutherland, A., Brunton-Smith, I., & Jackson, J. (2013). Collective efficacy, deprivation and violence in London. *British Journal of Criminology*, *53*(6), 1050–1074.
8 Fay-Ramirez, S. (2015). The comparative context of collective efficacy: Understanding neighbourhood disorganisation and willingness to intervene in Seattle and Brisbane. *Australian & New Zealand Journal of Criminology*, *48*(4), 513–542.
9 Sutherland, A., Brunton-Smith, I., & Jackson, J. (2013). Collective efficacy, deprivation and violence in London. *British Journal of Criminology*, *53*(6), 1050–1074.
10 Danielsson, P. (2021). Collective efficacy and violent crime in suburban housing estates. *European Journal of Criminology*, *18*(3), 345–365.
11 Butel, J., & Braun, K. L. (2019). The role of collective efficacy in reducing health disparities: A systematic review. *Family & Community Health*, *42*(1), 8.
12 Moolenaar, N. M., Sleegers, P. J., & Daly, A. J. (2012). Teaming up: Linking collaboration networks, collective efficacy, and student achievement. *Teaching and Teacher Education*, *28*(2), 251–262.
13 Barth, M., Jugert, P., & Fritsche, I. (2016). Still underdetected–Social norms and collective efficacy predict the acceptance of electric vehicles in Germany. *Transportation Research Part F: Traffic Psychology and Behaviour*, *37*, 64–77.

14 Merchant, R., Goldin, A., Manjanatha, D., Harter, C., Chandler, J., Lipp, A., ... & Naslund, J. A. (2022). Opportunities to expand access to mental health services: a case for the role of online peer support communities. *Psychiatric Quarterly*, *93*(2), 613–625.
15 Akers, R. L., & Jennings, W. G. (2019). The social learning theory of crime and deviance. *Handbook on crime and deviance*, 113–129.
16 Queensland. Defence Force & Queensland. (1885). *Regulations under the Defence Act of 1884* Retrieved July 26, 2023, from http://nla.gov.au/nla.obj-52800092
17 Casey, B. (2011). *Home on the Range: Queensland Rifle Association, 1861–2011*. Boolarong Press.
18 https://www.ag.gov.au/crime/publications/2017-national-firearms-agreement
19 https://www.ag.gov.au/crime/publications/2017-national-firearms-agreement
20 Gun oil, and most firearms cleaning equipment is not subject to regulations. This means that anyone can purchase something like gun oil without a licence.
21 Western Australia – Australia's western most state, in which the cities are geographically isolated from the rest of Australia's main cities and ports.
22 Akers, R. L., & Jennings, W. G. (2015). Social learning theory. *The handbook of criminological theory*, 230–240.
23 Barclay, E., Donnermeyer, J. F., & Jobes, P. C. (2004). The dark side of gemeinschaft: Criminality within rural communities. *Crime Prevention and Community Safety*, 6, 7–22.
24 Daly, K. (2014). *Redressing institutional abuse of children*. Springer.
25 Siuta, R. L., & Bergman, M. E. (2019). Sexual harassment in the workplace. In *Oxford research encyclopedia of business and management*.
26 Ahmad, Z., & Norhashim, M. (2008). The control environment, employee fraud and counterproductive workplace behaviour: An empirical analysis. *Communications of the IBIMA*, 3, 145–155.
27 Dempsey, S., Dutta, M., Frey, L. R., Goodall, H. L., Madison, D. S., Mercieca, J., ... & Miller, K. (2011). What is the role of the communication discipline in social justice, community engagement, and public scholarship? A visit to the CM Café. *Communication Monographs*, *78*(2), 256–271.
28 Blithe, S. J., & Lanterman, J. (2017). Camouflaged collectives: Managing stigma and identity at gun events. *Studies in Social Justice*, *11*(1), 113–135.
29 You can see a video that describes this activity with QRA here: https://qldrifle.com/university-partnership-program/
30 https://qldrifle.com/our-community/
31 https://qldrifle.com/strategic-plan-2022-2027/
32 https://www.ssaa.org.au/members/about-us/
33 https://www.abc.net.au/news/2023-02-18/qld-wieambilla-police-shooting-gun-licence-nathaniel-train/101987030

6

LEARNING FROM THE AUSTRALIAN EXPERIENCE OF GUN CONTROL

We are all working toward the same end as far as I'm concerned.

In Osmington, Western Australia, on May 11, 2018, a 61-year-old retired farmer took his own rifle and shot his wife, his daughter and his four grandchildren aged 13, 12, 10 and 8 before calling police and then turning the gun on himself. In what has been considered publicly to be Australia's worst shooting since the Port Arthur Massacre, this incident not only invigorated debate about effective gun control, but it also highlighted the important gap in mental health services, particularly in rural areas, and the normative barrier for men in seeking mental health support.

In 2019, about 10 months after the incident in Osmington, I attended, as a keynote speaker, the state annual meeting of the shooter's association. I always enjoyed these events, primarily because it was a good way to remember that even though I was not a part of the shooting community, their members were just like me in many different ways. When we sat at dinner, we talked about our families, the concerns and worries we had about our kids, the state of the economy and what our summer holidays might look like later this year. What I also enjoyed learning about is how the members of this organisation often talk about problems and gripes, firearms regulation-related or not, as well as what they could do to solve them. Being together in a community appeared to give them resolve. Some suggestions, in my opinion, were too simplistic, and others were too complicated. Others showed promise, consideration of research

DOI: 10.4324/9781003271642-7

evidence that they could find and genuine motivation to solve problems that face the gun-owning community and the Australian community as a whole.

As I sat next to the State President of this organisation while the table spoke about the shooting incident in Osmington the year before, he told me about his concerns for rural shooters and farmers. He talked about the pressure they were under economic pressure, pressure due to the impact that Australian weather conditions had on their livelihoods and the limited resources for medical and mental health services in remote and regional areas of Australia. His organisation had started an initiative that planned to commit over $30,000 to bring mental health services to rural areas in his state. When I asked him why, he said that even though not all farmers are members of his organisation, they are shooters and they are experiencing higher levels of depression without regular and easily accessible services. He also recognised how difficult it can be for men to ask for mental health help, a phenomenon supported by mental health research in Australia and abroad. He wanted to be part of that solution. More importantly, he wanted the firearms organisation he represented to be part of that solution. He said that we know they have guns out there, and there needs to be more resources for people undergoing mental health crises to prevent the development of coping mechanisms that rely on using firearms.

We have to accept that firearms are part of the fabric of life. Be it war, farming or shooting sports, there are socially agreed upon, legitimate and reasonable uses for firearms in Australian life as there are in other nations. The question for policymakers, law enforcement and even researchers is to understand how to ensure that they are regulated safely, used responsibly and kept away from people who present a risk to society. Australian gun dealers and their role in the gun control compliance process hold important knowledge and wisdom not only for Australian gun policy improvements but principles for effective gun control in other places around the world. Not only are those lessons helpful for understanding why compliance with regulations is high in Australia, but they are also important for understanding how to bridge the divide between the gun-owning community and the broader public that often dominates debate and policy creation.

The narratives that generalise concerns about irresponsible people and their access to firearms to the gun-owning community may highlight the concerns of the broader public who have limited contact with gun-owning communities, but they also obscure the possibility of seeing the contributions that the gun-owning community can make to gun regulation.

In this chapter, I summarise, as a reminder, the common ground we share with the gun-owning community as articulated by gun dealers across Australia. I summarise their concerns and dissatisfaction too and use those to highlight the lessons learned from their experiences that have implications for gun control creation, revision and implementation. Understanding what motivates compliance in the gun-owning community also helps us understand how to create and sustain that compliance and provides practical suggestions for how to engage with communities even when limited relationships exist. However, there is also so much more we can learn. As researchers, members of the public and policymakers, engagement with the gun-owning community to understand and share their knowledge is important for understanding how to achieve effective gun control here and other places around the world.

What Motivates Gun Control Compliance?

When I set out to interview gun dealers across Australia, I wanted to understand their perspectives on and experiences of gun control as well as explore their critical role in the gun control compliance process. For me, their perspective was of interest because their participation on the front lines of gun control reflects a critical component of gun control implementation and is therefore critical for understanding how and why gun control has worked in Australia. There appears to be general consensus across researchers, policymakers and the public that the 1996 gun control measures put in place after the Port Arthur massacre have been successful.[1] And if they are successful, then gun dealers, as members of the gun-owning community who have an integral role in everyday compliance tasks, play a large part in how we can understand their success.

By using Gezelius's and Hauck's compliance motivation framework,[2] I was able to incorporate an understanding of the gun-owning community and its role in motivating compliance that moves beyond common criminological notions of deterrence and perceptions of legitimacy. I have found that their framework has been helpful in thinking about ways to reduce the division between gun owners and the public generated by the media and political narratives of gun control debates. For example, traditional criminological frameworks for exploring why people obey the law might help us better understand how, why and to what extent gun dealers find the law legitimate and perceive it to be procedurally just. However, it is not as helpful as having a framework for understanding whether their views on legitimacy and procedural justice are embedded in a broader social identity and capacity for informal social control. This enables us to have different kinds of conversations about gun control. The understanding that there is underlying common ground between the gun-owning community, the public and policymakers regarding safety, reduction in violence and ensuring that risky people are not able to access firearms. Findings from gun dealers suggest that all three of Gezelius and Hauck's compliance motivations are driving compliance with gun law.

While the vast majority of our legal system is based on the principles of deterrence, early criminologists recognised that when the law is overly strict or harsh, it can undermine any deterrent outcome that policymakers are hoping to achieve.[3] While penalties that are small do not tend to motivate compliance, penalties that are too high make it difficult for organisations and businesses to continue if non-compliance is detected.[4] Most scholars of regulation and deterrence would argue that harsh deterrence-based motivators for compliance should be used as a *last resort* and only when other normative and cooperative methods have been attempted.[5] Recent criminological research on models of policing recognises this and suggests that the best practice policing approach for encouraging legal compliance should be cooperative in nature and good quality relationships between communities and law enforcement be prioritised.[6] In the case of gun dealers in Australia, fostering these cooperative relationships is challenging given their role as part of the compliance process and simultaneously as subjects to be monitored.

Motivations based on deterrence imply that compliance is driven by avoiding the costs and consequences of non-compliance when it is detected. With the level of surveillance gun dealers experience as a result of their integral role in the compliance process, not only would non-compliance be easily detected, but it could have serious implications for their business. There is no question that gun dealers are motivated by wanting to avoid these possibilities, even if they do not agree with the law. The threat of detection clearly weighs heavily on the minds of dealers, but this is not because they are attempting to break the law. This is because the regulation process is fraught with errors, misunderstandings and frequent changes, and gun dealers feel that they are at risk of bearing the brunt of these errors even if they do not make them and even when they attempt to correct them.

It is via their interactions with law enforcement that gun dealers also tend to report where they feel the stigmatisation that comes with being a gun owner. Those interactions with police run the risk of reinforcing labels of "risky", "vilent" and "dangerous" on gun dealers and the gun-owning community more widely. Lipsky's work[7] on street-level bureaucrats also suggests that these interactions are part of a socialisation process, embedding expectations about behaviour and what to expect in treatment from others. The concern for police gun dealer relations that are characterised as "us versus them" is that it runs the risk of socialising this as the normal relationship between the gun-owning community and law enforcement. Alternatively, a more cooperative relationship would likely socialise a more collaborative and productive relationship between the gun-owning community and regulators, thus easing the angst and potentially easing compliance fatigue when problems and difficulties can be solved in a more collaborative way. Scholars of regulation have pointed out how important it is to separate stigmatising labels from the group as a whole, even when non-compliance is detected.[8] In other words, in the event of finding out a dealer has broken the law, it is important not to label all gun dealers as rulebreakers or approach future interactions with gun dealers with the assumption that they are automatically non-compliant. To do so would potentially undermine enforcement practices as well as existing moral support for the overarching aims of regulation.

Sociological scholarship on deviance and crime has consistently suggested that informal social control is more effective in fostering behavioural change and motivating compliance with the law than formal social control strategies.[9] Informal social control is developed through processes of learning and socialisation via our interactions with family, friends and other members of our communities. These interactions are critical for teaching us what is expected of us and how to behave. For the gun-owning community, gun dealers are important leaders in their community that contribute to that socialisation process, especially in terms of communicating regulation requirements and legal expectations. Gun dealers naturally fill this socialisation role with respect to their positionality in the compliance process and in their communities. This is supported by their general agreement with the moral aims of gun control and their strong identities as law-abiding citizens, which can flow through to the broader community via their work and their position in the gun-owning community.

Gun dealers take their leadership role in the community seriously, and they demonstrate their commitment to the moral foundations of the NFA via their passion for educating new and existing clients about safe and responsible use. The importance they place on safety and responsibility and the core elements of the NFA, such as background checks and compulsory training, counter the more popular narrative that gun dealers and the gun-owning community do not support gun control regulations.[10] Their identities as law-abiding citizens are so much a part of how they approach their work that I suspect that even if support for the moral content of the laws was more limited than what I have found, compliance would still be a high priority. The moral support for the aims of the NFA and the strong law-abiding identity that gun dealers share demonstrate that motivation for compliance is driven by much more than deterrence alone. I would argue that these normative motivations – moral support for the law's content as well as legislators authority – are likely the primary reasons why gun control compliance is so high in Australia and why that compliance has been maintained even when gun control debates are contentious.

The primary concerns that gun dealers shared about gun control in Australia were related to the implementation of the NFA rather than its purpose or content. Gun dealers believed that the regulations that flow from the legislation change too rapidly, leading to uncertainty about what compliance regulations are. They report that the regulations are overly complex, making it difficult for clients to understand, and that the technology is out of date, leading to human error and slow processing times for licences and registrations. The bureaucratic and administrative burdens that gun dealers carry in their everyday compliance task carry social and financial costs for legitimate firearms owners and their communities. These concerns have implications for understanding compliance and the risks to compliance.

Compliance is likely to be easier when the rules for how to be compliant are well communicated, easy to follow and easy to understand.[11] We run the risk of increasing non-compliance when it is not clear what the expectations of behaviour look like. Research on regulatory compliance in other areas where livelihoods are regulated, such as tax systems, suggests that the more complicated a system, the less likely people will comply.[12] Complex compliance processes may even create *disincentives* to comply because they increase the financial burdens that businesses must carry. These administrative burdens not only create frustration and financial costs for dealers and the gun-owning community, but they also run the risk of creating negative feelings and attitudes towards the law. This may undermine the current support that we find within the community for gun control.

Governable Preconditions for Compliance

Each of Gezelius and Hauck's compliance motivations was paired with governable preconditions that are thought to cause or help to develop the motivations of deterrence, moral support for the law and legislators' authority.[13] While there have been few empirical studies that have investigated the mechanisms by which these preconditions work, they nonetheless provide a useful starting point for understanding how governments and policymakers can reinforce or create motivations for compliance. In other words, they may be helpful in generating support for gun control laws even when those laws appear to be unpalatable to the gun-owning community. According to Gezelius and Hauck, enforcement is the precondition that drives deterrence motivations, empowerment drives motivations based on moral support for the law and civic identity drives belief in legislative authority.

Enforcement refers to the use of formal institutions like the police to monitor, investigate and penalise non-compliance. It is founded on the idea that regulated citizens are rational actors wanting to avoid punishment, which then drives motivations to comply. Enforcement is the most common way governments motivate compliance with the law, including criminal and civil regulations. In regard to gun control compliance, Australian State and Territory policed-based weapons inspection units act as a formal enforcer whose role is to detect and punish non-compliance with gun legislation and regulations. However, given that the role of these inspection units hinges on the collaboration of dealers to provide critical information to inspectors, law enforcement needs to be wary of overly relying on enforcement as a way to deter individuals from breaking the law. To do so would undermine the role that gun dealers provide and potentially undermine the two other normative compliance motivators: empowerment and civic identity.

Empowerment provides an opportunity for agency and voice to be used by those who are impacted most by regulations. When the government authentically offers opportunities for empowerment to the regulated, it helps to ensure that the needs, rights and concerns of those citizens are considered during regulatory decision-making. According to this perspective, when gun dealers are given a chance to have their needs considered as part of the regulatory process, it increases the likelihood that they will agree with the moral content of the law. Ensuring that the gun-owning community has a seat at the decision-making table when implementing and creating gun laws ensures that they will be able to co-create and remain willing participants who are invested in compliance, lending their expertise and knowledge at the same time.

While there have been specific advisory boards in relation to gun control in Australia that have invited gun dealers and leaders of gun communities to be a part of the regulatory process, there is still considerable concern that this type of consultation is token in form. At best, gun dealers tend to suggest that consultation committees are primarily used for information sharing rather than discussion. This means it tends to be a one-way process whereby law enforcement communicates what they want gun dealers to know, but there is limited opportunity or desire to discuss and debate. That is, they are invited to the table, but gun dealers find they rarely see their views, concerns, or suggestions taken up and actioned. A continued lack of voice, coupled with compliance fatigue and heavy surveillance, carries the inherent danger of undermining both deterrence and moral support for the law as motivations for compliance. Authentic consultation that recognises that gun dealers have expertise to contribute is necessary in order to promote moral support for the content of gun laws.

In order to promote and reinforce legislators' authority, a strong civic identity is necessary that situates individuals and their communities inside and as a part of a broader society. A social identity that goes beyond that of being a member of the gun-owning community is necessary to drive that willingness to obey the law, even when it is disliked. Gun dealers have demonstrated this identity throughout my observations and interviews. Their identity as law-abiding citizens is the first thing they often speak about in terms of who they are as individuals and as a community. This broader social identity ensures that individuals understand their obligations to the state and society as a whole rather than only focusing on their obligations to their specific community.

What threatens this strong sense of civic identity is the perception that there is an "us versus them" mentality between gun dealers and police. Civic identity ensures that the regulated and policymakers identify as members of a collaborative group – a "we" instead of "us versus them". That means that the partnership between gun dealers, law enforcement and policymakers is key to ensuring that a strong civic identity continues to reinforce the value that the law should be obeyed no matter what. Gun dealers in Australia already have a strong foundation of civic identity and demonstrate compliance motivated by legislators' authority. To maintain this, or to create a strong identity and sustain it, gun dealers and the gun-owning community can't be put in a catch-22 position whereby they maintain their law-abiding status while also feeling as though they are blamed for gun violence and penalised inappropriately when compliance tasks go awry.

One way to minimise this is to ensure that deterrence is not overly relied on as a motivator for compliance and that gun dealers and other leaders in gun-owning communities are invited to consult on what regulations should look like.

Moving towards a National Gun Registry in Australia?

Each time I interviewed gun dealers, range officers or gun safety trainers, I asked them what changes to the NFA or state legislation and regulations, if any, they wanted to see. I wanted to know that if they could change aspects of the NFA or its implementation, what would be their first priority. Some responses wreaked of hyperbole and appeared to be borne out of frustration with the burden of administration or the way in which law enforcement has treated them. But even those responses gave way to more thoughtful, reasonable and realistic suggestions of how the NFA can be improved to make the system work more efficiently, minimise errors in the system and improve community safety. When this project first started, I had initially prepared myself for a barrage of remarks suggesting the NFA be torn down and regulations be removed entirely, but I quickly learned that when it comes to thinking about the regulatory system that they participate in on a daily basis, their expertise and knowledge of firearms and safety and their commitment to being law-abiding tend to outweigh any negative feelings about the laws themselves. Their thoughts and ideas should be taken seriously as experts in their field who also have a stake in reducing gun violence.

One of the most frequent complaints from gun dealers was in regard to the problems they encountered doing business between states and territories within Australia. While similar, states and territories have implemented the NFA in their own ways. To those reading the legal codes in each of those states, we probably wouldn't see much difference, but the regulations that flow from this legislation have a real impact on dealers and the gun-owning community more broadly, and those differences are much more visible when it comes to the process of complying. When I asked gun dealers about the changes that they would like to see, they often expressed that more unity and consistency between state legislation and regulations would be helpful.

> *If all firearms was taken from the states and was done [processed]federal. I don't think that would be a bad thing. As long it's consistent with probably everything that we've already got already, right. Like, we wouldn't want any additional impacts our shoulders.*

However, they often expressed this with hesitation. The dealer below expressed hesitation about supporting national regulations after detailing the problems he encountered with state and territory differences.

> *But the reason I'm not suggesting for a moment that I want national firearms regulation because I'm worried that if they ever put a set together they will contain the worst parts of all the state legislations instead of the best parts.*

While dealers could see the value in more national consistency, they often felt that this would be problematic in terms of giving the police more power or that changing the system would require them to once again shoulder the burden of change financially and even make their interactions with police more problematic and administrative burdens more onerous. As a result, they often stopped short of giving full support to a more national approach to regulations, despite that they recognised that it presented an opportunity to make the process of compliance easier on them and their clients. The mistrust between gun dealers and the government appears to be driving these hesitations.

In 2023, Australia's Labour Prime Minister announced that the natural next step to the 1996 gun reforms brought in by the conservative government would be a national gun registry. Currently, states and territories operate their own gun registries that contain information on gun sales and acquisitions, gun owner information, as well as information on gun licence suspensions and revocations. A national gun registry would allow law enforcement to access firearm information from anywhere in the country in real time, thereby reducing the likelihood that key information can be missed when guns travel across state borders. Public consultation has already begun on the national registry, and police ministers in Australia have already provided feedback and agreed to its next steps. The gun-owning community has been more tentative in their support.

When I read about the implementation of a national gun registry, my immediate reaction was that it sounded like a great solution to what gun dealers had been complaining about. While nothing I read would ensure gun dealers would have access to this registry, I thought it represented progress in being able to have quicker responses to potential problems and provide an opportunity to reduce some of the administrative burden associated with populating the registries in respective states. However, gun organisations were quick to respond by reminding the government to engage in authentic consultation with the gun-owning community and not to rush the process to ensure that it is properly funded and resourced. While hesitant, a leading gun organisation remained hopeful.

> *A working relationship that would allow the government to consult on workable solutions, communicate with the wider firearms community and prevent the occurrence of unintended consequences from policy decisions is increasingly important considering recent events.*
>
> *(SSAA Legislative Action, April 2023)*[14]

Gun-owning organisations also expressed the need for privacy for gun owners to ensure that the information included in the registry could not be targeted by criminals or used for purposes other than what the registry was designed for. I could feel both the hesitation and the hope in some of the responses to the national gun registry. However, I interpreted the hesitation as a consequence of the fraught relationships that the gun-owning community often reports to law enforcement and understood why there may be some mistrust. Yet, there appears to be a willingness to cooperate and be part of the process of ensuring that gun owners are fairly represented and that gun industry expertise is part of the decision-making process for the setup of the national registry. If this kind of authentic consultation and participation were possible, it would likely carry additional benefits such as reinforcing the civic identity of the gun-owning community as law-abiding citizens, as well as reinforcing the socialisation process towards compliance that gun dealers are already doing.

Lessons Learned from Australian Gun Dealers

While Australian gun control measures are often held up as a global example of a swift and firm response to gun violence, there are a number of learnings that would help improve the efficacy of Australian gun control measures as well as provide important principles for gun control creation elsewhere. The governable preconditions that stem from Gezellius and Hauck's compliance framework provide a helpful understanding of how to motivate compliance even when the laws themselves are unpopular, but the principles below borrow from existing literature to embed a starting place in which to engage with those preconditions and connect them to best practices in law enforcement, stigma reduction and community engagement. The principles below build on gun dealers' most consistent and impassioned pleas for improvements by providing concrete starting points on how these can be accomplished.

Build and Improve the Collaborative Relationships Between Gun Dealers and Regulators

I often found myself thinking about how much more successful the regulatory process could be if gun dealers and police regulators had a more collaborative relationship. There are, of course, instances of excellent collaboration and partnership that can and do occur between dealers and police officers. From gun dealers willingly helping and supporting police compliance tasks, to being able to build collaborative relationships with local police who they interact with regularly, the potential for collaboration is there. But it's more difficult for gun dealers to develop these relationships with gun registry staff. They are further removed than the local area and often only interact over the phone or email. Building more collaboration requires more intentional effort from both sides. But police and gun registry units are in a more powerful position, and therefore, I suggest that improving collaboration starts with them.

Research on best practices in policing suggests that community policing models are best for building collaborative relationships between police and community members.[15] Community policing as a strategy generally puts building collaborative relationships and partnerships with the people they serve at the centre of police organisational practice. This model requires police to engage with those they serve in order to gain trust and increase perceptions of legitimacy, which often results in easier information sharing between police and the community, as well as empowering community members to have a voice in how they are policed. In turn, this also helps aid policing in being effective in responding to and preventing criminal activity.

Community policing strategies are not new to Australian policing. There are a number of community policing strategies employed to help enhance community relations and thus increase police effectiveness. For example, police collaboration with Neighbourhood Watch allows for positive relationships to develop between community members and police in order to keep the neighbourhood safe – these initiatives are already in operation in various capacities across Australia.[16] School liaison officers embed or pair police officers with schools not only to increase safety but to build positive relationships between children, the community and police.[17] And there are multiple examples of consultative groups designed to ensure that community members have a say in police operations and priorities. Each of these strategies is based on the principles of community policing and is thought of as best practice for reducing tension between police and the community and increasing police effectiveness in the communities they police.

There has been no specific empirical testing the community policing model in the context of gun control compliance and enforcement processes. However, there is no specific reason that the principles of community policing can't be adopted for police processes outside of typical policing roles. A community policing approach to gun control may help to reduce the *us versus them* mentality as well as provide positive examples of interacting with police, which are likely to reduce tensions and build better partnerships aimed at the same common goals – protecting the community from crime and violence and ensuring that legal owners are responsible citizens. To do this, l*aw enforcement could ensure that there is limited staff turnover in gun registry police* units to help provide continuous relationships between the gun-owning community and police, as well as proving opportunities to interact with the gun-owning community that are not solely based on compliance tasks. There appears to be some appetite from gun dealers to do this. One gun dealer told me that he had routinely invited police to special event days at the gun shop, such as grand opening events, but police always declined to participate. The gun dealer was told by police that they couldn't attend because they didn't want to be seen playing favourites with gun dealers. While it's important that police don't "play favourites" with gun dealers, it's equally important to get to know them. Perhaps law enforcement is not well resourced enough to be able to attend these kinds of events or spend time building these relationships. But if they don't, the community policing model suffers. Maintaining more personal contact is one of the core principles of the community policing model.

Expanding the police mandate by increasing the hours of availability is another way to increase the community-based policing approach to gun control. At present, gun registry units often have limited windows in which gun dealers or members of the gun-owning community and the public are able to contact them, making them difficult to access and difficult to get information or help from in a timely manner. A properly resourced gun registry that is more responsive to the needs of the community will likely reduce the administrative burden faced by dealers and, at the same time, being responsive to their questions, concerns, ability to carry out their daily compliance tasks. Overall, increasing the use of community policing techniques would not only help to build better collaboration but also provide opportunities to build a stronger partnership that works to fulfil the common goals of community safety.

Provide Opportunities for Authentic Consultation so That Gun Dealer Voice and Expertise Can Be Heard

Many of my friends and colleagues have shared experiences with inauthentic consultation in their respective workplaces. This occurs when we are asked to move through the process of consultation without any evidence of our voice, our concerns or our ideas being taken up. This tokenistic consultation runs the risk of undermining any support for what needs to be achieved. Gun dealers are experts. They know the firearms industry, sports, trade and safety better than anyone. And they want to share that expertise. Over and over again, gun dealers shared with me their frustration with the lack of authentic consultation when they have immeasurable expertise in the area being regulated. They find this insulting, and I suspect it reinforces the feelings of stigmatisation they feel from outsiders in their community.

Consultation does happen with gun dealers across the country. Police often hold information sessions called "consultative meetings", but gun dealers expressed that these were underwhelming, and they did not provide opportunities for them to partner with police or even have their concerns addressed. In order to empower gun dealers to continue to invest in the compliance process and reinforce the informal social control capacity they have for the gun-owning community, real and authentic consultation, cooperation and connection are necessary. A codesign process would help achieve this and help build cooperative relationships between police and gun dealers that are necessary to ensure that compliance motivations continue to work effectively. Codesign processes are rapidly becoming useful mechanisms to help bring together different industries and groups that have an interest in or are affected by decision-making.

Co-design practices are a helpful way of ensuring buy-in from those who are affected most by the decisions made by regulators. But codesign is more about just consultations. It requires having community members at the table from beginning to end: regulations design, implementation, evaluation and review. According to scholars of co-design practices, codesign requires people to come together to share expertise, knowledge and connect in order to discuss and design a vision what they want a process or initiative to look like and consider what aspects of the present pose opportunities for improvement or barriers to reaching that shared vision.[18] This codesign process assumes that there will be disagreement, but through discussion and negotiation, a shared vision can be reached. Researchers are quickly realising that codesign practices are far more effective in getting cooperation and buy-in from stakeholders – those who are most impacted by our research.[19] Engaging in the codesign process from the conception of research to the implementation of it ensures that we are focusing our research on real-world problems, increasing validity by ensuring that we include those who work most intimately with those on the ground and ensuring that the implications of our research can be taken up.

While I advocate for codesign practices being adopted in the Australian context of gun control, it is the American context in which a codesign process may be most effective and most needed. Where the development of reasonable gun laws in the USA has been inconsistent across states, volatile in some and slow to respond to incidents of violence in others, a codesign process may help to bring different perspectives together in order to develop a future that is based on shared and common values. These are processes that value and respect the expertise of gun dealers and the gun-owning community. Codesign processes used in areas of food justice to reduce food inequality and increase sustainability have been helpful in reducing the distance between different groups and finding ways to negotiate based on existing common ground.[20] Perhaps codesign processes would allow for new and innovative ways to engage the gun-owning community in helping to design the future, including gun control that they can get behind. Future research and policymaking should prioritise these practices if they want to ensure that the gun-owning community and its leaders are continuing to support the compliance process, not because they have to but because they agree that the aims of gun control are important and shared among the community.

Reduce Stigmatisation by Finding Opportunities to Increase Contact Between the Gun-Owning Community and the Broader Community

One of the most effective ways to reduce stigmatisation is to increase education and contact between society and stigmatised groups.[21] Increased contact helps to break down stigmatisation by increasing interpersonal relationships that help to realign our understanding of people and groups where we previously only had limited or uninformed perceptions. In addition, increased education also helps to break down stigmatisation by increasing our understanding of particular people and groups. A number of stigma reduction programmes have been based on these two core mechanisms, *contact* and *education*, with some success; however, these have primarily been tests in areas of stigma reduction for mental illness and other vulnerable groups.

Contact-based programmes rest on the understanding that when we have positive interactions with members of a stigmatised group, it helps to minimise the use of negative labels and replace them with more positive ones. Psychologists, sociologists and criminologists have used the idea of the contact hypothesis to improve relationships among groups in which there is considerable tension, prejudice and stigma.[22] There is generally good empirical evidence that contact or positive interactions help to reduce stigma in the short and medium term.[23] Long-term effects of contact-based programs need more evaluation, but even short-term changes in perceptions may help to alleviate the frustration and stress caused by feeling stigmatised.

For a long time, knowledge and education of any topic in the world have been important in understanding one's attitudes towards any social or criminal policy. Gun control appears to be no different. Understanding something about firearms, the gun-owning community, crime trends and crime policy appears to be useful in understanding what kinds of policies people are willing to support. In one study, researchers in the USA found that those who had more accurate knowledge about the state of gun crime were far less likely to support gun control in the form of bans.[24] But they were more likely to support other forms of gun regulation.

Where does one get their knowledge of guns? Media? Upbringing? News? Media influence on crime views has long been documented in criminology.[25] For example, those who watch crime dramas are more likely to support gun control, most likely because they are exposed to more violent depictions of gun crime, no matter how fictional they might be. In contrast, those who read print media are less likely to support gun control. Perhaps representative of an older generation who still uses newspapers for daily news – a generation also liked conservative politics.

The gun community already offers a number of opportunities for the public to learn, participate and observe shooting sports, training and even seminars about the law. These opportunities can be valuable not only because they offer contact with the firearms community, but they also seek to educate. These interactions not only help to reduce stigma and prejudice but also aid in the socialisation of responsible gun use, which helps to support the compliance process.

Find Ways to Value the Expertise And Services That the Gun-Owning Community Can Provide to Others

The gun-owning community, or communities, are critical. Our deterrence-based and administrative processes carried out by law enforcement to licence and register firearms owners in order to ensure that only the most responsible and legitimate people have access to firearms are not error-free. Decisions to licence gun owners are made on the basis of the available information at the time of the licence application. In cases of gun violence incidents in Australia that do, on occasion, involve licenced shooters, they are often those who were experiencing acute mental health issues. Those mental health issues were unknown at the time of approval for gun ownership. The licencing system, no matter how it is implemented, is unlikely to always be able to know when an individual may be dangerous if it is not already in the system. But the community can. Members of the gun-owning community are in the best position (other than family and friends) to be able to identify problematic behaviours and shifts in behaviour from regular community members, and intervene. However, this only works if the gun-owning community has good and collaborative ties with law enforcement and law enforcement takes seriously what gun dealers tell them.

The gun-owning community's expertise is not just limited to knowledge about firearms. Their skills in hunting are used in pest control – a critical service for Australian farmers. They volunteer and work at large-scale sporting events like the Olympics and Commonwealth Games and are routinely relied on to provide critical firearms training to police. Their value to society has potential beyond just the firearms community alone. Recognising this value is important not only to reduce stigma and build better community relations, but when we see that value at work in a broader society, it acts as another way to reinforce responsible firearms use and socialise current and new members on the importance of community engagement. Finding additional ways to utilise the skills of the gun-owning community as well as recognising their value in intervening when things go wrong are critical components for understanding how to do gun control well.

Reduce the Administrative Burden of Compliance to Reduce Compliance Fatigue

If we want people to comply with regulations, especially if these regulations are fraught with disgruntled communities, then we need to make compliance easy to understand, easy to follow and communicated effectively to those who need to comply. Australian gun control could be substantially improved in terms of community safety as well as community buy-in, just in terms of lessening the burden of compliance. Real-time access to the firearms registry for gun dealers would ensure that they can perform their compliance tasks effectively and efficiently, as well as act on information in real time to understand who they should and should not sell firearms and ammunition to. Gun dealers need to be supported in their compliance task with a willingness to solve the problems they encounter, especially while they are willing to correct errors and solve those problems voluntarily.

Compliance figure, as I have articulated it in this book, has received limited empirical attention in regards to gun dealers.

This work is ongoing and necessary to increase our understanding of why compliance doesn't happen when it should. For example, continued investigation into known cases of noncompliance suggests that people choose to circumvent or break the law because the compliance process is too long, too experienced or too difficult. While non-compliance appears to be relatively rare, there is concern from gun dealers that compliance is a hard status to maintain when regulations change so quickly, are not communicated clearly and difficult to understand and navigate.

Can Australian Gun Control Work Elsewhere?

One of the most common questions I get asked about Australian gun control is whether I think it would work in the American context, where federal and state governments have struggled to provide clear and consistent guidelines on the regulation of firearms. These questions require consideration of whether these recommendations paint an overly ambitious and rosy view of the potential to work with the gun-owning community rather than against it. Is this kind of collaboration possible even in places where the tension between the gun-owning community is greater and the gun-owning community is less structured than it is in Australia? Or is the possibility of a collaborative codesign process a more reachable goal by changing our approach and assumptions about shared goals?

The answer to this question lies in future empirical research that looks at the success and failure of trying different approaches that bridge the divide between the gun-owning community and the public. In short, I cannot know for sure. I don't believe the kinds of gun bans and restrictions we have in Australia's NFA are an unhelpful place to start short of the bans already in place in North America – such as those for machine guns. The proliferation of firearms and the numbers of firearms in circulation across the USA may make the process of registration and tracking too onerous as a first port of call. However, we are already seeing some traction with background checks and regulations that attempt to keep firearms out of the hands of those who would harm themselves or others.

A possibly easier place to start might be increasing the regulations and restrictions on ammunition. Outside of supervised gun clubs, perhaps it is time to think about whether waiting periods and caps on the amount of ammunition purchased in a particular time period might be useful as a quick win for reducing the gun violence that the USA experiences. I suspect members of the gun-owning community would recoil at that suggestion – both here and in the USA – but I suspect reform might be best achieved by including some quick wins while working on solutions that work towards longer term success, like building trust, reducing stigma and increasing collaborative relationships between the gun-owning community and policymakers.

Too little research, in Australia and abroad, has focused on the normative roles that the gun-owning community does or could play in socialising responsible gun owners and contributing to legal compliance. Quantitative studies demonstrate the gun-owning community holds diverse views about the merits of gun control, and more moderate members of the gun-owning community likely support reasonable gun control regulations. Qualitative research, whereby researchers and policymakers are spending time within the gun-owning community to better understand their concerns and determine where there is common ground, is needed to find out if collaboration is possible – especially in places where it seems division dominates and undermines any effort to reduce the risks posed by firearms. I suspect this kind of research will remain challenging. It requires us as researchers to step back from our own assumptions about who the gun-owning community is and what they believe, and it requires the gun-owning community to trust us with their views.

I have often been asked about whether arming more people would reduce crime in the US context. While it might seem like a good idea to flood the country with the "good guy with a gun" in order to combat the "bad guy with the gun", there is limited evidence that this is borne out in reality. There are far too many instances in the USA where a well-intentioned citizen has fatally shot a person who was not the threat they first perceived them to be. Instead, we do have research that suggests that weapons in the home are much more likely to be used against the homeowners themselves rather than invaders or criminal.[26] This is not a good solution to this problem. I think we need to reconceptualise who the good guy with the gun is. Good guys with guns are not those who are ready and armed to take on the latest threat. Instead, they are the leaders of the gun-owning community who can socialise responsible and safe firearms use and encourage compliance with the law. We need them to be partners in safe gun policies rather than solely the subjects of them. Their knowledge and expertise are invaluable to making gun control better, creating gun control that is effective and reducing the ongoing tension between gun owners and the public that seems to permeate each and every incident of violence where a firearm is used. Unless we are sure that the gun-owning community is not on board with the values of safety and responsibility, it is time to recognise our common ground as a new way to approach gun control.

Chapter Summary

In May 2023, a US news source reported that there had been more mass shootings in the USA than days into 2023.[27] While I'm not convinced that each of those incidents would qualify for the official definition of a mass shooting, it was a news headline indicative of the ongoing work around gun control and gun violence that needs to happen in the USA. Lessons can be learned from the Australian experience of gun control by Australian gun dealers. Australia's response to the Port Arthur massacre in 1996 has been considered a successful and strong gun control response. One that has a high rate of compliance and that I have found shares its moral underpinnings of community safety with the gun-owning community. Acknowledging the important role that gun dealers have and can play in the compliance process is critical. Developing strong cooperative ties between police and gun dealers ensures a smoother compliance process that does not undermine the moral support for the underlying aims of gun laws that gun dealers share. Acknowledging gun dealers' value and expertise opens new possibilities for approaching gun laws, and recognising the benefits that the gun-owning community does and can provide to broader society, especially in socialising people into responsible gun owners, is critical for success. These can be achieved by utilising strategies that already exist: community policing, codesign, stigma reduction initiatives and community engagement. These provide a valuable starting point for changing the nature of divisive gun debates that ultimately risk support for gun control and prevent good quality and reasonable policy from developing where we need it most.

Notes

1 Klieve, H., Barnes, M., & De Leo, D. (2009). Controlling firearms use in Australia: Has the 1996 gun law reform produced the decrease in rates of suicide with this method? *Social Psychiatry and Psychiatric Epidemiology*, *44*, 285–292.

2 Gezelius, S. S., & Hauck, M. (2011). Toward a theory of compliance in state-regulated livelihoods: A comparative study of compliance motivations in developed and developing world fisheries. *Law & Society Review*, *45*(2), 435–470.

3 Young, D. B. (1983). Cesare Beccaria: Utilitarian or retributivist? *Journal of Criminal Justice*, *11*(4), 317–326.

4 Parker, C. (2006). The "compliance" trap: The moral message in responsive regulatory enforcement. *Law & Society Review*, *40*(3), 591–622.

5 Winter, S. C., & May, P. J. (2015). Street-level bureaucrats and regulatory deterrence. In *Understanding street-level bureaucracy* (pp. 133–152). Policy Press.

6 Mazerolle, L., Antrobus, E., Bennett, S., & Tyler, T. R. (2013). Shaping citizen perceptions of police legitimacy: A randomized field trial of procedural justice. *Criminology*, *51*(1), 33–63.

7 Lipsky, M. (2010). *Street-level bureaucracy: Dilemmas of the individual in public service*. Russell Sage Foundation.

8 Tyler, T. R., & Huo, Y. J. (2002). *Trust in the law: Encouraging public cooperation with the police and courts*. Russell Sage Foundation.

9 Bazemore, G., & Erbe, C. (2004). Reintegration and restorative justice: Towards a theory and practice of informal social control and support. *After crime and punishment: Pathways to offender reintegration*, 27–56.

Becker, G. S. (1968). Crime and punishment: An economic approach. *Journal of Political Economy*, *76*(2), 169–217.

Groff, E. R. (2015). Informal social control and crime events. *Journal of Contemporary Criminal Justice*, *31*(1), 90–106.

Sampson, R. J. (2012). *Great American city: Chicago and the enduring neighborhood effect*. University of Chicago Press.

10 Cook, P. J., & Ludwig, J. (2019). The social costs of gun ownership: A reply to Hayo, Neumeier, and Westphal. *Empirical Economics*, *56*, 13–22.

11 Alm, J., Martinez-Vazquez, J., & Torgler, B. (Eds.). (2010). *Developing alternative frameworks for explaining tax compliance*. Routledge.

12 Alm, J. (2019). What motivates tax compliance? *Journal of Economic Surveys*, *33*(2), 353–388.

13 Gezelius, S. S., & Hauck, M. (2011). Toward a theory of compliance in state-regulated livelihoods: A comparative study of compliance motivations in developed and developing world fisheries. *Law & Society Review*, *45*(2), 435–470.

14 https://www.ssaa.org.au/?ss_news=ssaa-national-responds-to-national-firearms-register-consultation

15 Braga, A. A., Brunson, R. K., & Drakulich, K. M. (2019). Race, place, and effective policing. *Annual Review of Sociology*, *45*, 535–555.

16 McCarthy, M. M., Porter, L. E., Townsley, M., & Alpert, G. P. (2019). The effect of community-oriented policing on police use of force: Does community matter? *Policing: An International Journal*, *42*(4), 556–570.

17 Asquith, N. L., Bartkowiak-Théron, I., Asquith, N. L., & Bartkowiak-Théron, I. (2021). Police Liaison. *Policing Practices and Vulnerable People*, 129–146.

18 Zamenopoulos, T., & Alexiou, K. (2018). *Co-design as collaborative research*. Bristol University/AHRC Connected Communities Programme.

19 Bevan Jones, R., Stallard, P., Agha, S. S., Rice, S., Werner-Seidler, A., Stasiak, K., ... & Merry, S. (2020). Practitioner review: Co-design of digital mental health technologies with children and young people. *Journal of Child Psychology and Psychiatry*, *61*(8), 928–940.

20 Smith, K. (2022). Pluralising food justice in Australia: insights from 'fair food futures'.

21 Heijnders, M., & Van Der Meij, S. (2006). The fight against stigma: An overview of stigma-reduction strategies and interventions. *Psychology, Health & Medicine*, *11*(3), 353–363.

22 Fuochi, G., Voci, A., Veneziani, C. A., Boin, J., Fell, B., & Hewstone, M. (2020). Is negative mass media news always associated with outgroup prejudice? The buffering role of direct contact. *Group Processes & Intergroup Relations*, *23*(2), 195–213.

23 Maunder, R. D., & White, F. A. (2019). Intergroup contact and mental health stigma: A comparative effectiveness meta-analysis. *Clinical Psychology Review*, 72, 101749.

24 Kruis, N. E., Wentling, R. L., Frye, T. S., & Rowland, N. J. (2021). Firearm ownership, defensive gun usage, and support for gun control: Does knowledge matter? *American Journal of Criminal Justice*, 1–30.

25 Croitoru, A., Kien, S., Mahabir, R., Radzikowski, J., Crooks, A., Schuchard, R., ... & Stefanidis, A. (2020). Responses to mass shooting events: The interplay between the media and the public. *Criminology & Public Policy*, *19*(1), 335–360.

26 Schleifer, J. (1999). *Everything You Need to Know about Weapons in School and at Home*. The Rosen Publishing Group, Inc.

27 https://abcnews.go.com/US/mass-shootings-days-2023-database-shows/story?id=96609874

7

EPILOGUE

I have no doubt that some will read this book and arrive at the conclusion that I am just another gun-toting apologist. Over the course of this research, I have been called, accused of, and described as a gun owner, a right-wing NRA member, and a proponent of the anti-gun control lobby. I was once introduced by one of my colleagues to another academic as "this is Suzanna. She likes guns". Other academics were introduced by their full titles. While other gun researchers have shared similar experiences with me no matter on what side of the gun debate we might fall, the receiving death threats and even rape threats, particularly after engaging with the media, has been an eye-opening experience. Most often, those threats have been from what appears to be the political left, those who have recoiled at my unwillingness to demonise the gun-owning community. Those experiences only reassured me that the conversations about gun control need to change and that policymakers, the public and academics need to get better at learning how to hold dialogue with those we often disagree with. To be clear, I am not a gun owner, nor do I participate in shooting sports, and I fully support gun control as a measure for safety and reductions in violence. For those who want to know my political leanings, I voted for democratic candidates in the last US election and for labour candidates in the last Australian election. I am an outsider to the gun community in which the members have been so generous in sharing with me their time, their experiences, and their fears. I am grateful for that generosity and for

DOI: 10.4324/9781003271642-8

the opportunity to learn that they too care about reducing gun violence as much as I do.

My students have also paid the price for my choices in research. While they have voluntarily joined me on this research journey, I have often felt guilty for exposing them to potential threats and for the assumptions some of my fellow academics have made about them. During a PhD seminar in which one of my students was presenting their research on understanding gun control perceptions 20 years on after the 1996 massacre and the sweeping changes to gun laws the Australian government made, she was subject to muttered comments from academics – one senior academic said in deprecating tones "why do we care about this?". If this question had been asked in the spirit of getting the student to think about the "so what?" question of their research, I would not have thought much of it, and my student would have provided an answer. But muttering at the back of the room for just a few people was disrespectful. These experiences have made my students more resilient, but I've felt guilt and disappointment that they have had to shoulder that.

During presentations in which student teams presented their crime policy improvements in 2023, one group said they were a bit nervous to share with me their project findings. When I asked why, they said they were not sure how I would react. They said that they couldn't tell what side of the gun control debate I was on and were confused because, on the one hand, I had spoken so highly of the members of the gun community while also talking about how better gun control could be created in places that needed it. I took this as a big win – to be able to talk about my research and stay away from views that are divisive in nature is part of how I believe better and more collaborative dialog about gun control is possible.

The writing of this book was inherently difficult. In part because I wanted to write a different kind of research monograph than those that present findings of long-term research – a more typical model I have seen in social science here in Australia. I wanted to inspire more critical thinking and encourage a different kind of conversation about gun control than we are used to having. That required me to include more of how this project has challenged my own thinking. Much of that comes from the time I have spent on the road traveling to visit and talk with gun dealers across the country.

While Chapters 2 through 4 focus squarely on answering the research questions I sought to answer at the beginning; what do gun dealers really think about the gun laws in Australia and how do they navigate their roles as subjects to the laws they help to enforce, Chapter 5 has less to do with specific project findings and more to do with thinking about the possibilities of what might be. Studies in how communities encourage and/or prevent crime have been so much a part of my academic career and training that it was impossible for me not to think about the implications for their community and the possibilities that could be leveraged if we thought about gun-owning communities differently than we have been socialised to do.

In the lead-up to my student's visits to the gun range in Queensland, they often tell me how nervous and scared they are. When they write about those concerns in their journals for class, they say they are afraid of being around people with guns and that they were concerned about the dangerousness of the class activity at the range. It has become clear over the years of running this activity how much the gun-owning community has been linked to violence and danger in the eyes of those outside the gun-owning community.

There is part of me that suspects that many are not ready to hear the message of this book. That's ok; I understand. There are real emotions that sit behind this kind of policy debate that are legitimate. People from both inside and outside the gun-owning community say that my vision of a more collaborative policy environment is unrealistic or downright impossible. There are times that I have felt I'm kidding myself too. However, I stand by what I've learned so far; there are more similarities between us than we realise, and the goals of community safety are goals that unite us rather than drive us apart. Surely, that could be a useful start.

If you have read this far and still believe that this work is designed to support a single anti-gun control agenda, I understand that. I have been there. And I know that taking my word for it isn't enough. However, I do ask that you consider this one question: What do we lose by having a conversation with those different from us?

BIBLIOGRAPHY

Ahmad, Z., & Norhashim, M. (2008). The control environment, employee fraud and counterproductive workplace behaviour: An empirical analysis. *Communications of the IBIMA*, *3*, 145–155.

Akers, R. L., & Jennings, W. G. (2019). *The social learning theory of crime and deviance. Handbook on Crime and Deviance*, Springer, pp. 113–129.

Alm, J. (2019). What motivates tax compliance? *Journal of Economic Surveys*, *33*(2), 353–388.

Alm, J., Cherry, T., Jones, M., & McKee, M. (2010). Taxpayer information assistance services and tax compliance behavior. *Journal of Economic Psychology*, *31*(4), 577–586.

Alm, J., Martinez-Vazquez, J., & Torgler, B. (Eds.). (2010). *Developing alternative frameworks for explaining tax compliance*. Routledge.

Altman, J. (2009). The hybrid economy and anthropological engagements with policy discourse: A brief reflection 1. *The Australian Journal of Anthropology*, *20*(3), 318–329.

Asquith, N. L., Bartkowiak-Théron, I., Asquith, N. L., & Bartkowiak-Théron, I. (2021). "Police Liaison." *Policing Practices and Vulnerable People*, pp.129–146. Palgrave Macmillan.

Australian Crime Commission (2015). *Organised crime in Australia*. Commonwealth Government of Australia.

Barclay, E., Donnermeyer, J. F., & Jobes, P. C. (2004). The dark side of gemeinschaft: Criminality within rural communities. *Crime Prevention and Community Safety*, *6*, 7–22.

Barth, M., Jugert, P., & Fritsche, I. (2016). Still underdetected–social norms and collective efficacy predict the acceptance of electric vehicles in Germany. *Transportation Research Part F: Traffic Psychology and Behaviour*, *37*, 64–77.

Bazemore, G., & Erbe, C. (2004). "Reintegration and restorative justice: Towards a theory and practice of informal social control and support." *After Crime and Punishment: Pathways to Offender Reintegration*, pp. 27–56. Willan Publishing.

Becker, G. S. (1968). "Crime and punishment: An economic approach"." In The economic dimensions of crime, pp. 13–68. Palgrave Macmillan

Berry, H., Hogan, A., Owen, J., Rickwood, D., & Fragar, L. (2011). Climate change and farmers' mental health: Risks and responses. *Asia-Pacific Journal of Public Health*, *23*(2), 119S–132S.

Bevan Jones, R., Stallard, P., Agha, S. S., Rice, S., Werner-Seidler, A., Stasiak, K., ... & Merry, S. (2020). Practitioner review: Co-design of digital mental health technologies with children and young people. *Journal of Child Psychology and Psychiatry*, *61*(8), 928–940.

Blithe, S. J., & Lanterman, J. (2017). Camouflaged collectives: Managing stigma and identity at gun events. *Studies in Social Justice*, *11*(1), 113–135.

Bradshaw, D., & Muldoon, O. T. (2020). Shared experiences and the social cure in the context of a stigmatized identity. *British Journal of Social Psychology*, *59*(1), 209–226.

Braga, A. A., Brunson, R. K., & Drakulich, K. M. (2019). Race, place, and effective policing. *Annual Review of Sociology*, *45*, 535–555.

Braithwaite, J. (1989). *Crime, shame and reintegration*. Cambridge University Press.

Braithwaite, J. (2002). *Restorative justice & responsive regulation*. Oxford University press on demand.

Bricknell, S. (2012). Firearm trafficking and serious and organised crime gangs, Sage.

Burgess, E. W. (2008). The growth of the city: An introduction to a research project, pp. 71–78. Springer US.

Burton, A. L., Logan, M. W., Pickett, J. T., Cullen, F. T., Jonson, C. L., & Burton, V. S. Jr. (2021). Gun owners and gun control: Shared status, divergent opinions. *Sociological Inquiry*, *91*(2), 347–366.

Butel, J., & Braun, K. L. (2019). The role of collective efficacy in reducing health disparities: A systematic review. *Family & Community Health*, *42*(1), 8.

Carswell, S. M. (2022). Have we surrendered to gun violence in urban America? Federal neglect stymies efforts to stop the slaughter among young Black men. *Race and Justice*, 12(1), 126–140. https://doi.org/10.1177/2153368719865306.

Casey, B. (2011). *Home on the range: Queensland Rifle Association, 1861–2011*. Boolarong Press.

Celinska, K. (2007). Individualism and collectivism in America: The case of gun ownership and attitudes toward gun control. *Sociological Perspectives*, *50*(2), 229–247.

Chapman, S. (2013). *Over our dead bodies: Port Arthur and Australia's fight for gun control*. Sydney University Press.

Chapman, S., Alpers, P., Agho, K., & Jones, M. (2006). Australia's 1996 gun law reforms: Faster falls in firearm deaths, firearm suicides, and a decade without mass shootings. *Injury Prevention*, *12*(6), 365–372.

Chriss, J. J. (2022). *Social control: An introduction*. John Wiley & Sons.

Cook, P. (1978). *The effect of gun availability on robbery and robbery murder: A cross-section study of 50 cities*. Center for the Study of Justice Policy, Institute of Policy Sciences and Public Affairs, Duke University.

Cook, P. J., & Goss, K. A. (2020). *The gun debate: What everyone needs to know®*. Oxford University.

Cook, P. J., & Ludwig, J. (2019). The social costs of gun ownership: A reply to Hayo, Neumeier, and Westphal. *Empirical Economics*, *56*, 13–22.

Crenshaw, K. W. (2017). *On intersectionality: Essential writings*. The New Press.

Croitoru, A., Kien, S., Mahabir, R., Radzikowski, J., Crooks, A., Schuchard, R., ... & Stefanidis, A. (2020). Responses to mass shooting events: The interplay between the media and the public. *Criminology & Public Policy*, *19*(1), 335–360.

Daly, K. (2014). *Redressing institutional abuse of children*. Springer.

Danielsson, P. (2021). Collective efficacy and violent crime in suburban housing estates. *European Journal of Criminology*, *18*(3), 345–365.

Decker, S. H., Ortiz, N., Spohn, C., & Hedberg, E. (2015). Criminal stigma, race, and ethnicity: The consequences of imprisonment for employment. *Journal of Criminal Justice*, *43*(2), 108–121.

Dempsey, S., Dutta, M., Frey, L. R., Goodall, H. L., Madison, D. S., Mercieca, J., ... Miller, K. (2011). What is the role of the communication discipline in social justice, community engagement, and public scholarship? A visit to the CM Café. *Communication Monographs*, *78*(2), 256–271.

Duggan, M.. (2001). More guns, more crime. *Journal of Political Economy*. 109. 1086–1114. https://doi.org/10.1086/322833

Duwe, G. (2020). Patterns and prevalence of lethal mass violence. *Criminology & Public Policy*, *19*(1), 17–35.

Every-Palmer, S., Cunningham, R., Jenkins, M., & Bell, E. (2021). The Christchurch Mosque shooting, the media, and subsequent gun control reform in New Zealand: a descriptive analysis. *Psychiatry, Psychology and Law*, 28(2), 274–285.

Fay, S. (2022). Gun dealer motivations for complying with the law: Lessons from the Australian experience of gun control. *Sociological Perspectives*, *65*(1), 154–176.

Fay-Ramirez, S. (2015). The comparative context of collective efficacy: Understanding neighbourhood disorganisation and willingness to intervene in Seattle and Brisbane. *Australian & New Zealand Journal of Criminology*, *48*(4), 513–542.

Fay-Ramirez, S. (2016). Therapeutic practice through restorative justice: Managing stigma in family treatment court. *QUT Law Review*, *16*, 50.

Feeley, M. M. (1979). *The process is the punishment: Handling cases in a lower criminal court*. Russell Sage Foundation.

Fuochi, G., Voci, A., Veneziani, C. A., Boin, J., Fell, B., & Hewstone, M. (2020). Is negative mass media news always associated with outgroup prejudice? The buffering role of direct contact. *Group Processes & Intergroup Relations*, *23*(2), 195–213.

Furst, R. T., & Evans, D. N. (2017). Renting apartments to felons: Variations in real estate agent decisions due to stigma. *Deviant Behavior*, *38*(6), 698–708.

Gezelius, S. S., & Hauck, M. (2011). Toward a theory of compliance in state-regulated livelihoods: A comparative study of compliance motivations in developed and developing world fisheries. *Law & Society Review*, *45*(2), 435–470.

Goffman, E. (2009). *Stigma: Notes on the management of spoiled identity*. Simon and Schuster.

Gorrey, M. (January 12th 2016). Gun ownership increase with more than 19,000 firearms in the ACT. The Sydney Morning Herald.

Groff, E. R. (2015). Informal social control and crime events. *Journal of Contemporary Criminal Justice*, *31*(1), 90–106.

Hahn, R. A., Bilukha, O., Crosby, A. M., Fullilove, T., Liberman, A., Moscicki, E., ... Briss, P. A. (2005). Firearms laws and the reduction of violence: A systematic review. *American Journal of Preventive Medicine*, *28*, 40–70.

Heijnders, M., & Van Der Meij, S. (2006). The fight against stigma: An overview of stigma-reduction strategies and interventions. *Psychology, Health & Medicine*, *11*(3), 353–363.

Hill, T. D., Dowd-Arrow, B., Burdette, A. M., & Warner, T. D. (2020). Gun ownership and life satisfaction in the United States. *Social Science Quarterly*, *101*(5), 2121–2136.

Jacobs, J. B., & Fuhr, Z. (2019). *The toughest gun control law in the nation: The unfulfilled promise of New York's SAFE Act*. NYU Press.

Judd, F., Jackson, H., Fraser, C., Murray, G., Robins, G., & Komiti, A. (2006). Understanding suicide in Australian farmers. *Social Psychiatry & Psychiatric Epidemiology*, *41*(1), 1–10.

Kennedy, A., Adams, J., Dwyer, J., Rahman, M. A., & Brumby, S. (2020). Suicide in rural Australia: Are farming-related suicides different? *International Journal of Environmental Research and Public Health*, *17*(6), 2010.

Killias, M., van Kesteren, J., & Rindlisbacher, M. (2001). Guns, violent crime, and suicide in 21 countries. *Canadian Journal of Criminology*, *43*, 429–448.

Kleck, G. (2013). Gun control after Heller and McDonald: What cannot be done and what ought to be done. *Fordham Urban Law Journal*, *39*, 1383–1420.

Kleck, G., Kovandzic, T., & Bellows, J. (2016). Does gun control reduce violent crime? *Criminal Justice Review*, *41*(4), 488–513.

Klieve, H., Barnes, M., & De Leo, D. (2009). Controlling firearms use in Australia: Has the 1996 gun law reform produced the decrease in rates of suicide with this method? *Social Psychiatry and Psychiatric Epidemiology*, *44*, 285–292.

Kopel, D. B. (1993). Japanese gun control. *Asia Pacific Law Review*, 2(2), 26–52.

Kruis, N. E., Wentling, R. L., Frye, T. S., & Rowland, N. J. (2021). Firearm ownership, defensive gun usage, and support for gun control: Does knowledge matter? *American Journal of Criminal Justice*, 48, 21–50. https://doi.org/10.1007/s12103-021-09644-7

Lignier, P., Evans, C., & Tran-Nam, B. (2014). Tangled up in tape: The continuing tax compliance plight of the small and medium enterprise business sector. In *Australian Tax Forum*.

Lipsky, M. (2010). *Street-level bureaucracy: Dilemmas of the individual in public service*. Russell Sage Foundation.

Lott, J. R. (2013). *More guns, less crime: Understanding crime and gun control laws*. University of Chicago Press.

Ludwig, J., & Cook, P. J. (Eds.). (2004). *Evaluating gun policy: Effects on crime and violence*. Brookings Institution Press.

Maunder, R. D., & White, F. A. (2019). Intergroup contact and mental health stigma: A comparative effectiveness meta-analysis. *Clinical Psychology Review*, 72, 101749.

May, P. J. (2004). Compliance motivations: Affirmative and negative bases. *Law & Society Review*, *38*(1), 41–68.

Mazerolle, L., Bennett, S., Davis, J., Sargeant, E., & Manning, M. (2013). Procedural justice and police legitimacy: A systematic review of the research evidence. *Journal of Experimental Criminology*, *9*, 245–274.

McCarthy, M. M., Porter, L. E., Townsley, M., & Alpert, G. P. (2019). The effect of community-oriented policing on police use of force: Does community matter? *Policing: an International Journal*, 42(4), 556–570.

McGloin, J. M., & Thomas, K. J. (2019). Peer influence and delinquency. *Annual Review of Criminology*, 2, 241–264.

McPhedran, S. (2016). A systematic review of quantitative evidence about the impacts of Australian legislative reform on firearm homicide. *Aggression and Violent Behavior*, *28*, 64–72.

Melzer, S. (2012). *Gun crusaders: The NRA's culture war*. NYU Press.

Merchant, R., Goldin, A., Manjanatha, D., Harter, C., Chandler, J., Lipp, A., ... Naslund, J. A. (2022). Opportunities to expand access to mental health services: A case for the role of online peer support communities. *Psychiatric Quarterly*, *93*(2), 613–625.

Moolenaar, N. M., Sleegers, P. J., & Daly, A. J. (2012). Teaming up: Linking collaboration networks, collective efficacy, and student achievement. *Teaching and Teacher Education*, *28*(2), 251–262.

Nagin, D. S., Koper, C. S., & Lum, C. (2020). Policy recommendations for countering mass shootings in the United States. *Criminology & Public Policy*, *19*(1), 9–15.

Newman, J., & Head, B. (2017). The national context of wicked problems: Comparing policies on gun violence in the US, Canada, and Australia. *Journal of Comparative Policy Analysis: Research and Practice*, *19*(1), 40–53.

Pager, D. (2003). The mark of a criminal record. *American Journal of Sociology*, *108*(5), 937–975.

Papachristos, A. V., Meares, T. L., & Fagan, J. (2009). Why do criminals obey the law? The influence of legitimacy and social networks on active gun offenders. *The Influence of Legitimacy and Social Networks on Active Gun Offenders (January 12, 2009). Yale Law & Economics Research Paper*, (373), 09–199.

Papachritos, A. V., Meares, T. L., & Fagan, J. (2012). Why do criminals obey the law-the influence of legitimacy and social networks on active gun offenders. *Journal of Criminal Law and Criminology*, *102*, 397.

Parker, C. (2006). The "compliance" trap: The moral message in responsive regulatory enforcement. *Law and Society Review*, *40*(3), 591–622.

Parsons, T. (1968). *The structure of social action.* (Vol. 491). Free press.

Paternoster, R., & Bachman, R. (2012). Perceptual deterrence theory.

Paternoster, R., & Sally, S. (1996). Sanction threats and appeals to morality: Testing a rational choice model of corporate crime. *Law and Society Review*, 549–583.

Pescosolido, B. A. (2013). The public stigma of mental illness: What do we think; What do we know; What can we prove? *Journal of Health and Social Behavior*, *54*(1), 1–21.

Pratt, T. C., Cullen, F. T., Blevins, K. R., Daigle, L. E., & Madensen, T. D. (2006). The Empirical Status of Deterrence Theory: A Meta-Analysis Taking stock: The status of criminological theory (pp. 367–395). Piscataway, NJ, US: Transaction Publishers.

Pryor, J. B., Reeder, G. D., & Monroe, A. E. (2012). The infection of bad company: Stigma by association. *Journal of Personality and Social Psychology*, *102*(2), 224.

Quinn, D. M., & Earnshaw, V. A. (2013). Concealable stigmatized identities and psychological well-being. *Social and Personality Psychology Compass*, *7*(1), 40–51.

Restivo, E., & Lanier, M. M. (2015). Measuring the contextual effects and mitigating factors of theory. *Justice Quarterly*, *32*(1), 116–141.

Robertson, J. (March 9th, 2016). *Gun control lobby raises alarm over silencers*. The Sydney Morning Herald.

Rosenbaum, D. P., & McCarty, W. P. (2017). Organizational justice and officer "buy in" in American policing. *Policing: an International Journal of Police Strategies & Management*, *40*(1), 71–85.

Rosenhan, D. L. (1973). On being sane in insane places. *Science*, *179*(4070), 250–258.

Sampson, R. J., Raudenbush, S. W., & Earls, F. (1997). Neighborhoods and violent crime: A multilevel study of collective efficacy. *Science*, *277*(5328), 918–924.

Schildkraut, J., Gruenewald, J., Gilliam, M., & Novak, M. (2021). Framing mass shootings as a social problem: A comparison of ideologically and non-ideologically motivated attacks. *Aggression and Violent Behavior*, *60*, 101533.

Schleifer, J. (1999). *Everything you need to know about weapons in school and at home*. The Rosen Publishing Group, Inc.

Senate Legal and Constitutional Affairs Committee (2015). *Ability of law enforcement authorities to eliminate gun-related violence in the community*. Commonwealth Government of Australia.

Shaw, C. R., & McKay, H. D. (1942). *Juvenile delinquency and urban areas*. University of Chicago Press.

Siuta, R. L., & Bergman, M. E. (2019). *Sexual harassment in the workplace. In Oxford research encyclopedia of business and management*. Oxford University Press.

Skeem, J., & Mulvey, E. (2020). What role does serious mental illness play in mass shootings, and how should we address it? *Criminology and Public Policy*, *19*(1), 85–108.

Smadi, H., Obeidat, M., & Haider, A. S. (2022). Paratextual (re) framing of media coverage of Christchurch Mosque Shootings: A translation-oriented study. *Cogent Social Sciences*, *8*(1), 2029251.

Smith, K. (2022). Pluralising food justice in Australia: insights from 'fair food futures'.

Stiles, B. L., & Kaplan, H. B. (1996). Stigma, deviance, and negative social sanctions. *Social Science Quarterly*, 77(3), 685–696.

Sugie, N. F., Zatz, N. D., & Augustine, D. (2020). Employer aversion to criminal records: An experimental study of mechanisms. *Criminology*, *58*(1), 5–34.

Sunshine, J., & Tyler, T. R. (2003). The role of procedural justice and legitimacy in shaping public support for policing. *Law and Society Review*, *37*(3), 513–548.

Sutherland, A., Brunton-Smith, I., & Jackson, J. (2013). Collective efficacy, deprivation and violence in London. *British Journal of Criminology*, *53*(6), 1050–1074.

Thomson, S., Stancich, L., & Dickson, L. (1998). Gun control and snowdrop. *Parliamentary Affairs*, *51*(3), 329+. https://link.gale.com/apps/doc/A21099997/AONE?u=anon~d540027c&sid=googleScholar&xid=5b813927

Tyler, T. R. (1990). Justice, self-interest, and the legitimacy of legal and political authority. In J. J. Mansbridge (Ed.), Beyond self-interest (pp. 171–179). University of Chicago Press.

Tyler, T. R., & Fagan, J. (2008). Legitimacy and cooperation: Why do people help the police fight crime in their communities. *Ohio State Journal of Criminal Law*, 6, 231.

Tyler, T. R., & Huo, Y. J. (2002). *Trust in the law: Encouraging public cooperation with the police and courts*. Russell Sage Foundation.

Wallace, L. N. (2017). Concealed ownership: Americans' perceived comfort sharing gun ownership status with others. *Sociological spectrum*, *37*(5), 267–281.

Winter, S. C., & May, P. J. (2015). "Street-level bureaucrats and regulatory deterrence." In *Understanding street-level bureaucracy*, pp. 133–152. Policy Press.

Wondemaghen, M. (2014). Media construction of a school shooting as a social problem. *Journalism*, *15*(6), 696–712.

Young, D. B. (1983). Cesare Beccaria: Utilitarian or retributivist? *Journal of Criminal Justice*, *11*(4), 317–326.

Zamenopoulos, T., & Alexiou, K. (2018). *Co-design as collaborative research*. Bristol University/AHRC Connected Communities Programme.

Zoller, H. M., & Casteel, D. (2021). #March for our lives: Health activism, diagnostic framing, gun control, and the gun industry. *Health Communication*, *37*(7), 1–11.

INDEX

Note: Page numbers in *italics* refer figures and **bold** tables in the text.

For Product Safety Concerns and Information please contact our EU
representative GPSR@taylorandfrancis.com
Taylor & Francis Verlag GmbH, Kaufingerstraße 24, 80331 München, Germany

www.ingramcontent.com/pod-product-compliance
Lightning Source LLC
LaVergne TN
LVHW021125300926
849160LV00010B/868
9781032222226